Improving Reading Achievement Through Professional Development

Improving Reading Achievement Through Professional Development

Dorothy S. Strickland

AND

Michael L. Kamil

EDITORS

Christopher-Gordon Publishers, Inc.
Norwood, Massachusetts

Copyright Acknowledgments

Every effort has been made to contact copyright holders for permission to reproduce borrowed material where necessary. We apologize for any oversights and would be happy to rectify them in future printings.

Figure 12-1 from *Guiding Readers and Writers, Grades 3-6: Teaching Comprehension, Genre, and Content Literacy* by Irene C. Fountas and Gay Su Pinnell. Copyright © 2001 by Irene C. Fountas and Gay Su Pinnell. Published by Heinemann, a division of Reed Elsevier, Inc., Portsmouth, NH. Used by permission.

Material from *Language Arts, Learning and Teaching* (with CD-ROM and InfoTrac) 1st edition by Strickland/Cullinan/Galda © 2004. Reprinted with permission of Wadsworth, a division of Thomson Learning: www.thomsonrights.com. Fax 800-730-2215.

Material from *Speaking and Listening for Preschool through Third Grade* (2001) and *Reading and Writing Grade by Grade* (1999). New Standards c/o National Center on Education and the Economy. Reprinted by permission.

All names and vignettes from The Benchmark School reprinted by permission.

Christopher~Gordon Publishers, Inc.
Bridging Theory and Practice

1502 Providence Highway, Suite #12
Norwood, Massachusetts 02062

800-934-8322 • 781-762-5577

Printed in the United State of America
10 9 8 7 6 5 4 3 2 1   08 07 06 05 04

ISBN: 1-929024-68-1
Library of Congress Catalogue Number: 2003109067

Content

Preface

Reports and Recommendations From the National Invitational Conference "Improving Reading Achievement Through Professional Development"

Dorothy S. Strickland, Michael L. Kamil, Herbert J. Walberg, and JoAnn B. Manning

The causes of reading failure are numerous and complex. Until recently, ineffective teaching was rarely cited as a cause of reading problems. Nevertheless, it is reasonable to assume that if the instruction provided by the school is ineffective or insufficient, even some otherwise capable learners will have difficulty learning to read. Throughout the country, people are recognizing that excellence as a teacher of reading is not attained upon graduation from a teacher preparation program followed by occasional participation in a district's inservice day activities, nor is it attained through graduate coursework. Improving literacy instruction through professional development is an ongoing process involving all of the members of a schoolwide literacy team in activities that will help them become more effective in what they do. Fortunately, the importance of career-long, high-quality professional development has not gone unnoticed. It has become a priority in the many efforts enlisted to reform schools and improve student performance in reading, including the recent No Child Left Behind legislation.

This emphasis on professional development has come relatively late in the current reform movement, however. The National Reading Panel report (NICHHD, 2000) concludes that professional development is a largely untested solution for widespread improvement in literacy instruction. Although much has been learned about what constitutes effective professional development, there is little research-based evidence about how to design professional-development programs and activities such that changes in teacher instructional practices can be linked to better student performance. Fortunately, the current climate of reform offers an ideal time to initiate exemplary professional-development programs and to systematically study them as a means to improve student performance.

Unfortunately, the dismal reputation of professional development is both widespread and well deserved. Instead of a history characterized by steady progress based on advances in knowledge and understanding, staff development is characterized primarily by disorder, conflict, and criticism. Teachers complain that their district's entire professional-development program consists of one or two inservice days each year, which they refer to as "one-shot" or "drive-by" workshops. Very often, the workshop topics are not the ones about which they care most. Even when the topics are relevant and the ideas well presented, there is little or no follow-up. In addition to the ineffectiveness of annually scheduled inservice days, teachers say they are frustrated by the lack of sufficient professional development when new materials, technologies, and curriculum initiatives are introduced. Moreover, these issues are only part of the problem.

Many teachers believe that professional development would be greatly improved if *they* were more involved in the decision making and planning. Teachers understand that there are many factors and many people to be considered; they simply want some input. If, indeed, the school district is operating on the basis of a larger vision, it is not always evident to them. They do not share in that vision. These concerns are extremely pertinent in the area of literacy instruction, since it is an area where much of the professional-development programming is targeted and it is often the focal point of reform.

To address these and other important professional-development issues, the National Invitational Conference, "Improving Reading Achievement Through Professional Development," cosponsored by Rutgers University, the Carnegie Corporation of New York, and the Laboratory for Student Success (LSS), the Mid-Atlantic Regional Educational Laboratory at Temple University, was convened in Washington, DC, November 13–14, 2002. The purpose of the conference was to bring together teachers, principals, reading specialists, teacher educators, and other education professionals to discuss the current best thinking on what teachers and administrators need to know and do to provide quality literacy instruction for optimum student performance. The conference papers, which were distributed to the participants prior to the conference to facilitate discussion, were commissioned to address professional-development strategies for improving literacy instruction at various educational levels. The conference discussions included topics such as teacher preparation standards, what teachers need to know and do to elicit the best reading performance from their students, how to engage students in reading and writing activities, training self-reflective teachers who translate reflections on classroom practices into strategies for high-quality instruction, and the role of principals in leading professional-development efforts and improving reading instruction.

Throughout the conference, the participants were organized into small work groups. The work groups were designed to elicit next-step recommendations for improving reading achievement through professional development, the ultimate goal of the conference attendees. The recommendations can be organized into the following topics.

Content and Process

The participants agreed that professional development should be the following:

- Research-based
- Thoughtfully planned and ongoing for all teachers, no matter their level of education or experience
- An integral part of the infrastructure of the school (e.g., included in teacher contracts)
- Collaborative, such that teachers, other school staff, and outside literacy professionals participate in the transfer of knowledge, skills, and learning
- Determined by student needs (derived from assessments, classroom observations, and student reflections on their progress), teacher needs, and the needs of parents and the larger community
- Encouraging of teachers to recognize individual student differences, strengths, and weaknesses, and adjust their instruction accordingly.

Tailoring Professional Development

The professional-development needs of individual school staff members will differ. Participants' recommendations for tailoring professional development to meet diverse needs include the following:

- Professional development should be grounded in children's learning processes.
- The school's vision for reform should be shared by all in the school community, including principals, teachers, and other staff members.
- Professional development should be designed to attend to individual teacher needs and encourage teachers to reflect on and evaluate their teaching practices.
- Professional development should encourage the formation of teacher study groups in which teachers can discuss their goals, needs, and perceptions of student needs.

Building a Community of Learners

One of the important by-products of high-quality professional development is the creation of a community of learners in which the transfer of knowledge, ideas, and skills abound. The participants agreed that:

- Professional development should include opportunities for multidisciplinary collaboration among teachers and support the shared vision of the school.
- Teachers' classroom practices should be grounded in research. Research findings should be linked to the shared vision, and teachers should keep abreast of current best thinking and practices in their field (e.g., professional library in the school).
- Special education and regular education teachers should seek and conduct separate research.
- Teachers should be included in data-driven decision making regarding professional development and reform efforts.
- Teachers should be encouraged to offer and accept criticism and other feedback from their colleagues.
- Professional development should be deliberate and structured (scheduled meetings and planning times).
- "Master teacher" leaders that teachers trust should be appointed to focus on coaching and staff development.

Role of Administrators in Accomplishing Professional Development Goals

Administrators should do the following:

- Support professional development for teachers, encourage principal participation in professional development, and participate in professional development themselves, especially literacy professional development
- Be aware of teachers' needs and share observations with appropriate personnel. Be creative with scheduling and planning preparation time
- Share leadership and coordinate efforts with teachers and principals

- Be effective leaders of instruction and use the services of specialists and resource teachers
- Focus on *coaching* teachers rather than criticizing and evaluating
- Include principals and other school staff in coaching and scaffolding teachers after professional-development training
- Be aware that they share the responsibility (accountability) for student outcomes with teachers and principals
- Along with principals, be aware of their particular school environments, situations, and classroom needs and encourage partnerships with parents to meet these needs
- Develop the infrastructure to maintain professional-development efforts when leadership changes or support is withdrawn
- Think about and be prepared for (future) planning with a limited budget or no budget

Principals should be involved in professional networks and collaborate with other principals.

Reference

National Institute of Child Health and Human Development (NICHHD). (2000). *Report of the National Reading Panel. Teaching children to read: An evidence-based assessment of the scientific research literature on reading and its implications for reading instruction.* (NIH Publication No. 00-4769). Washington, D.C.: U.S. Government Printing Office.

Introduction

What do we know about the relationship of teacher education and professional development to student achievement? We can turn to the research literature to provide guidance in answering this question. In 2000 the National Reading Panel (NRP) surveyed the research literature on teacher education and professional development. In that analysis, they examined experimental and quasi-experimental research. As they did so, they made several requirements of the research in order to answer this question: Studies had to measure teacher changes (as a result of the intervention), and they had to measure student outcomes in reading as well. This is important because teacher education or professional development is effective only if it leads to improvement in student achievement. Consequently, if teachers don't change their teaching as a result of professional development, it would be inappropriate to attribute changes in student achievement to teacher education.

The results were quite striking. First, only a very small set of studies met the criteria established by the NRP. Of the 21 studies that met the criteria, 17 measured teacher outcomes, 15 of these reported at least moderate or greater improvement in teaching. That is, teachers learned and applied what was being taught in professional development sessions. Of the 21 studies, 15 measured student outcomes, and 13 of these reported improvements in student reading achievement. More important was the finding that if there were no gains for the teachers, there were no gains for the students. Although this is a very small sample of studies, the consistency is extremely high.

Unfortunately, there was little or no consensus about the content of the professional development programs that were used to produce these gains. Four areas of concentration were found: comprehension and strategy instruction, general teaching methods (e.g., language experience, whole language, phonics), classroom management, and improvement of teachers' attitudes. One striking absence was that there were no studies that examined programs that focused on standards-based instruction.

In a separate analysis, the NRP looked at ways in which teachers were prepared to teach comprehension. The conclusions were that teachers did benefit from professional development in this area but that support was necessary to sustain the programs. Sustained resource allocation became a focus of the long-term efforts. Teachers do need to be prepared to help students learn comprehension strategies and, in particular, to be able to apply them in content area reading. In addition, NRP concluded that laying the groundwork for these teaching skills should begin in preservice programs.

Where does this leave the field? This is tantalizing evidence that professional development for teachers *is* effective, but more detail is needed, as is a broader range of studies in a wide range of contexts. These efforts are being mounted and are beginning to demonstrate effective ways of conducting professional development with teachers. Moreover, there has been a renewed focus on teacher education at the preservice level.

A recent publication on the topic of teacher education is *Preparing Our Teachers: Opportunities for Better Reading Instruction* (Strickland et al., 2002). This book focuses on what teachers need to know and be able to do to help young children become accomplished readers. The book is unique in that it goes beyond providing the knowledge base for understanding key content and instructional strategies related to the development of oral and written language, reading comprehension, learner motivation, and appropriate classroom intervention. It also provides strategies to be used in the context of preservice teacher education and professional development in order to help teachers develop and improve the teaching of reading. By building in activities for action and reflection by its readers, the book's use is facilitated in teacher education classrooms and in study groups where teachers gather to inform and improve their practice.

The conference on which this volume is based stemmed from a feeling we had that it was time to address the current state of research in professional development in a more systematic manner. We approached the Carnegie Corporation and the Laboratory for Student Success (LSS) at Temple University with the proposal for the conference. An agreement was reached to have the conference follow the pattern of other successful LSS conferences: Papers were to be prepared and distributed ahead of time. At the conference, authors were given only a short time to summarize their findings. Respondents to each paper were charged with stimulating discussion of the issues. Authors were allowed to respond to the comments of the respondents, but the intent of the conference was to generate discussion of critical ideas related to professional development.

The conference was held in Washington, DC, on November 12–13, 2002. About 75 people were in attendance, a diverse group of individuals bound by their concern for reading. Represented in this group were teachers, administrators, researchers, parents, and policy makers. Small-group sessions were held during the two days to allow discussions to pursue topics in more detail.

This volume represents a wide range of topics and research projects that span the field of reading and literacy instruction. It has no hierarchical structure but is meant to be sampled by topic. We do not envision the reading starting at the beginning and proceeding to the end. Rather, topics related to professional development should be read as needed.

To facilitate that end we have included an overview of Key Ideas and Audiences as an introduction. For each chapter we asked authors to identify three major concepts that were contained in the chapter. This will allow the reader to make choices about which of the chapters is relevant to a particular topic. A second feature of the overview is that the chapters are identified by target audiences. Some are designed for administrators, others are designed for reading specialists, still others are of interest to more general audiences. These features of the overview will allow efficient access to those topics of immediate interest.

One other element of this volume is worth noting. At the conference, participants were asked to submit short descriptions of their most memorable professional development experiences. We have collected a number of these personal reflections and they are included as Part IV.

We believe that we are on the verge of making great strides in research concerning professional development. The conference and this volume are but early steps to assist in those new developments. We hope we have initiated a dialogue around these important issues and that this volume will help to sustain the momentum from the conference.

Dorothy S. Strickland
Michael L. Kamil

Reference

Strickland, D. S., Snow, C., Griffin, P., Burns, M. S., & McNamara, P. (2002). *Preparing our teachers: Opportunities for better reading instruction.* Washington, DC: National Academy of Education, Joseph Henry Press.

Acknowledgments

This project was cosponsored by the Laboratory for Student Success, the Carnegie Corporation of New York, and Rutgers University of New Jersey.

The editors would like to express their thanks to JoAnn Manning and the staff at the Laboratory for Student Success for the opportunity to work with them on the National Invitational Conference, which served as the platform for this volume. A special thanks to Marilyn Murphy for her help in making the arrangements for the conference, to Dana Jones Robinson for her deft editorial skills, and to Mikki O'Connor, assistant to Dorothy Strickland, for her efforts to keep things moving along day by day. We are grateful to the conference particpants for their participation and feedback. The comments helped to strengthen this volume in many ways. Thanks to Sue Canavan and Hiram Howard at Christopher-Gordon for guiding this project to publication. Our thanks to Kate Liston of Christopher-Gordon for her guidance in the preparation of this manuscript and to Helen Kim of Stanford University for her help in the final editing process.

This publication was made possible in part by a grant from Carnegie Corporation of New York. The statements made and views expressed are solely the responsibility of the authors. We are particularly grateful to Andres Henriquez, Program Officer, Education Division for his thoughtful comments and support.

Key Ideas
and Audiences

Part I. Teacher Preparation

Chapter 1. Teachers Who Improve Reading Achievement: What Research Says About What They Do and How to Develop Them *by Gerald G. Duffy*

Key Ideas

The key to high achievement in reading is thoughtfully adaptive teachers who select strategies and practices in response to student and curricular needs.

"Training" teachers to follow certain routines or practices is not effective because it encourages teachers to be compliant followers of prescribed practices rather than creators of instruction that is responsive to different students.

Professional development must promote autonomous and independent decision making, which in turn requires changes in what we teach teachers, how we teach teachers, and when we teach teachers.

For

Teacher educators and persons responsible for staff development in public schools

Policy makers

Chapter 2. Sources of Standards for Teacher Preparation
by Cathy M. Roller and James V. Hoffman

Key Ideas

Standards-based reform that began in the K–12 arena is now moving into teacher preparation.

There are four sources of standards for teacher preparation: consensus, student standards, instructional research on best practices, and research.

The extant research is not sufficient for strong research-based teacher preparation standards.

For

Teacher educators

Teachers

Part II. Professional Development Across Instructional Levels

Chapter 3. Introduction *by Dorothy S. Strickland*

Chapter 4. Establishing the Basis for Improved Reading Achievement: Prekindergarten and Kindergarten
by M. Susan Burns and Robert A. Stechuk

Key Ideas

Prekindergarten and kindergarten teachers need to understand and apply knowledge and skills related specifically to literacy and possess more general knowledge of the language systems that underlie reading and writing.

Telling does not equal understanding; professional development ought to encourage teachers to enact, assess, analyze, and reflect upon the principles and practices they are being taught.

Being an effective teacher of reading and writing is a lifelong learning process, and professional development should address the needs of teachers at different career and skill levels (e.g., preservice, beginning teacher, experienced teacher, and master teacher).

For

Early childhood professional development providers, both preservice and inservice

Early childhood teachers

Key Ideas

Educators need to attend to content and process as they plan effective professional development for teachers.

Primary-grade teachers benefit from a deep understanding of theory and practice in the five components of reading: phonemic awareness, phonics, fluency, vocabulary, and comprehension.

Primary-grade teachers benefit from professional development that includes demonstrations and guided practice with feedback through in-class coaching.

For

Professional development providers

Administrators, curriculum coordinators, teacher educators

Key Ideas

The knowledge and skills that teachers need for helping children to fulfill their potential cannot be achieved in the short time that professors have with preservice teachers.

If we want all students to receive the education they deserve, it is imperative that professional development be part of the fabric of the school and that a menu of professional development opportunities be available at each school.

To ensure that this happens, it is the job of the instructional leader of the school to recognize and understand classroom expertise, to keep current on instructional research and theory, and to know how to orchestrate meaningful opportunities for teachers to collaborate and grow.

For

K–12 teachers

K–12 administrators

Chapter 7. **Professional Development Content for Reading Educators at the Middle and High School Levels**
by Donna E. Alvermann and Allison Nealy

Key Ideas

The focus of this chapter is on the content of professional development for reading educators at the middle and high school levels.

A learning specialist discusses her collaboration with social studies and science middle school teachers.

A university professor examines some assumptions underlying the reading profession's knowledge base and invites a reexamination of what constitutes the content of professional development for reading educators.

For

Teachers, teacher educators, and administrators responsible for secondary (middle and high school) and special education

Part III. Issues in Professional Development

Chapter 8. **Building Capacity for the Responsive Teaching of Reading in the Academic Disciplines: Strategic Inquiry Designs for Middle and High School Teachers' Professional Development** *by Cynthia L. Greenleaf and Ruth Schoenbach*

Key Ideas

For all students to continue to develop as readers beyond the early grades, plentiful opportunities to read and to learn strategic approaches to reading, with the support and guidance of knowledgeable teachers, are necessary. Yet for many reasons, secondary teachers are reluctant to teach reading in their subject area classes.

Those of us responsible for teachers' professional learning must design effective learning environments for teachers, providing strategic opportunities, tools, resources, and collaborations to assist teachers in developing key capacities necessary to "teach for understanding" in the complexity and diversity of modern classrooms.

By engaging secondary teachers in a variety of inquiries into their own and their students' reading practices, we can assist teachers in constructing richer and more complex theories of reading, in seeing in new and more generous ways their students' capacities to read and learn, in drawing on and developing their own resources and knowledge as teachers of reading, and in transforming their classrooms into places where students develop new identities as capable, academic readers.

For

Teacher educators

Administrators, teachers, researchers

Chapter 9. Reengaging Youngsters With Reading Difficulties by Means of Innovative Professional Development
by Susan Florio-Ruane, Taffy E. Raphael, Kathy Highfield, and Jennifer Berne

Key Ideas

The Teachers' Learning Collaborative (TLC), organized in 1996 as part of the Center for the Improvement of Early Reading Achievement (CIERA), involved literacy teachers in Michigan in collaborative, inquiry-based professional development of struggling young readers from school literacy by grade 3.

The members of TLC designed and piloted a curriculum framework called Book Club *Plus.* This aimed to scaffold youngsters' reengagement in authentic and challenging literacy, both individually, at their instructional level, and as a community, with age-appropriate texts in small-group and whole-class peer-led literacy activities.

As part of their own professional development, the TLC teachers used multiple methods of data collection and analysis to research the curriculum framework and found that the third graders who were initially working below grade level in TLC classrooms showed increased engagement when it was used and at least a year's growth in reading during a yearlong pilot.

For

Teacher educators, literacy researchers

Teachers, policy makers

Chapter 10. Professional Development in the Uses of Technology *by Elizabeth S. Pang and Michael L. Kamil*

Key Ideas

Video technology is the most widely utilized technology for modeling effective teaching.

There has been a sharp rise in research on Internet-based technologies in literacy teacher education.

Future research should examine the connection between technology-based teacher education and student learning outcomes.

For

Teacher educators, literacy researchers

Teachers, policy makers

Chapter 11. Reflective Inquiry As a Tool for Professional Development *by Gay Su Pinnell and Emily M. Rodgers*

Key Ideas

We describe a multifaceted model of professional development that provides opportunities for reflective inquiry in three different contexts: collaboratively with a group of teachers, individually with a coach, and independently.

Effective reflective inquiry requires opportunities for collaborative problem solving with peers with a focus on children's behavior as evidence of learning.

Professional development initiatives must be complex—nested within a comprehensive school reform effort that brings classroom teachers and literacy specialists together for further learning.

For

Teacher educators and graduate classes with a focus on teacher education

Researchers and those engaged in the professional development of teachers

Chapter 12. Professional Development at Benchmark School *by Irene W. Gaskins*

Key Ideas

The knowledge and skills that teachers need to help children fulfill their potential cannot be achieved in the short time that professors have with preservice teachers.

If we want all students to receive the education they deserve, it is imperative that professional development be part of the fabric of the school and that a menu of professional development opportunities be available at each school.

To ensure that this happens, it is the job of the instructional leader of the school to recognize and understand classroom expertise, to keep current on instructional research and theory, and to know how to orchestrate meaningful opportunities for teachers to collaborate and grow.

For

K–12 teachers

Administrators

Key Ideas

The essence of educational leadership is the improvement of learning.

School leadership that improves learning is a shared enterprise, distributed across many actors, not the sole domain of the principal.

An analysis of two school cases illustrates the nature of leadership practices employed by principals who seek to improve learning, including (1) a persistent, public focus on learning, (2) the use of inquiry, (3) the development of enabling structures, (4) shared responsibility for decision making, and (5) personal participation as a learner.

For

Pre-K–12 school and system leaders

Pre-K–12 policy makers and those who prepare pre-K–12 educational leaders

Part *I*

Teacher Preparation

Teachers Who Improve Reading Achievement: What Research Says About What They Do and How To Develop Them

Gerald G. Duffy

Key Ideas

✓ The key to high achievement in reading is thoughtfully adaptive teachers who select strategies and practices in response to student and curricular needs.

✓ "Training" teachers to follow certain routines or practices is not effective because it encourages teachers to be compliant followers of prescribed practices rather than creators of instruction that is responsive to different students.

✓ Professional development must promote autonomous and independent decision making, which in turn requires changes in what we teach teachers, how we teach teachers, and when we teach teachers.

For

• Teacher educators and persons responsible for staff development in public schools

• Policy makers

There is much current debate about how to develop reading teachers. This chapter attempts to clarify the debate by describing research on effective reading teachers and on how to develop them, and by recommending changes we must undertake if we are to translate these research findings into practice.

Because the teacher development debate is spurred largely by perceptions about America's literacy problem, we must start there. At the extremes, the debate pits critics who claim we have a pervasive literacy crisis (e.g., Lyon, 1997; Moats, 2000) against others who cite a decade of National Assessment of Educational Progress scores, as well as recent international comparisons, as evidence that there is no literacy decline among American fourth graders (Allington, 2001; Berliner & Biddle, 1996; Bracey, 1997). Snow, Burns, and Griffin (1998) provide a more balanced assessment: "Current difficulties in reading largely originate from *rising demands for literacy,* not from declining absolute levels of literacy" (p. 1; emphasis added).

Eisner (1999) describes the nature of these rising demands:

> our educational aspirations have been influenced by the fact that our children will inhabit a world requiring far more complex and subtle forms of thinking than children needed three or four decades ago.... No longer will most jobs ... require the use of routine skills and rote memory. (p. 658)

These rising societal demands translate into two specific literacy needs:

1. We do not adequately prepare children of poverty to handle rising societal demands, leaving them at risk of being unable to contribute productively in tomorrow's world (Allington, 2001; Grissmer, Kirby, Berends, & Williamson, 1994).

2. Students across the board are inadequately prepared to use text as a vehicle for higher order thinking, an ability essential in the coming decades (Elley, 1992; National Center for Educational Statistics, 2002).

Consequently, I cite research on teacher effectiveness and professional development with a particular emphasis on helping at-risk students and strengthening higher order thinking. What this research says is that we must develop teachers who adjust as situations change during the pursuit of instructional goals, and that doing so requires changes in how we teach teachers.

I embark on the task with mixed feelings, for three reasons. First, teacher education and professional development practices are culturally embedded in school and university tradition, so they are often difficult to change. Second, implementing the research I report here requires greater investment in teachers, but politicians, policy makers, and the public are reluctant to spend more money on education. Finally, the inflammatory nature of the current debate about reading often impedes progress. On the one hand, supporters of the No Child Left Behind Act (PL 107-110) make no bones about the fact that new federal legislation is intended to put an end to independent teacher decision making (e.g., Finn, 2002); charge that teacher educators and professional developers are themselves the root of the problem (Walsh, 2001); claim that better reading can be achieved simply by "taking people off the street and giving them scripts"; and argue for dismantling teacher education systems (U.S. Department of Education, 2002). On the other hand, defenders of teachers and of teacher development are equally vehement in charging that critics use flawed data (e.g., see Darling-Hammond, 2002; Darling-Hammond & Youngs, 2002); that the effort to dismantle teacher education institutions is motivated by a desire to cut costs, not by a desire to improve teaching (Cochran-Smith & Fries, 2001); that the new legislation is intended to enrich commercial companies having close ties to President Bush (Strauss, 2002); and/or that the real intent is to replace local control with a national reading curriculum (Allington, 2002). The result is a schism rather than a solution.

Consequently, we cannot be naive about the difficulties involved in improving reading achievement through professional development. Although the research findings reported below are compelling and could provide a foundation for moving reading instruction forward, it would be a mistake to underestimate the difficulty of overcoming enculturated practice, the money issue, or the inflammatory climate surrounding the whole issue of improving reading achievement through professional development.

What We Have Learned From Research

What Research on Effective Teaching Tells Us

There has long been a hope that research would reduce effective teaching to a discrete set of pedagogical techniques that all teachers could be taught to use. For a time, we thought the answer lay with time management and direct teaching practices associated with process-product studies of classroom teaching generally (Brophy & Good, 1986) and of reading in particular (Anderson, Evertson, & Brophy, 1979).

That hope was soon dashed, however. First, the classic First Grade Studies (Bond & Dykstra, 1967) found teaching effectiveness to be tied more to teachers and what teachers do than to programs or materials. Then, starting in 1975, studies coming out of the Center for the Study of Reading (at the University of Illinois), which was charged with the study of comprehension (e.g., Anderson & Pearson, 1984), and from the Institute for Research on Teaching (at Michigan State University), which was charged with getting inside teachers' minds to determine the nature of classroom teaching (e.g., Clark & Peterson, 1986), resulted in the collective realization that reading instruction, especially comprehension instruction, was not a matter of following routine procedures. As Buchmann (1990) has said:

> Teaching … routinely involves multiple pairs of obligations—binding claims on one's attention in which if one is satisfied, the other cannot be. … Such multiplying moral dilemmas are 'resolved' in an interconnected series of imperfect decisions that bypass one horn of each dilemma and deal with any residues in the network later. (p. 5)

Subsequent studies of the constructivist nature of learning (Prawat, 1991), of situated learning (Brown, Collins, & Duguid, 1989), and of the holistic nature of reading (Goodman & Goodman, 1979) pushed us further away from the idea that reading instruction can be proceduralized. Similarly, Bloome and Greene (1984), Brice-Heath (1994), Cazden (1986), Moll (1994), and others established that effective literacy learning is influenced by language, culture, and what Dillon (1989) called the "creation of culturally congruent social organizations" in classrooms, further illuminating the complexity of literacy teaching. As Elmore (1992) suggests, we began to understand that literacy involved managing different types of knowledge in order to perform complex tasks centered on concrete problems. So the picture became more complex still.

As researchers continued to study effective reading instruction from the late 1980s into the 1990s, we became aware that teacher adaptability is often more important than adherence to established procedures. For instance, although it was found that modeling reading strategies (Duffy et al., 1987) and coupling modeling with scaffolded assistance (Pressley et al., 1992) is effective, especially for struggling readers, it was also found that such techniques could not be scripted or proceduralized. On the contrary, teachers who produce the greatest achievement gains adjust and modify modeling and scaffolding techniques during lessons depending on how students respond (Duffy, 1993a).

Most recently, observational studies of exemplary teachers further supported the importance of adaptive and selective teacher judgment during instruction. For instance, Allington and Johnston (2002) note that fourth-grade teachers use explicit teaching when they need to, but not all the time. Langer (2001) describes how middle and high school teachers use a variety of activities and techniques. Wharton-McDonald, Pressley, and Hampston (1998) report that exemplary primary-grade teachers often employ several ideological and methodological practices, sometimes within a single lesson; and Mosenthal, Lipson, Mekkelsen, Russ, & Sartino (2001) report that no single approach or model accounts for success in schools where large numbers of students are successful in reading.

In sum, while effective reading teachers work within a framework of routine procedures and employ "best practices," the most effective teachers adapt and modify their practices when they encounter instructional problems. As Garrison (1997) says, effective teaching is "doing the right thing in the right way and at the right time *in response to problems posed by particular people in particular places on particular occasions*" (p. 271; emphasis added). This adaptive responsiveness is not unlike what airline pilots or doctors or other professionals do when things go awry—they modify their routines and procedures to fit the situation. The National Reading Panel (NICHHD, 2000) emphasized the adaptive aspect of good reading instruction in its summary of "Teacher Preparation and Comprehension Strategies Instruction":

> What we must remember is that reading comprehension instruction is extremely complex and that teaching reading comprehension is also extremely complex. The work of the researchers discussed here makes this clear. They have not recommended an "instructional package" that can be prescribed for all students. They have not identified a specific set of instructional procedures that teachers can follow routinely. Indeed, they have found that reading comprehension cannot be routinized. (p. 4-125)

Consequently, the lesson from the history of reading teacher effectiveness research is that improved reading achievement is associated with thoughtfully adaptive teachers. Even skills such as phonemic awareness require adaptive teaching and independent teacher decisions, simply because all children do not respond to instruction in predictable ways. As Snow et al. (1998) say: "If we have learned anything from this effort [the National Research Council report on preventing reading difficulties], it is that effective teachers are able to craft a special mix of instructional ingredients for every child they work with" (p. 2).

What Research on Teacher Development Tells Us

The current teacher development debate often proceeds as if teacher effectiveness were unrelated to teacher education and professional development (e.g., U.S. Department of Education, 2002). In fact, however, there is abundant evidence establishing the importance of teacher education and professional development (Anders, Hoffman, & Duffy, 2000; Darling-Hammond & Youngs, 2002). For instance, we know that increased amounts of professional development work are associated with better teaching performance (National Commission on Teaching and America's Future, 1997), and that graduates of traditional teacher education programs get better results than teachers certified through emergency certification procedures (Ashton & Crocker, 1987). In addition, we know that teachers perform as well academically as other college-educated adults (Bruschi & Coley, 1999); that there is a high level of teacher satisfaction with preservice teacher education (National Center for Educational Statistics, 1999); and that most new teachers do well on teacher tests and in the professional development associated with teacher induction programs (Hoffman, Edwards, O'Neal, Barnes, & Paulissen, 1986). I could find no credible data contradicting this generally positive pattern. Even the National Reading Panel (NICHHD, 2000), viewed by some as an instrument of federal efforts to impose restrictive teaching practices on teachers and to discredit teacher education (e.g., Allington, 2002; Snow, 2001), supports development of thoughtfully responsive teachers (see chapter 4, part III of the Summary Report).

One reason the teacher development debate persists is that we have not yet established a direct connection between teacher education and improved student reading performance. Fortunately, two current studies are now doing just that. First, Grossman and Valencia et al. (1999) followed their University of Washington graduates as they moved into their first and second years of teaching, documenting their performance as they put their preservice education to work. Second, Roller and Hoffman (2002), under the auspices of the International Reading Association, are conducting a study of the graduates of eight exemplary preservice reading education programs across the nation, observing their teaching during their first, second, and third years on the job. Both studies are yielding much-needed information about the relationship between various program characteristics, graduates' on-the-job performance, and student achievement.

In the meantime the debate continues. It is often described in terms of two polarized positions, one emphasizing a "training" model and the other an "educative" model (e.g., Hoffman & Pearson, 2000; Richardson & Placier, 2001). In a training model, teachers are told about a recommended practice, it is demonstrated to them, and they are expected to implement it in their classrooms. In its extreme form, training seeks to ensure teacher compliance with scripted procedures. This is the case with programs such as DISTAR and Success for All. Though differing in detail, both prescribe rigid adherence to certain procedures and actions.

While such training may develop skill-like behaviors associated with the early stages of decoding and low-level comprehension, the jury is still out regarding the lasting effects of such gains for at-risk students (e.g., Allington, 2001; Jones, Gottfredson, & Gottfredson, 1997), and I know of no data establishing that such programs develop higher order thinking.

Unlike training models, educative models seek to develop teacher autonomy and decision making. Voluntary involvement, collaboration, inquiry, reflection, and teacher construction of knowledge in a school setting are emphasized.

Research reports substantiate that educative approaches increase teacher thoughtfulness (e.g., Lytle & Cochran-Smith, 1992; McVee & Pearson, 1997) and that teachers become confident in their decision-making abilities, take responsibility for what happens in their classrooms, and develop a strong sense of individual autonomy (Richardson & Placier, 2001). Similarly, Anders and Richardson (1991) report that when teachers control professional development and are encouraged to take positions and debate them, beliefs as well as practices change; a result also substantiated by social psychology research (Petty, 1995). However, and less positively, educative professional development requires substantial time and effort, is costly, and does not result in steady growth (Hoffman & Pearson, 2000). Instead, progress is more a matter of ups and downs as teachers confront the complexities and dilemmas associated with making changes in their reading instruction (Duffy, 1993b). Hence, educative approaches do not offer a "quick fix."

As is the case with training models, it is currently unclear whether educative professional development has a positive impact on student achievement. However, a string of data has begun to emerge. For instance, one educative professional development effort documented at-risk students' gains in instructional reading levels and in metacognitive use of reading strategies (Duffy, 1993a, 1994); preliminary findings from the International Reading Association's study of exemplary teacher education programs document text-rich classroom environments that, in turn, suggest positive achievement (James Hoffman, personal communication, September 25, 2002); and the research on effective teachers reported earlier in this chapter indicates that student achievement is associated with thoughtfully adaptive teachers.

Training and educative approaches are not mutually exclusive. All good teaching is based on routines, procedures, and best practices. Few teachers could survive for long without such a foundation to carry the school day forward, and those routines, procedures, and best practices are often learned through training. For instance, both preservice and inservice programs often train teachers in the use of lesson-plan formats, in procedures for increasing student time on task, and in efficient ways to organize and manage the school day.

Having said this, however, it is crucial to also emphasize that the most effective teachers do not stick with routine procedures in all situations. Instead, when unanticipated problems arise during instruction, they respond appropriately. For instance, a teacher may be trained to teach a particular skill in a particular way, but when a student does not respond, the teacher adapts and changes as needed.

Consequently, the defining element of all professional development must be its capacity to create teachers who change their practices when student or environmental data says that what they are doing is not working. If teachers are to adjust instruction for non-standard students and for the subtle cognitive demands of higher order thinking, then autonomy, thoughtfulness, and adaptive behavior are essential. In contrast, teachers who are led to believe that they must not deviate from their training cannot adjust instruction and therefore cannot be as effective.

In the end, the question is not whether professional development should be rooted in training or educative models. It is whether the professional development goal is to authorize teachers to think for themselves when standard instructional procedures do not work. In short, adaptive teaching must be the centering focus of teacher development at all levels.

What We Need to Do to Put the Research Into Practice

Current teacher education and professional development, as practiced in many universities and school districts, is neither training nor educative. It is, rather, dissemination of professional knowledge in traditional ways and at specified times. If we are to prepare adaptive teachers who use judgment to change practices when necessary, we must change what we teach teachers, how we teach, and when we teach. Making these changes, as I show below, will be difficult.

Thinking Differently About *What* We Teach Teachers

Most professional development efforts, whether of the preservice or inservice variety, disseminate knowledge about various aspects of effective reading instruction. Yet while professional knowledge is essential, simply disseminating it does not prepare teachers to be adaptive when things go awry. Two elements are important.

"Knowing About" vs. "Transforming" Professional Knowledge

Traditionally, it has been assumed that knowledge is the key to improved teaching. Yet if knowledge alone were the key, we could script instruction. What makes scripts less effective than good teachers is that good teachers do what scripts cannot do—they take charge of professional knowledge, manipulate it, and adapt it to changing instructional situations. Hence, it is not enough to simply possess knowledge. As Coulter and Wiens (2002) say, the important thing is judgment and the ability to act on judgments. Shulman (1990) calls this the "critical interpretation and transformation" of professional knowledge. That is, as instructional situations change, teachers transform knowledge to fit the situation, often on a case-by-case basis. Consequently, our professional development goal should not be to simply disseminate knowledge to teachers; it should be to teach teachers to make judgments about how to modify or adapt professional knowledge to fit changing situations.

Two examples of transforming knowledge in reading are illustrative. First, research specified earlier in this chapter establishes that effective reading teachers are not disciples of a particular reading theory, philosophy, method, or set of materials, just as they are not compliant followers of instructional scripts. Rather, they "see the point" of various practices, use judgment to select from them when adjustments become necessary, and adaptively apply them rather than faithfully following certain tenets or procedures regardless of situational conditions. Although they may favor a particular philosophy, approach, or program, when "push comes to shove" they are eclectic, deciding what to do by reference not to a particular authority or procedure but to what students need in any given situation. For instance, the most effective reading teachers use whole-language practices when the situation calls for those and behaviorist practices when the situation calls for those.

Similarly, "standards" specifying what teachers should know are not adequate in themselves. Of course teachers should "know about" child development, learning, curriculum, the structure of language, literacy, and pedagogical techniques, to name just a few. Ultimately, however, teachers must be able to adapt and modify knowledge when situations change. In this sense, the most important "standard" for teachers is the ability to use professional knowledge in uniquely different ways when faced with different instructional situations and different students.

Developing Strength to Transform Knowledge

It takes mental and emotional strength to transform knowledge. Teachers transform knowledge in their classrooms by themselves and, as Cuban (1992) points out, it takes strength to act alone. This is especially true in classrooms, where making a judgment to choose one approach or method or technique over other alternatives invariably raises conflicts with competing values, commitments, expectations, and preferences. Dealing with these requires spirit, risk taking, courage, and a vision that sustains one (Duffy, 1998, 2002; Hammerness, 2001). Grossman and Valencia et al. (1999) observed this strength and spirit when they saw a neophyte graduate of their preservice program persist in using a particular literacy technique even after an authority figure in an inservice program "blasted" it. Cuban (1992) says that making such decisions is "a tightrope walk" because teachers walk the rope alone while juggling competing demands, pressures, and expectations. If we expect teachers to be autonomous decision makers, our professional development efforts must develop the strength to walk this tightrope.

Summary

To be adaptive and responsive to the needs of at-risk students and/ or the demands of teaching high-level thinking, teachers cannot faithfully implement knowledge associated with particular methods, materials, programs, or authority figures. Instead, they must be able to transform that knowledge to fit different situations. To do so, they must be convinced that power resides in their professional judgment. This does not result from simply "knowing." It comes when teachers (a) are freed from the expectation that they must emulate mentors or follow commercial prescriptions; (b) learn to transform knowledge in ways that meet the needs of students and of curricular goals; and (c) develop the inner strength to do so in the midst of a constantly changing, highly charged, dilemma-ridden classroom where accountability and high-stakes testing often make for a hostile environment. These should be emphasized at both the preservice and inservice levels.

However, we cannot be naive about the difficulty of doing this. It is much more difficult to develop teachers who make judgments than to simply disseminate knowledge and test for it. It requires more investment and support. Consequently, teacher educators and staff developers who are comfortable in the traditional role of dispensing answers will find it difficult to abandon that role in favor of teaching teachers to use knowledge in what Shanahan and Neuman (1997) call "methodologically eclectic" ways. Similarly, we can expect resistance from those policy makers who prefer fast, easy, and inexpensive answers.

Thinking Differently About How We Teach Teachers

Professional development typically employs lecture methods; information is "delivered" to a relatively passive audience of teachers. However, this approach encourages teachers to think of themselves as working *under* and complying *with* others, in the same way that scripts encourage teachers to think of themselves as passive and compliant. Collaborative models tend to be more effective than lectures in developing teachers who think for themselves. This is because in collaborative models teachers are not passive recipients of information. Rather, they work *with* experts to construct responses to problems of teaching. In doing so, they learn to adapt what experts say, rather than complying with what they say.

Collaboration is promoted when three conditions are in place. First, collaboration is promoted when professional development is rooted in field-based inquiry. This does not mean that there are no university classes. It does mean, however, that professors, staff developers, principals, and teachers wrestle together with professional knowledge within the context of real problems encountered in real teaching situations (e.g., Lytle & Cochran-Smith, 1992; Santa & Santa, 1995). As a result, the "ivory tower" element that often divides professors and teachers is eliminated. Most important, however, school-based inquiry puts the emphasis on "transforming" knowledge, because what counts is making knowledge work in real classroom situations.

Second, collaboration is promoted when reflection is the focus. An "intellectual community" of teachers, principals, staff developers and teacher educators share dilemmas, hypotheses, and alternatives in what Huberman (1990) calls "conceptually informed discussions" (see also Duffy, 1994). Policy mandates and instructional recommendations are interpreted, not followed, and teachers—together with colleagues in administration, teacher education, and staff development—debate, discuss, and challenge in a process of ongoing problem solving.

Finally, collaboration is promoted when professional development is rooted in a spirit of egalitarian searching. Because the basic assumption is that there is no "quick fix," leaders are not thought of as "answer-givers." Instead, all participants contribute as equals.

Summary

A collaborative approach to professional development often poses a dilemma for those of us who teach teachers. Because we are accustomed to being "experts," we want teachers to do things *our* way. We want teachers to be empowered and autonomous, but not if that means doing something other than what we recommend.

Similarly, many policy makers have little patience for collaborative approaches to the problems of teaching reading. They prefer cut-and-dried answers to reading instruction, and they look to "scientifically based" programs to provide those answers. Nevertheless, as we have learned from studies of effective teaching, reading instruction is not cut-and-dried. Things seldom go as planned during reading instruction, so judgment, adaptation, responsiveness, and creativity are required. Policy makers have difficulty dealing with this reality because it does not lend itself to clean and quick answers. Consequently, rather than freeing teachers to think for themselves in response to students' needs, policy makers tend to lock teachers down.

Thinking Differently About <u>When</u> We Teach Teachers

Training models often assume specific beginnings and endings. Educative models, in contrast, are ongoing. Ongoing professional development is desirable for three reasons.

First, it takes a long time to learn to be an effective teacher. Because teaching occurs in an ill-structured domain, things are always more difficult than had been anticipated. As Greene (1991) has said:

> when we have our initial experiences with teaching in public schools, … we become sharply aware of limits, of structures and arrangements that cannot easily be surpassed. No matter how practical, how

grounded our educational courses were, they suddenly appear to be totally irrelevant in the concrete situation where we find ourselves. This is because general principles never fully apply to new and special situations. (p. 7)

Second, ongoing professional development is desirable because reading instruction is context-bound, with teaching demands changing as changes occur in schools and school districts. This is an enduring characteristic of teaching. We saw it decades ago in the Follow-Through study in which contextual differences from site to site resulted in more variance in student achievement within programs than between programs (House, Glass, McLean, & Walker, 1978), and we see it today in the work of Grossman, Thompson, and Valencia (in press) and Place (2001). The former documents how first- and second-year teachers are impacted by the context of their schools, while the latter documents how school context influences implementation of statewide policy mandates. As Berliner (2002) has recently said, "schools are embedded in complex and changing networks of social interaction" (p. 19). Those changing networks make continuing professional development necessary.

Finally, ongoing professional development is necessary because of the interdependent nature of classrooms. As Hoffman (1998) demonstrated in a study of "why bad things happen to good ideas in literacy education," one good idea interacts with other conditions in the teaching environment, requiring that those then be adjusted. It is a constant process of one innovation making still other innovations necessary. The process goes on and on.

Summary

Professional development cannot be a "one-shot deal." On the contrary, perhaps the most important aspect of teaching is that one never reaches perfection, and that constant striving to learn and improve is part of the job. As Van Manen (1996) points out, change is a given in the life of a teacher. Therefore, ongoing professional development makes sense.

However, this idea, too, encounters resistance. First, it means that we must rethink roles, with principals and teachers carrying as much responsibility as teacher educators and staff developers. Second, we must think differently about whether achieving "permanent" certification means that there is no longer a need to learn how to teach.

This difficulty pales in comparison to policy makers' problems with ongoing professional development. They see immediately that it requires a significantly larger financial investment in teachers, and they know it will be difficult to convince politicians and tax payers of the importance of making such an investment.

Conclusion

The research evidence is clear. Although effective reading teachers operate from a base of routine procedures, their distinguishing feature is an ability to adapt instruction to fit situational needs. When the goal is improved achievement of at-risk children and development of higher order thinking, adaptive teaching is even more important.

Nevertheless, there is resistance to developing adaptive teachers, for two reasons. First, there is pressure to find a "quick fix" for children who currently fail in school. Because educating adaptive teachers is neither quick nor cheap, it is difficult to convince policy makers of the need to make the necessary investment. Second, the emotional nature of the literacy debate creates dissonance and resistance. As Cochran-Smith and Fries (2001) point out, teacher development debates are "driven by ideas, ideals, values, and assumptions about the purpose of schooling, the social and economic future of the nation, and the role of public education in a democratic society" (p. 3). Consequently, participants in the debate choose sides by reference to beliefs rather than data. Those who value simple concepts of literacy and quick-fix solutions are drawn to scripts and other highly directive forms of instruction because those programs promote their values; those who want taxes kept low are similarly drawn to highly directive commercial programs because they promise to eliminate the need for expensive teacher development; those who want to avoid the wrenching pain of change are drawn to maintaining traditional practices; and teachers and teacher advocates make teacher judgment a priority because they see teaching as a profession rather than as a technical endeavor. Consequently, while the research findings are compelling, both about what effective reading teachers do and about how to develop them, it will be difficult to translate these findings into practice because they conflict with values held by various and influential groups of stakeholders.

In sum, we cannot be naive. To improve reading achievement through professional development, we must start with the reality that the task is difficult, seek common ground to the extent that it is possible to do so, and then create a proactive agenda of what must be done, how to get started doing it, and how to muster the will and resources to sustain it. We hope that the following chapters in this book will provide a start toward achieving that goal.

References

Alllington, R. (2001). *What really matters for struggling readers: Designing research-based programs.* New York: Addison-Wesley.

Allington, R. (2002). Troubling times: A short historical perspective. In R. Allington (Ed.), *Big brother and the National Reading Curriculum: How ideology trumped evidence.* Portsmouth, NH: Heinemann.

Allington, R., & Johnston, P. (2002). *Reading to learn: Lessons from exemplary fourth-grade classrooms.* New York: Guilford.

Anders, P., Hoffman, J., & Duffy, G. (2000). Teaching teachers to teach reading: Paradigm shifts, persistent problems and challenges. In M. Kamil, P. Mosenthal, P. D. Pearson, & R. Barr (Eds.), *Handbook of reading research* (Vol. 3, pp. 719–742). Mahwah, NJ: Erlbaum.

Anders, P., & Richardson, V. (1991). Research directions: Staff development that empowers teachers' reflection and enhances instruction. *Language Arts, 68,* 316–321.

Anderson, L., Evertson, C., & Brophy, J. (1979). An experimental study of effective teaching in first grade reading. *Elementary School Journal, 79,* 193–223.

Anderson, R., & Pearson, P. D. (1984). A schema-theoretic view of basic processes in reading. In P. D. Pearson, R. Barr, M. Kamil, & P. Mosenthal (Eds.), *Handbook of reading research* (Vol. 1, pp. 255–291). New York: Longman.

Ashton, P., & Crocker, L. (1987). Systematic study of planned variations: The essential focus of teacher education reform. *Journal of Teacher Education, 38,* 32–38.

Berliner, D. (2002). Educational research: The hardest science of all. *Educational Researcher, 31,* 18–20.

Berliner, D., & Biddle, B. (1996). *The manufactured crisis.* New York: Longman.

Bloome, D., & Green, J. (1984). Directions in the sociolinguistic study of reading. In P. D. Pearson, R. Barr, M. Kamil, & P. Mosenthal (Eds.), *Handbook of reading research* (Vol. 1, pp. 395–421). New York: Longman.

Bond, G., & Dykstra, R. (1967). The cooperative research program in first-grade reading instruction. *Reading Research Quarterly, 2,* 1–142.

Bracey, G. (1997). The seventh Bracey report on the condition of public education. *Phi Delta Kappan, 79,* 120–137.

Brice-Heath, S. (1994). The children of Tracton's children: Spoken and written language in social change. In R. Ruddell, M. Ruddell, & H. Singer (Eds.), *Theoretical models and processes of reading* (4th ed). Newark, DE: International Reading Association.

Brophy, J., & Good, T. (1986). Teacher behaviors and student achievement. In M. C. Wittrock (Ed.), *Handbook of research on teaching* (3rd ed., pp. 328–375). New York: Macmillan.

Brown, S., Collins, A., & Duguid, P. (1989). Situated cognition and the culture of learning. *Educational Researcher, 18*, 32–42.

Bruschi, B., & Coley, R. (1999). *How teachers compare: The prose, document and quantitative skills of America's teachers.* Princeton, NJ: Educational Testing Service, Policy Information Center.

Buchmann, M. (1990). Beyond the lonely, choosing will: Professional development in teacher thinking. *Teachers College Record, 91*, 481–508.

Cazden, C. (1986). Classroom discourse. In M. Wittrock (Ed.), *Handbook of research on teaching* (3rd ed., pp. 432–463). New York: Macmillan.

Clark, C., & Peterson, P. (1986). Teachers' thought processes. In M. Wittrock (Ed.), *Handbook of research on teaching* (3rd ed., pp. 255–296). New York: Macmillan.

Cochran-Smith, M., & Fries, M. (2001). Sticks and stones, and ideology: The discourse of reform in teacher education. *Educational Researcher, 30*, 3–15.

Coulter, D., & Wiens, J. (2002). Educational judgment: Linking the actor and the spectator. *Educational Researcher, 31*, 15–25.

Cuban, L. (1992). Managing dilemmas while building professional communities. *Educational Researcher, 21*, 4–11.

Darling-Hammond, L. (2002, September 6). Research and rhetoric on teacher certification: A response to "Teacher certification reconsidered." *Education Policy Analysis Archives, 10* (36), 1.

Darling-Hammond, L., & Youngs, P. (2002). Defining "highly qualified teachers": What does "scientifically based research" actually tell us? *Educational Researcher, 31*, 13–25.

Dillon, D. (1989). Showing them what I want them to learn and that I care who they are: A microethnography of the social organization of a secondary low-track English-reading classroom. *American Educational Research Journal, 26*, 227–261.

Duffy, G. (1993a). Re-thinking strategy instruction: Teacher development and low achievers' understandings. *Elementary School Journal, 93*, 231–247.

Duffy, G. (1993b). Teachers' progress toward becoming expert strategy teachers. *Elementary School Journal, 94*, 109–120.

Duffy, G. (1994). How teachers think of themselves: A key to mindfulness. In J. Mangieri & C. Collins-Block (Eds.), *Creating powerful thinking in teachers and students: Diverse perspectives.* Fort Worth, TX: Holt, Rinehart & Winston.

Duffy, G. (1998). Teaching and the balancing of round stones. *Phi Delta Kappan, 79*, 777–780.

Duffy, G. (2002). Visioning and the development of outstanding teachers. *Reading Research and Instruction, 41*, 331–343.

Duffy, G., Roehler, L., Sivan, E., Rackliffe, G., Book, C., Meloth, M., Vavrus, L., Wesselman, R., Putnam, J., & Bassiri, D. (1987). Effects of explaining the reasoning associated with using reading strategies. *Reading Research Quarterly, 22*, 347–368.

Eisner, E. (1999). The use and limits of performance assessment. *Phi Delta Kappan, 80*, 658–661.

Elley, W. (1992). *How in the world do students read? IEA study of reading literacy.* The Hague, Netherlands: International Association for Evaluation of Educational Achievement.

Elmore, R. (1992). Why restructuring alone won't improve teaching. *Educational Leadership, 49*, 44–48.

Finn, C. (2002, October 6). Teachers vs. better schools. *New York Post* [On-line]. Available: http://www.nypost.com/cgibin/printfriendly.pl

Garrison, J. (1997). *Dewey and Eros: Wisdom and desire in the art of teaching.* New York: Teachers College Press.

Goodman, K., & Goodman, Y. (1979). Learning to read is natural. In L. Resnick & P. Weaver (Eds.), *Theory and practice of early reading* (Vol. 1, pp. 137–154). Hillsdale, NJ: Erlbaum.

Greene, M. (1991). Teaching: The question of personal reality. In A. Lieberman & L. Miller (Eds.), *Staff development for education in the 90's: New demands, new realities, new perspectives* (pp. 3–14). New York: Teachers College Press.

Grissmer, D., Kirby, S., Berends, M., & Williamson, S. (1994). *Student achievement and the changing American family.* Santa Monica, CA: RAND Institute on Education and Training.

Grossman, P., Thompson, C., & Valencia, S. (in press). Focusing the concerns of new teachers: The district as teacher educator. In M. Knapp, M. McLaughlin, J. Marsh, & A. Hightower (Eds.), *School districts and instructional renewal: Opening the conversation.* New York: Teachers College Press.

Grossman, P., Valencia, S., Evans, K., Thompson, C., Martin, S., & Place, N. (1999, December). *Transitions into teaching: Learning to teach writing in teacher education and beyond.* Paper presented at the annual conference of the National Reading Conference, Orlando, FL.

Hammerness, K. (2001). Learning to hope or hoping to learn? The role of vision in teachers' early professional lives. *Journal of Educational Change, 2*, 143–163.

Hoffman, J. (1998). When bad things happen to good ideas in literacy education: Professional dilemmas, personal decisions and political traps. *The Reading Teacher, 52*, 102–113.

Hoffman, J., Edwards, S., O'Neal, S., Barnes, S., & Paulissen, M. (1986). A study of state-mandated beginning teacher programs. *Journal of Teacher Education, 37*, 16–21.

Hoffman, J., & Pearson, P. D. (2000). Reading teacher education in the next millennium: What your grandmother's teacher didn't know that your granddaughter's teacher should. *Reading Research Quarterly, 35*(1), 28–44.

House, E., Glass, G., McLean, L., & Walker, D. (1978). No simple answer: Critique of follow through evaluation. *Harvard Educational Review, 48*, 128–160.

Huberman, M. (1990). Linkage between researchers and practitioners: A qualitative study. *American Educational Research Journal, 27*, 363–391.

Jones, E., Gottfredson, G., & Gottfredson, D. (1997). Success for some: An evaluation of the Success for All Program. *Evaluation Review, 21*, 643–670.

Langer, J. (2001). Beating the odds: Teaching middle school and high school students to read and write well. *American Educational Research Journal, 38*, 837–880.

Lyon, G. R. (1997). Statement of G. Reid Lyon, Ph.D., before the Committee on Education and the Workforce, U.S. House of Representatives, National Institute of Child Health and Human Development, National Institute of Health, Bethesda, MD.

Lytle, S., & Cochran-Smith, M. (1992). Teacher research as a way of knowing. *Harvard Education Review, 62*, 447–474.

McVee, M., & Pearson, P. D. (1997, December). *Exploring alternative assessments in an ESL setting: Researchers, teachers and students learning to use portfolios.* Paper presented at the annual conference of the National Reading Conference, Scottsdale, AZ.

Moats, L. (2000). *Whole language lives on: The illusion of "balanced" instruction.* New York: Thomas Fordham Foundation.

Moll, L. (1994). Literacy research in community and classrooms: A sociocultural approach. In R. Ruddell, M. Ruddell, & H. Singer (Eds.), *Theoretical models and processes of reading* (4th ed.). Newark, DE: International Reading Association.

Mosenthal, J., Lipson, M., Mekkelsen, J., Russ, B., & Sartino, S. (2001). *Elementary schools where students succeed in reading.* Providence, RI: LAB at Brown.

National Center for Educational Statistics. (1999). *The condition of education, 1997.* Washington, DC: U.S. Department of Education.

National Center for Educational Statistics. (2002). *Highlights from the 2000 program for international student assessment.* (NCES 2002-116). Washington, DC: U.S. Department of Education.

National Commission on Teaching and America's Future (1997). *Doing what matters most: Investing in quality teaching.* New York: Author.

National Institute of Child Health and Human Development (NICHHD). (2000). *Report of the National Reading Panel. Teaching children to read: An evidence-based assessment of the scientific research literature on reading and its implications for reading instruction.* (NIH Publication No. 00-4769). Washington, D.C.: U.S. Government Printing Office.

Petty, R. (1995). Attitude change. In A. Tesser (Ed.), *Advanced social psychology* (pp. 195–256). Boston: McGraw-Hill.

Place, N. (2001, December). *Policy in action: The influence of mandated early reading assessment on teachers' thinking and practice.* Paper presented at the annual conference of the National Reading Conference, San Antonio, TX.

Prawat, R. (1991). The value of ideas: The immersion approach to the development of thinking. *Educational Researcher, 20,* 3–10.

Pressley, M., El-Dinary, P., Gaskins, I., Schuder, T., Bergman, J., Almasi, L., & Brown, R. (1992). Beyond direct explanation: Transactional instruction of reading comprehension strategies. *Elementary School Journal, 92,* 511–554.

Richardson, V., & Placier, P. (2001). Teacher change. In V. Richardson (Ed.), *Handbook of research on teaching* (4th ed.). Washington, DC: American Educational Research Association.

Roller, C., & Hoffman, J. (2002, May). *National Commission on Excellence in Elementary Teacher Preparation in Reading Instruction: An update.* Paper presented at the annual meeting of the International Reading Association, San Francisco.

Santa, C., & Santa, J. (1995). Critical issues: Teacher as researcher. *Journal of Reading Behavior: A Journal of Literacy, 27,* 3.

Shanahan, T., & Neuman, S. (1997). Conversations: Literacy research that makes a difference. *Reading Research Quarterly, 32,* 202–211.

Shulman, L. (1990, April). *The transformation of knowledge: A model of pedagogical reasoning and action.* Paper presented at the annual conference of the American Educational Research Association, San Francisco.

Snow, C. (2001). Preventing reading difficulties in young children: Precursors and fallout. In T. Loveless (Ed.), *The great curriculum debate* (pp. 229–246). Washington, DC: Brookings Institution.

Snow, C., Burns, M., & Griffin, P. (Eds.). (1998). *Preventing reading difficulties in young children: A report of the National Research Council.* Washington, DC: National Academy Press.

Strauss, V. (2002, September 10). Phonics pitch irks teachers: U.S. denies it's pushing commercial products. *The Washington Post,* A1.

U.S. Department of Education. (2002). *Meeting the highly qualified teachers challenge: The Secretary's annual report on teacher quality.* Washington, DC: U.S. Department of Education, Office of Postsecondary Education, Office of Policy, Planning and Innovation.

Van Manen, M. (1996). Fit for teaching. In W. Hare & J. Portelli (Eds.), *Philosophy of education: Introductory readings* (2nd ed., pp. 29–50). Calgary, Alberta, Canada: Detselig.

Walsh, K. (2001). *Teacher certification reconsidered: Stumbling for quality.* Baltimore, MD: Abell Foundation.

Wharton-McDonald, R., Pressley, M., & Hampston, J. (1998). Literacy instruction in nine first grade classrooms: Teacher characteristics and student achievement. *Elementary School Journal, 99,* 101–128.

• •

The author wishes to thank the following persons for their helpful contributions during the writing of this paper: Richard Allington, Auleen Duffy, James Hoffman, Michael Kamil, Misty Sailors, and Sheila Valencia.

• •

Chapter **2**

Sources of Standards for Teacher Preparation

. . . .

Cathy M. Roller and James V. Hoffman

Key Ideas

✓ Standards-based reform that began in the K–12 arena is now moving into teacher preparation.

✓ There are four sources of standards for teacher preparation: consensus, student standards, instructional research on best practices, and research.

✓ The extant research is not sufficient for strong research-based teacher preparation standards.

For

- Teacher educators
- Teachers

What do teachers and administrators need to know and be able to do in order to provide quality literacy instruction at various educational levels? How do we determine what it is that teachers and administrators need to know and be able to do? These questions raise issues that were the focus of the National Invitational Conference on Improving Reading Achievement Through Professional Development. Our task in this chapter is to examine the implications of what we know about standards and professional development for addressing these critical questions. In order to do that we will first review the course of standards-based reform and how it arrived at teacher professional development as central to the success of reform. Then we will turn specifically to the issue of teacher standards and the various sources for grounding them. Finally, we will argue that research specifically focused on teacher preparation and student achievement is essential to moving the field forward.

The Course of Standards-Based Reform

The standards-based movement is in full swing at the public school level. The logic of standards-based reform is deceptively simple. Set clear goals (i.e., standards) and assess them. If standards and assessments are aligned, teachers and students will achieve the goals—meet the standards. Standards determine what students should learn; the assessments determine whether the students have learned it. If they haven't learned it, then the system must change to allow students to meet the standards. The logic is intuitively appealing and easy to illustrate. For example, consider the following goal: children will identify the 50 state capitals. Assume also that students will take a written test that involves providing the capitals for each of the 50 states. Given such a standard and knowledge of the written test, teachers and students would work together to learn the capitals of the 50 states, and after instruction the test would determine if the children could supply the 50 state capitals. Most likely, the children would learn the 50 state capitals. They might even be better at the task than adults who have been confused by the knowledge of more than one large city in each state.

However, standards-based reform may not be the panacea that some have promised. As witnessed by the current reform movement, what is simple and logical is not always realistic (Strickland, 2001). Despite a decade and more of work with standards and assessments, reading achievement is only slightly improved, and the achievement gap between majority and minority students continues. Two of the important targets of standards-based reform seem quite resistant to improvement. Standards-based reform is much more complicated than learning the 50 state capitals.

The problem with the simple logic of standards-based reform is that none of the seemingly simple tasks—setting standards, teaching students, assessing students, and making corrections—is simple. Deciding what children should know and be able to do, setting standards, is a values-fraught enterprise that almost certainly involves political conflict and compromise. There are many stakeholders who want to decide what children should know and be able to do. There are often conflicts over whether students should be responsible for knowing facts and information or whether they should be able to evaluate information, solve problems, and make well-informed decisions. There is much that would be useful for students to know, and certainly there is much more to know than can actually be learned. The task of writing standards is the task of prioritizing, and there are many different stakeholders with priorities—parents, professional organizations, businesspeople, policy makers, and so forth.

A second issue is the development of assessments. Assuming that the standards are developed (and indeed they have been developed, in 49 of the 50 states), valid and reliable standards-based assessments are difficult and expensive to develop. Many educators would prefer to use authentic performance-based assessments, whereas others argue that such assessments are too costly both in time and money and that group standardized multiple-choice tests are adequate for the purposes of standards-based reform. Most states choose to evaluate particular standards at particular intervals (e.g., math and reading at 3rd, 5th, 8th, and 10th grades). However, current federal law requires yearly evaluation of math and reading achievement, and yearly assessment of science will be added in 2006. One of the clear issues in assessment is whether the states have the capacity to implement these yearly assessment programs. Recent errors in scoring (e.g., hundreds of Minnesota students were mistakenly denied a diploma due to test scoring mistakes [*Examiner,* 2000]) and test companies' inability to provide results in a timely manner (e.g., a national testing company nearly lost its contract with Georgia last year because it returned Stanford 9 results so late that they were virtually useless for assessing student performance [Salzer, 2002]) suggest that capacity is a very real issue.

Finally, making corrections when assessments indicate that standards are not being met is a complex process. Rarely do the assessments provide adequate information for locating the difficulties and addressing them. There is a general assumption that instruction must be changed, but there is little in either the standards or the assessments to guide instructional change. Until recently teaching and instruction received little attention from reformers:

> Reformers have initiated school reforms without thinking about teaching reforms. Reformers too often incorrectly assume that reducing class sizes, raising student standards, or creating small schools could be accomplished in a vacuum without teachers. However, studies confirm that the quality of teaching is the single most important factor in closing the student achievement gap. (Nogura & Brown, 2002)

Because of the lack of progress and the accompanying frustration with standards-based reform, there is now a strong consensus that teachers and instruction are crucial to successful reform, and the quality of teacher preparation programs and professional development programs are now in the spotlight. There is recognition that if teachers do not have a good understanding of standards and do not know how to teach to them, then neither standards nor any amount of assessment will improve the situation. Earlier models of reform that presumed a simple causal relationship from content standards to assessment and improved achievement have been replaced by more complex conceptualizations that focus on curriculum and instruction and include roles for professional development, standards for teacher licensure, and standards for teacher education accreditation (Pearson, 2001). There is a strong consensus that teacher quality makes a difference (Whitehurst, 2002). Consistent with the pattern of standards-based reform, once the focus shifted to teachers and instruction, standards for teacher preparation and professional development became an important object of the reform movement.

Sources for Teacher Standards

We began this chapter with two questions: What do teachers and administrators need to know and be able to do in order to provide quality literacy instruction at various educational levels? How do we determine what it is that teachers and administrators need to know and be able to do? There is a peril, for both students and the profession, in rushing to answer the first question without careful exploration of the second. In other words, before we set standards and move, we must be certain that standards are valid. To ensure that our initiatives for reform will result in the changes we all desire, we must create a plan for developing standards that considers all possible knowledge sources. Pearson (2001) has argued, and we concur, that there are four plausible sources for teacher standards: (a) professional consensus, (b) student standards, (c) instructional research on best practices, and (d) research. We now turn to exploring each of these sources for developing teacher standards for preparation and professional development.

Relying on Professional Consensus

Historically, the field has relied on consensus processes to develop standards. The International Reading Association produced the first set of standards for reading teachers in 1986 (*Guidelines for the Specialized Preparation of Reading Professionals*). These have been revised periodically, most recently in 2003. In addition, the National Council for Accreditation of Teacher Education (NCATE) has produced standards for elementary school teachers that include standards for the teaching of reading. There are Interstate New Teacher Assessment and Support Consortium (INTASC) standards and National Board for Professional Teaching Standards (NBPTS) guidelines. In each state, there are licensure and certification regulations that essentially are standards prescribing the content of teacher preparation programs. The National Council of Teachers of English (NCTE) also has standards for the preparation of English teachers that include the teaching of reading. In addition, several recent publications include lists and specifications for what teachers of reading should know and be able to do: *Every Child Reading: A Professional Development Guide* (Learning First Alliance, 2000); *Preventing Reading Difficulties in Young Children* (Snow, Burns, & Griffin, 1998); *Excellent Reading Teachers: A Position Statement of the International Reading Association* (International Reading Association, 2000); *Characteristics of Teachers Who Are Effective in Teaching All Children to Read* (Taylor, 2002), *Preparing Teachers to Teach Reading Effectively* (California State University, 2002); and *Reading Instruction and Assessment: Understanding the IRA Standards* (Armbruster & Osborn, 2002).

Our problem is not that we have no teacher standards but rather that we have a plethora of standards and a cacophony of voices answering the question "What do teachers and administrators need to know and be able to do in order to provide quality literacy instruction at various educational levels?" We have many groups of knowledgeable professionals coming together to negotiate a set of proposed standards or guidelines, producing draft documents to be sent to many different groups and people for feedback, repeating the process until consensus is declared and a document is published. However, as the long but not exhaustive list of teacher standards documents above suggests, the notion of consensus may be hyperbolic in this context.

What we have is many alternative lists of standards all vying for recognition. For many years reading professionals were content to have the International Reading Association use a consensus process to develop standards for reading professionals. Many teacher educators turned to those standards for guidelines in developing their teacher preparation programs. The proliferation of standards documents suggests that the consensus process is simply no longer convincing. Reading instruction and the professional development of reading teachers is suddenly so important that it cannot be left to reading professionals.

Instead, we have influential panels convened by the National Academy of Sciences, panels legislated by the United States Congress, and groups of professional associations such as the Learning First Alliance (which does not include the International Reading Association, although the IRA was invited to provide feedback and endorsed *Every Child Reading: A Professional Development Guide*), all claiming the right to produce standards for reading teachers. Each of the national teachers' unions has documents related to reading teacher professional development, and indeed the American Federation of Teachers is providing professional development for reading teachers. Even the International Reading Association felt it necessary to develop a position paper about the characteristics of excellent reading teachers. The problem of answering important questions by consensus is that consensus works only when there really *is* a consensus and when there is a recognized entity with the authority to determine the answers.

Aligning Teacher Standards With Student Standards

The second source of insight from Pearson's list, aligning teacher standards with student standards, makes good sense. When teacher standards are derived from student standards, teacher licensure and teacher education accreditation standards ensure that teachers will know and be able to do whatever is required for students to meet standards. There is some indication from very specific studies, such as those of the National Reading Panel (NICHHD, 2000), that such alignment can produce improvement in student achievement. In addition, Cohen and Hill (cited in Whitehurst, 2002) found positive effects of alignment in mathematics instruction. They

compared the effects of teacher participation in professional development specifically targeted to a mathematics reform initiative in
California and issues workshops that were not linked to the content
of the mathematics initiative. The more time teachers spent in targeted training on the framework and curriculum of mathematics reform, the more their classroom practices changed in ways that were
consistent with the mathematics reform, and the more they learned
about the content and standards for that reform. Teachers who participated in the focused training and whose classroom practice moved
towards incorporating the framework of the new math initiative had
students who scored higher on a test of the math concepts imparted
by the new curriculum. (p. 7)

However, we should note that most student standards are developed through a process of consensus (often of parents, politicians,
businesspeople, and educators). Turning to student standards as
sources for teacher standards makes eminent good sense, but the
derived teacher standards will be no more convincing than the consensus behind the student standards themselves. In many cases
the student standards reflect the input of conflicting stakeholders,
and the resulting standards represent compromise reflected in general language that makes standards very difficult to interpret
(Placier, Walker, & Foster, 2002). Aligning teacher standards to
such general student standards may not be effective.

Drawing on Best Practices

The third potential source for developing teacher standards is
grounded in the work on effective practices. Given that we know
effective practices for teaching reading, teacher standards require
that teachers know and are able to do whatever is necessary to
implement those practices. Most recently, in the implementation of
Reading First (Part B of the No Child Left Behind Act, P.L. 107-
110), the federal government has opted for the use of this source.
Drawing on the findings of the National Reading Panel (NICHHD,
2000) on effective practices in the areas of phonemic awareness,
phonics, fluency, vocabulary, and comprehension, the law mandates
that states receiving Reading First funds must offer professional
development and technical assistance grounded in scientifically
based research and must include professional development related
to five essential components: phonemic awareness, phonics, fluency, vocabulary, and comprehension. The Panel concluded that
certain instructional practices improve student performance in reading, and thus the law requires professional development that enables teachers to use the identified practices. The law also includes

a state review of teacher preparation programs to determine if the programs are based on scientifically based reading research and include appropriate preparation in the five essential elements.

However, the Panel did not claim that the list of practices identified in their report was exhaustive or represented sufficient knowledge for the delivery of optimal reading instruction. Because of the large domain involved in reading research, they were able to investigate only a portion of the topics they had identified as worthy of study. The Panel's report tells us that knowledge of the identified practices should be included in teachers' knowledge base and implemented in their practice, but it does not say either how these practices should be combined or what additional knowledge and practices are necessary. Best practices in the five essential components may be a necessary aspect of teacher knowledge, but the argument that they are sufficient cannot be supported. In the long run, knowledge of best practices cannot be sufficient for defining teachers' knowledge base.

Grounding Teacher Standards in Research

Ideally, following Pearson's scheme, we would also draw on research for developing standards for teacher licensure and teacher education accreditation. To do this, we would need research documenting that teachers who possess a certain body of knowledge (what teachers know), and who demonstrate the use of best practices (what teachers should be able to do) actually do promote higher levels of student learning. Although we would like to rely on such research, the existing studies that have been recently reviewed (Anders, Hoffman, & Duffy, 2000; Darling-Hammond, 1999; Hoffman & Pearson, 2000; Pearson, 2001) have highlighted the paucity of research in the area of teacher preparation and professional development. We have a recent survey of the state of practice (Hoffman & Roller, 2001). We also have several groundbreaking studies, such as those conducted by the National Commission on Teaching and America's Future (Darling-Hammond, 2000a, 2000b, 2000c), which have provided case studies of excellent teacher preparation programs. Grossman et al. (2000) have extended that work by following teachers from two preparation programs through the first four years of their teaching careers. These provide rich descriptions of excellence in teacher preparation that are highly useful in program design, program evaluation, and program revision. However, none of the extant case studies connect teacher preparation ultimately to student reading achievement.

To date the research addressing the relationship between teacher preparation and student achievement is at either a very general or a very specific level. For example, there are large correlational studies examining such proxies for teacher knowledge as teacher major in content area, general knowledge and ability, certification and licensure, experience, and master's degree. Most of these studies work with extant data, and there is no attempt to actually specify the knowledge base represented by major, content area, general knowledge and ability, certification and licensure, experience, or master's degree. In a paper delivered at the White House Conference on Preparing Tomorrow's Teachers, Whitehurst (2002) concluded that, with the exception of certification and licensure, there is evidence that these proxies are associated with higher student achievement. Recently, Laczko-Kerr and Berliner (2002) reported that students of fully certified teachers had higher achievement scores than those students who had teachers licensed through alternative certification paths. The general conclusion is that teacher knowledge as represented by these proxies does affect student achievement. However, the large data bases used in these studies do little to specify the knowledge represented by those proxy variables, and the results are aggregated across subject areas and often do not address reading instruction.

At the other extreme there are very specific studies, such as the four studies reviewed by the National Reading Panel (NICHHD, 2000). These studies focused on the preparation of teachers for conducting reading comprehension strategy instruction. The Panel concluded that "intensive instruction of teachers can prepare them to teach reading comprehension strategically and that such teaching can lead students to greater awareness of what it means to be a strategic reader and to the goal of improved comprehension" (p. 125). However, even in these four specific studies the teacher knowledge base varied greatly depending on the particular approach to comprehension strategy instruction used. The findings were similar for the 32 studies reviewed in the teacher education chapter of the Report. Based on these very general and very specific studies, we conclude that teacher knowledge and preparation can make a difference, but both types of studies leave us far from actually specifying the essential teacher knowledge and practices that lead to improved student reading achievement.

The International Reading Association's National Commission on Excellence in Elementary Teacher Preparation is conducting one promising effort in this area. It is alone in examining the relationship between teachers' preparation for reading instruction and their students' reading achievement. The study followed beginning reading teachers from eight excellent reading teacher preparation programs through their first three years of teaching, and in the third year collected reading achievement data from these teachers' students. At three of the sites there were existing general teacher preparation programs to provide comparison with teachers whose programs were not focused on reading instruction. In addition, comparison teachers were recruited from the schools where the program's beginning teachers were teaching. In the first year of the study the Commission collected interview data at the beginning, middle, and end of the year, and did a cross-site analysis of the features of the eight teacher preparation programs. In the second year, data collection included both interviews and classroom observations, and in the third year the data collected included interviews, observations, and student achievement data.

The "Features of Excellence"—features of the Commission programs that were present in the various programs to some extent (Harmon et al., 2001)—characterize the content and practices that the beginning teachers encountered in their programs. The data collected from the first-year interviews found that program teachers talked quite differently about their children's reading progress. Rather than referring to student progress in general terms (e.g., "they're doing great," "they really love reading") the program's beginning teachers used the specific vocabulary of reading instruction (e.g., "I have one group that still has decoding problems") and talked about individual and small groups of children rather than answering the questions of progress at the class level (Maloch et al., 2003).

The second-year observation data indicated that the program teachers' classrooms were richer in print environments and that the children and teachers from the program classrooms had a deeper understanding of the uses of the texts in their classrooms. The third-year data are currently being analyzed. The design of the study will allow us to make some specific statements about what reading teachers know and are able to do and how that relates to student reading achievement.

Setting the Research Agenda

The logic of this chapter suggests that research-proven teacher standards are crucial to achieving consensus and moving the field forward. We would like to know that a certain body of knowledge and practice ultimately leads to higher student reading achievement.

The present proliferation of standards has no arbiter. Instead we have competing voices declaring that their standards are "the" standards. What is required is a research program that identifies crucial teacher knowledge and practices in reading and then systematically tests whether teachers with that knowledge produce better reading achievement in controlled experiments, quasi-experiments, and planned variation studies.

Clearly there is great interest and significant funding for improving teacher preparation programs. However, there does not seem to be a commitment to testing a variety of approaches selected by an empirical analysis of teacher preparation programs and the knowledge bases and practices they include in their preparation programs. Although there is ample rhetoric, deep conviction, in some cases vitriolic criticism, and even substantial funds devoted to improving teacher preparation, there is currently no major funding for research on teacher preparation for reading instruction. Given the high focus on reading instruction, the continual commentary on the importance of teacher quality, the focus on professional development in reading in the No Child Left Behind Act (Public Law 107-110), and the frequent disparagement of teacher preparation programs, it is perhaps reasonable to predict that significant funding for research on teacher preparation for reading instruction is imminent. We hope so.

We are not arguing that the field should stand still until a research program on teacher preparation and its effects on student reading achievement can be completed. There is much that we know about excellent reading instruction, and reading professionals do have enough knowledge at hand to prepare teachers to teach reading well. We must move forward. There are too many children in school now who must be taught to read. They cannot be allowed to endure poor reading instruction until we have an unequivocal answer to the question "What do teachers and administrators need to know and be able to do in order to provide quality literacy instruction at various educational levels?" What we are arguing is that we must simultaneously have a major research effort that in the end will provide a convincing answer to this question.

Formulating, implementing, and interpreting a basic research agenda for teacher education that has the potential to guide reform will take time and money and a commitment from the teacher education community. Unfortunately, there is no time, there is little money, and there is division within the teacher education community about the best way to proceed. We are left to choose from three options:

1. Initiate a plan for reform in teacher education that represents our best guess at what works. Design and implement programs, gather baseline and follow-up data, and evaluate the effectiveness of the reform effort. The problem with this plan is that it is an all-or-nothing proposition that ignores existing effective practices and traditions. It is guided by ignorance and politics—not a promising formula for success and not something on which you want to risk the intellectual lives of children. It also relegates to the sidelines all of the teacher educators and teacher education programs that may follow a different philosophy and plan.

2. Identify two or three competing plans for reform and initiate a reform effort around a study that will once and for all determine the best way to prepare teachers. We have ample evidence from the past (e.g., first-grade studies in reading) that such a "horserace" comparison mentality yields little value and even less in the way of a consensus among teacher educators that can support reform on a national scale.

3. Identify multiple models for teacher preparation that are in operation and that show evidence of effectiveness. Initiate reform efforts with multiple models and conduct a planned variation study that is focused not just on which model is the best but on the identification of program features that contribute to teacher learning and student achievement.

This third option holds the most promise to address the need for evidence-based reform that is timely to the issues of reform in teacher preparation. This research model would follow the design of the Follow-Through Evaluation Studies (Stallings & Kaskowitz, 1974). The Follow-Through research study involved 108 first-grade and 58 third-grade classes taught by experienced teachers who were implementing one of seven Follow-Through models. This study is regarded by experts in the field of research in teaching (e.g., Brophy & Good, 1986) as foundational to process-product research. This model was effective because of its broad focus on effective processes nested within particular program contexts (e.g., direct instruction models). It was less a case of competition between models than it was a case of examining the links to student outcomes. Each of the models in the Follow-Through study had an existing research, intellectual, and practice base on which to build. Those implementing the models had an investment in its success, but the research team operated independently of the particular models.

This same model for research could be applied to reform in teacher education. It would build a knowledge base around effective practices. It would be consensus building, not dividing, within the teacher education community because it would value our traditions and our excellence, as these exist today. We have, through the International Reading Association study of teacher preparation, developed a framework for teacher preparation that shows evidence of promise. It is a model that we believe merits further exploration and scrutiny through a follow-through—a planned variation research investigation. We do not take the position that our framework is perfect or nearly complete, only that it is worthy of building upon. We believe that there are other models that should be examined similarly, with the goal of eventually building a new consensus on effective teacher preparation.

Models of Teacher Preparation

It is illustrative at this point to suggest the range of possible models for teacher preparation that might be explored through a planned variation study. These models might include the following:

1. **A Standards Model.**   Several states are pursuing the idea the idea that reform in teacher education should be focused on the infusion of the content of the state curriculum for elementary school-age students into the teacher education curriculum. Alignment of the content and processes of the teacher education program with the content and processes of the public school curriculum is key here. Teacher education programs and graduates are held accountable for their knowledge and skill in these areas (chiefly through the testing and certification requirements for students, but also through program accreditation standards).

2. **A Fifth-Year Post-Baccalaureate Model.**   Although the elements of the programs vary, they tend to focus on a year of academic coursework and some field experience, leading to certification. These programs might be tied to a Masters (MAT) degree that is offered through a university. We would consider here not a blanket post-baccalaureate certificate requirement as exists in the state of California, but specific programs of preparation that are guided by theory and research. Valencia's University of Washington experimental program for teacher education is representative of a research-based program.

3. **A Four-Year Baccalaureate/Clinical Model.** This model is represented best in the work and findings of the International Reading Association. This program emphasizes the crucial role that carefully supervised and articulated field-clinical experiences play in the development of teaching expertise. The model foregrounds the "program" as a correlated and coordinated set of educative experiences and puts "coursework" in a place that serves the needs of the program. The model stresses the importance of collaboration between universities and public schools but also maintains the autonomous responsibility of the university in initial teacher preparation.

4. **An Academic Model.** This model places emphasis on the reform of the academic content of the preparation program. The belief here is that there is insufficient preparation in information basic to teaching. This model would follow suggestions for reform, for example, advocated by Snow and Fillmore (2000) in expanding the preparation of teachers in the areas of linguistics. Their suggestions call for increasing the number of courses and the content focused on the future teacher's understanding of the structure of English.

5. **A Professional Development Model.** This model is one that emphasizes the shared and collaborative work of public schools and teacher education institutions in preparing teachers. These programs are best represented by the Holmes Group reform effort, which emphasizes the post-baccalaureate or five-year plan for teacher preparation. It is possible to see evidence of this plan in four-year programs as well.

6. **An Alternative Certification Model.** This model is one that is typically managed by state agencies, although there may be elements of collaboration with teacher preparation institutions. The model deemphasizes course preparation (typically a summer of coursework and institutes) followed by full-time teaching responsibilities.

These are six models that we could begin to consider in a planned variation type study. There may be others, and some of these would require greater specificity to achieve "model" status. The models are not mutually exclusive in terms of their features. In fact, it is exactly this point of overlap that makes a planned variation model for research more appropriate than a traditional experimental design study that would look for the "best" program. What would emerge from this study would be the identification of the program features that are tied directly to learning and teaching effectiveness.

We have argued here (as we have elsewhere; see Roller, 2001) that research is the best potential guide for excellence and that it is crucial to invest now in a strong research program that will inform the quest for quality reading-teacher standards. We have cautioned against a quick rush into standards-based reform of teacher education without a careful exploration of the validity of the standards we use. We must be mindful of the many high-quality teacher preparation programs around the country, and we must build on and not ignore that practice. There is no need to proceed as if there were a vacuum. Although we would like to know more, there is much that we already know about excellent teacher preparation in reading. Finally, we have pleaded for an inclusive model of reform that encourages dialogue, values divergent views, and respects the responsibility of professional teacher educators as participants in the process.

References

Anders, P., Hoffman, J., & Duffy, G. (2000). Teaching teachers to teach reading: Paradigm shifts, persistent problems, and challenges. In M. Kamil, P. Mosenthal, P. D. Pearson, & R. Barr (Eds.), *Handbook of reading research* (Vol. 3, pp. 719–742). Mahwah, NJ: Lawrence Erlbaum.

Armbruster, B. B., & Osborn, J. H. (2002). *Reading instruction and assessment: Understanding the IRA standards.* Boston: Allyn & Bacon.

Brophy, J., & Good, T. (1986). Teacher behavior and student learning: In M. C. Wittrock (Ed.), *Third handbook of research on teaching.* Chicago: Rand McNally.

California State University. (2002). *Preparing teachers to teach reading effectively.* Long Beach, CA: Author.

Darling-Hammond, L. (1999). *Teacher quality and student achievement: A review of state policy evidence.* Seattle, WA: University of Washington Center for Teaching Policy.

Darling-Hammond, L. (Ed.). (2000a). *Studies of excellence in teacher education: Preparation at the graduate level.* Washington, DC: American Association of Colleges for Teacher Education.

Darling-Hammond, L. (Ed.). (2000b). *Studies of excellence in teacher education: Preparation in a five-year program.* Washington, DC: American Association of Colleges for Teacher Education.

Darling-Hammond, L. (Ed.). (2000c). *Studies of excellence in teacher education: Preparation in the undergraduate years.* Washington, DC: American Association of Colleges for Teacher Education.

Examiner. (2000). Polls show skepticism about tests. *Examiner, 14*, 4.

Grossman, P. L., Valencia, S. W., Evans, K., Thompson, G., Martin, S., & Place, N. (2000). Transitions into teaching: Learning to teach writing in teacher education and beyond. *Journal of Literacy Research, 32* (4), 631–662.

Harmon, J., Hedrick, W., Martinez, M., Perez, B., Keehn, S., Fine, J. C., Eldridge, D., Flint, A. S., Littleton, D. M., Bryant-Shanklin, M., Loven, R., Assaf, L., & Sailors, M. (2001). Features of excellence of reading teacher preparation programs. In J. V. Hoffman, D. L. Schallert, C. M. Fairbanks, J. Worthy, & B. Maloch (Eds.), *50th yearbook of the National Reading Conference.* Chicago: National Reading Conference.

Hoffman, J., & Pearson, P. D. (2000). Reading teacher education in the next millennium: What your grandmother's teacher didn't know that your granddaughter's teacher should. *Reading Research Quarterly, 35* (1), 28–44.

Hoffman, J. V., & Roller, C. M. (2001). The IRA Excellence in Reading Teacher Preparation Commission's Report: Current practices in reading teacher education at the undergraduate level. In C. M. Roller (Ed.), *Learning to teach reading: Setting the research agenda* (pp. 32–79). Newark, DE: International Reading Association.

International Reading Association. (1986). *Guidelines for the specialized preparation of reading professionals.* Newark, DE: Author.

International Reading Association. (2000). *Excellent reading teachers: A position statement of the International Reading Association.* Newark, DE: Author.

Laczko-Kerr, & Berliner, D.C. (2002). The effectiveness of "Teach for America" and other undercertified teachers on student academic achievement: A case of harmful public policy. *Education and Policy Analysis Archives* [On-line], *10* (37). Available: http://epaa.asu.edu/epaa/v19n37/

Learning First Alliance. (2000). *Every child reading: A professional development guide.* Washington, DC: Author.

Maloch, B., Flint, A. S., Eldridge, D., Harmon, J., Loven, R., Fine, J. C., Bryant-Shanklin, M., Martinez, M. (2003). Understandings, beliefs, and reported decision making of first-year teachers from different reading teacher preparation programs. *The Elementary School Journal, 103,* 431–457.

National Institute of Child Health and Human Development (NICHHD). (2000). *Report of the National Reading Panel. Teaching children to read: An evidence-based assessment of the scientific research literature on reading and its implications for reading instruction.* (NIH Publication No. 00-4769). Washington, D.C.: U.S. Government Printing Office.

Nogura, P. A., & Brown, E. M. (2002, September 20). Educating America's new majority. *The Boston Globe* [On-line]. Available: http://www.boston.com/dailyglobe2/263/oped/Educating_America_s_new_majority+.shtml

Pearson, P. D. (2001). Learning to teach reading: The status of the knowledge base. In C. M. Roller (Ed.), *Learning to teach reading: Setting the research agenda* (pp. 4–19). Newark, DE: International Reading Association.

Placier, M., Walker, M., & Foster, B. (2002). Writing the "Show-Me" Standards: Teacher professionalism and political control in U.S. state curriculum policy. *Curriculum Inquiry, 32*, 281–310.

Roller, C. (2001). A proposed research agenda for teacher preparation in reading. In C. M. Roller (Ed.), *Learning to teach reading: Setting the research agenda* (pp. 198–205). Newark, DE: International Reading Association.

Saltzer, J. (2002, June 26). Stanford 9 test results being thrown out. *Atlanta Journal-Constitution* [On-line]. Available: http://www.accessatlanta.com/ajc/metro/0602/26stanford.html

Snow, C. E., Burns, M. S., & Griffin, P. (Eds.). 1998. *Preventing reading difficulties in young children: A report of the National Research Council.* Washington, DC: National Academy Press.

Snow, C. E., & Fillmore, L. (2000). *What teachers need to know about language.* Paper prepared for the U. S. Department of Education Office of Educational Research and Improvement, Center for Applied Linguistics, Washington, DC.

Stallings, J., & Kaskowitz, D. (1974). *Follow-Through classroom observation evaluation 1972–1973.* Stanford, CA: Stanford Research Institute.

Strickland, D. S. (2001). The interface of standards, teacher preparation, and research: Improving the quality of teachers. In C. M. Roller (Ed.), *Learning to teach reading: Setting the research agenda* (pp. 20–29). Newark, DE: International Reading Association.

Taylor, B. M. (2002). *Characteristics of teachers who are effective in teaching all children to read.* Washington, DC: National Education Association.

Whitehurst, G. J. (2002, March 5). *Research on teacher preparation and professional development.* Paper presented the White House Conference on Preparing Tomorrow's Teachers. Washington, DC. Available: http://www.ed.gov/inits/preparingteachersconference/whitehurst.html

Part II

Professional Development Across Instructional Levels

Chapter 3

Introduction

Dorothy S. Strickland

The primary purpose of this volume is to provide the best thinking about what is known about the professional development of reading educators. To that end, we stress the research and current best thinking of how quality professional development should be planned and implemented. Thus our main focus is on the processes surrounding professional development. We are aware, however, that the content of professional development is no less important. In this section, we present syntheses of the current best thinking on what should be the content of the professional development of teachers and administrators working with students at various levels or stages of reading. This section contains four chapters, one per instructional level: prekindergarten and kindergarten, primary grades, upper elementary and intermediate grades, and middle and secondary school. At each level we provide a sense of what children are like at this stage of development and the special challenges faced by their teachers. In addition, we address issues related to the content of instruction, assessment, and management. The following standards for teachers, adapted from Strickland, Galda, and Cullinan (2003), help to establish a framework of knowledge and skills teachers need in order to be effective.

Standard 1.   Effective teachers of reading are knowledgeable about the major theoretical understandings, research findings, policy issues, and practices that help to shape contemporary instructional decision making. Such teachers do the following:

✓ Understand how humans learn and develop reading abilities and provide learning opportunities that support a range of individual variation

✓ Know the importance of social, cultural, linguistic, and cognitive differences among learners and use this information to inform their instructional decisions

✓ Understand how technology influences communication, language, and composition, and make appropriate use of it throughout the curriculum

✓ Are familiar with the educational goals and standards for reading instruction of the school district in which they teach and apply that knowledge to their practice

Standard 2.   Effective teachers of reading provide students with opportunities to learn in a literate and supportive environment that addresses individual needs and backgrounds. Such teachers do the following:

✓ Use a variety of instructional formats, including whole- and small-group instruction and personalized one-on-one instruction, and make use of focused direct instruction along with indirect opportunities for independent learning and application

✓ Use a variety of methods and teaching strategies to accommodate learner differences, such as linguistic and cultural differences, differences in abilities and background experiences, and differences in interests and motivation

✓ Use a combination of materials, including textbooks, trade books, and instructional and informational technologies, to stimulate interest and promote growth in reading

✓ Coordinate school and community resources, such as schoolwide intervention programs, allied professionals, and parents, in order to plan and support instruction

Standard 3.   Effective teachers use a variety of literature throughout the curriculum to encourage students to appreciate the written word, inspire them to use interesting language in their own writing, and motivate them to love literature. Such teachers do the following:

✓ Use literature to create learner-centered classrooms that motivate students to read, write, speak, listen, and develop a lifelong interest in reading and books

✓ Are knowledgeable about books and other literature for children and the ways to foster appreciation for the written word

✓ Employ strategies that increase the motivation of learners to read widely and independently for information, pleasure, and personal growth

✓ Provide opportunities for creative and personal response to literature

✓ Provide experiences with a wide variety of literature throughout the curriculum

Standard 4. Effective teachers of reading are knowledgeable about children's language and reading development, the importance to personal, social, and cognitive development, and the application to the curriculum. Such teachers do the following:

✓ Are knowledgeable about how children learn and develop language and understand its role in learning

✓ Understand the relationship between language and thought processes

✓ Understand and respect language variation and the function of the home language in the development of children and take these into account in their instructional planning

✓ Use their knowledge of effective communication to foster active inquiry, collaboration, and supportive interaction in the classroom

Standard 5. Effective teachers of reading are knowledgeable about the nature of young children's literacy development and have the skills to support young learners as emerging and conventional readers and writers. Such teachers do the following:

✓ Help students to develop concepts about print, alphabet recognition, phonemic awareness, sound-letter correspondences, and sight word vocabularies

✓ Are knowledgeable about the various language components of literacy development, including phonemes (sounds of language), morphemes (words and meaningful parts of words), semantics (meaning), syntax (sentence structure, parts of speech), and pragmatics (how language works in social context)

✓ Understand and implement strategies that support the inter-related development of word recognition, reading fluency, and comprehension

Standard 6. Effective teachers of reading provide opportunities for students to gain competence in their abilities to enjoy and learn from a variety of literary and informational texts. Such teachers do the following:

✓ Help students to understand that people read for a variety of purposes

✓ Help students to develop the skills needed to effectively respond to texts

✓ Help students to use a variety of strategies for comprehending texts

✓ Provide opportunities for students to read from a wide variety of reading materials and genres

Standard 7. Effective teachers of reading have the knowledge and ability to help students link reading with writing. Such teachers do the following:

✓ Build students' awareness of various text structures, literary devices, and writing conventions for their use as readers and writers

✓ Provide well-crafted trade books from all genres that can be used as models for student writing

✓ Help students to build competence in various skills and strategies associated with the writing process to become effective writers

✓ Help students to recognize the techniques and strategies used by successful writers in all genres

Standard 8. Successful teachers of reading help students to acquire and apply enriched vocabularies and knowledge about English language structures in order to read and spell with competence. Such teachers do the following:

✓ Understand how the written language system works and how to apply that knowledge to ensure a sound program of word study for children

✓ Understand the importance of vocabulary development in students' overall language development and reading comprehension

✓ Understand basic principles related to spelling development and its relationship to reading

✓ Implement a balance of both direct and contextual approaches to word study, vocabulary, and spelling instruction

Standard 9.   Effective teachers of reading are knowledgeable about a variety of assessment tools and strategies; they skillfully use the results of assessment to make instructional decisions and to encourage student self-assessment. Such teachers do the following:

✓ Understand and use assessment as a means to determine what their students know and are able to do in meeting national, state, and local standards and what kinds of experiences they must offer students to further their growth and development

✓ Are knowledgeable about assessment-related issues and the purposes, characteristics, and limitations of various types of assessments

✓ Use the results of assessments to reflect on student learning and to modify their own teaching and instructional practices

✓ Maintain accurate and useful records and work samples of student performance and communicate student progress responsibly to parents, appropriate school staff, and the students themselves

Standard 10.   Effective teachers of language arts and reading are skillful in the ways they integrate instruction within the language arts (listening, speaking, reading, writing, representing, and viewing) and with content area subjects across the curriculum. Such teachers do the following:

✓ Are knowledgeable about methods of inquiry

✓ Know how to plan for the integration of oral and written language through thematic units across the curriculum

✓ Use a variety of techniques to build and capitalize on student interest and enthusiasm

✓ Build on and extend students' background knowledge

✓ Help students to generate their own questions relevant to a unit of study

✓ Systematically teach research skills and other tools of inquiry

✓ Systematically provide opportunities for the use of oral language, reading, writing, listening, viewing, and visually representing what they know

✓ Help students to find ways to share what they have learned with others

Reference

Strickland, D. S., Galda, L., & Cullinan, B. (2003). *Language arts: Learning and teaching.* Belmont, CA: Wadsworth.

Chapter 4

Establishing the Basis for Improved Reading Achievement: Prekindergarten and Kindergarten

M. Susan Burns and Robert A. Stechuk

Key Ideas

✓ Prekindergarten and kindergarten teachers need to understand and apply knowledge and skills related specifically to literacy and possess more general knowledge of the language systems that underlie reading and writing.

✓ Telling does not equal understanding; professional development ought to encourage teachers to enact, assess, analyze, and reflect upon the principles and practices they are being taught.

✓ Being an effective teacher of reading and writing is a lifelong learning process, and professional development should address the needs of teachers at different career and skill levels (e.g., preservice, beginning teacher, experienced teacher, and master teacher).

For

• Early childhood professional development providers, both preservice and inservice

• Early childhood teachers

During a planning period in early October, three teachers at Barrett Elementary School meet to discuss their shared knowledge of a group of kindergarten children.

Mary, a kindergarten teacher working in a full-day program, is beginning her second year in the profession. Kathy, the lead teacher for the preschool special education classroom, has seven years of experience and was selected by the principal to mentor Mary. Beth is a teacher in one of several Head Start classrooms in the school and has been working with young children for more than 20 years. The trio is discussing Mary's class of 18 children, of whom 6 were enrolled in Beth's classroom and 3 in Kathy's classroom last year.

Kathy: So, tell us, how has this year gone so far? Any different from last year?

Mary: Well, you know that last year was such a learning experience for me. It all seems like a blur now. This year it's sinking in how much work it is to plan and carry out everything that you want to do.

Kathy: Tell us about the children in your room this year.

Beth: Yeah, how are my kids doing?

Mary: You know, I almost don't know where to begin. Out of 18 children, your 6 Head Start children from last year are at least somewhat similar. I can see that they all had instruction on language and early literacy. One girl is keeping a journal, writing down words and a few phrases, and sounding out some easily decodable words. Kathy, of your three children with IEPs [Individual Educational Program] one is using adaptive equipment and writing a fair amount. The other two are still developing their verbal language at this point. Those are the children that you two already know about. The nine children "new to the system," are all over the place—you know I don't mean wild. One is a beginning reader. Two children barely speak and don't seem to *want* to write or read anything. The rest are somewhat on track, I guess. Several don't seem to be able to focus for even one minute.

Kathy: What are you doing to cope?

Mary: I've been reluctant to ask for help from the main office. Last year I only saw the principal and the assistant a couple of times—and then at the end of the year. After this year's push for "accountability" I'm afraid to ask for help.

Kathy: We'll just have to take this "accountability" stuff as it comes. As long as you align your lessons to the standards, you're set—but you know that already.

Mary: The funny thing is that I go back and forth on how comfortable I feel in the classroom. Sometimes I think that I'm really getting the hang of it, that I can really see that the light bulbs are going on. Then at other times I'm struggling. Sometimes I'm glad I became a teacher, at other times—

Beth: How do you feel that your college coursework prepared you for all of this?

Mary: Actually, they did a fairly good job with the basics. I remember their emphasis on "prior knowledge" and its importance. Now that I've been in the classroom, I can really see the importance. I know what outcomes are expected for my kids, and understand how I need to use assessment data in my instruction. The problem is in addressing such a wide variety of prior knowledge and current skills for a group of 18. Just think of the variety of reading skills my students have on standards. I just feel that all of my children have not met the prekindergarten standards related to literacy. Also, there are so many other things competing for attention—screenings, assemblies, class photos.

Beth: So tell us what we can do to help. You know that you just have to work through the interruptions and make the best use of the time you have.

Mary: Well, there are three children in particular that I have real concerns about, and I think making a plan for them will help me with many of the other children, too!

First there is Pat. He was in Beth's Head Start class. You know how he really caught on to a good understanding of the language system—he reached all the listening and speaking expectations. For example, he playfully manipulates language, using nonsense words, rhymes, and silly songs; he can identify a favorite book and tell why he likes it in great detail; he seems to learn new words every day. He is independently writing words that I can decipher and is reading simple text. How do I provide him with challenging experiences when he's so far ahead of most of the class?

Then there is Anabelle—she has never been to school before. Her mother says she does everything for her. Although she seems interested in learning to read and write, she just doesn't seem to have the ability to concentrate or to direct her attention to an activity. At times she doesn't even seem to remember what she is doing halfway through an activity. How do I begin to work on her attention level? When would I have time, when there is so much content to get through every week?

Finally, there is Caroline from your class, Kathy. Although she now has hearing aids and seems to comprehend most of what I say, she does seem to miss some sounds. For example, the other day I was talking about "girls" and she thought I said "curls." How can I improve her phonological awareness when she is not hearing all the letter sounds correctly?

Kathy: Well, these children sure are different!

Beth: Yes, but I can see what Mary means by thinking that if she addresses the instructional needs of these three, she can probably apply the information to all the other kids in her room.

Mary: Let's get started.

In considering the competencies teachers need to effectively support the literacy development of Pre-K and kindergarten children, the complex natures of language, literacy, and learning are all too evident. Our review of research-based best practices was guided by two basic questions: (a) What knowledge do teachers need to implement best practices? (b) What knowledge do administrators and supervisors need to ensure that professional development opportunities support teachers to understand and implement best practices?

Unfortunately, it appears to be the case that knowledge of how to provide maximum support for children's early literacy development is not widespread among Pre-K and kindergarten teachers. Recent reviews of the literature have demonstrated that many teachers are unaware of how literacy skills emerge in preschool-age children (Snow, Burns, & Griffin, 1998). It may be the case that a variety of perspectives exist at the practitioner level. For example, some Pre-K teachers may believe that children are "not ready" to receive instruction related to literacy skills, thereby ignoring valuable opportunities for learning. Some kindergarten teachers may believe that literacy skills can be advanced only by creating a formal academic environment that incorporates phonics lessons, assigned writing tasks, and drill (Mason & Sinha, 1993). Children are expected to function within a "one size fits all" curriculum that may fail to acknowledge or address children's individual differences. Neither of these two approaches appears to offer optimal benefits for children.

How do early literacy opportunities relate to later literacy? Although a few children seem to learn to read without instruction, for most children, becoming a "conventional" reader is not easy (NICHHD, 2000). It is an acquired skill involving considerable time and substantial effort. Pre-K and kindergarten literacy experiences provide a foundation to facilitate beginning reading and writing (Snow et al., 1998). Pre-K and kindergarten children need easy access to books and other print material and to learn a wide range of skills, including knowledge of letters and their sounds, phonemic awareness, and listening comprehension strategies (Burns, Griffin, & Snow, 1999; Resnick & Tucker, 1999, 2001). To be an effective teacher—to match appropriate instruction to individual children's competence—requires that teachers have knowledge of word structure, sentence structure, and lexical development and how these combine to support conventional reading. Teachers, therefore, need to understand specific skills related to reading as well as more general knowledge of the language systems that underlie reading (Moats, 2000).

These initial observations of the nature of language, literacy, and learning provoke additional questions. How are Pre-K and kindergarten teachers prepared to support the early literacy of the children with whom they work? Do they have sufficient knowledge of how reading develops and of the language systems that underlie reading outcomes? Is their knowledge of teaching methods based on current research findings on effective reading instruction? How effective are professional development programs for improving reading achievement? How can professional development be presented in a manner that is usable in Pre-K and kindergarten classes?

Knowledge and Skills for Teaching Pre-K and Kindergarten Children

In effective school systems there are expectations for how Pre-K and kindergarten children should perform in the areas of language and literacy. Teachers must be prepared to examine and critique the child outcomes used in their school and understand how they are related to the instruction they provide in the classroom. We have examined several documents that focus on language and literacy expectations for Pre-K and kindergarten children and suggest that the reader review *Speaking and Listening for Preschool Through Third Grade: New Standards* (Resnick & Tucker, 2001), *Reading and Writing Grade by Grade: New Standards* (Resnick & Tucker, 1999), and *Starting Out Right: A Guide to Promoting Children's Reading Success* (Burns et al., 1999). Table 4-1 includes a few examples from the New Standards.

Table 4-1. New Standards for Listening, Speaking, Reading, and Writing[1]

Examples of Listening and Speaking Standards (Pre-K)

Standard 1: Habits

Talking a Lot (Resnick & Tucker, 2001, p. 48)

Children should experiment and play with language daily in the following ways:

- Talk daily for various purposes
- Engage in play, using talk to enact or extend a story line (e.g., taking on roles, using different voices, solving problems)
- Playfully manipulate language (including nonsense words, rhymes, silly songs, repetitious phrases)
- Express ideas, feelings, and needs
- Listen and respond to direct questions
- Ask questions
- Talk and listen in small groups (during playtime or mealtime or more formally at workshop areas or craft tables)
- Share and talk daily about their experiences, products, or writing (e.g., explaining their pictures or "reading" their writing attempts)

Standard 2: Kinds of Talk and Resulting Genres

Explaining and Seeking Information (Resnick & Tucker, 2001, p. 82)

Although preschoolers may still use personal narratives to provide information, explanatory talk should begin to appear. They may do the following:

- Seek or provide information by observing; looking at books; or asking teachers, parents, and peers
- Request or provide explanations of their own or others' actions, speech, or feelings
- Explain their own or others' intentions and thinking when asked (e.g., "Why is the milk out?" "For cereal. I want some cereal.")
- Give simple, one-sentence explanations, with supporting details or evidence (e.g., "I cut my knee because I fell.")
- Request or provide explanations of word meanings (e.g., "What's 'your highness'?")
- Use all their senses to describe physical characteristics of objects, self, and others
- Describe objects, self, and others in terms of location and position
- Use gestures and sounds when they don't have descriptive words (e.g., describing an accident scene, "They took him in that … that … RRRR-RRRR, it was LOUD!")

Table 4-1.   New Standards for Listening, Speaking, Reading, and Writing[1]
(Continued)

Standard 3: Language Use and Connections

Vocabulary and Word Choice (Resnick & Tucker, 2001, p. 112)

There is a direct correlation between vocabulary development and academic development. At the preschool level children are expected to do the following:

- Add words to familiar knowledge domains
- Sort relationships among words in knowledge domains
- Add new domains from subjects and topics they are studying (e.g., in math, shapes like circle and triangle, or in science, reptiles like snake and lizard)
- Learn new words daily in conversation
- Learn new words daily from what is being explored or read aloud
- Show a general interest in words and word meanings, asking adults what a word means or offering definitions
- Recognize that things may have more than one name (e.g., "Fluffy is a cat, the cat is a pet, the pet is an animal.")
- Categorize objects or pictures and tell why they go together (e.g., group the following objects into toy or food categories: ball, skates, grapes, kite, bread, milk)
- Increase vocabulary of verbs, adjectives, and adverbs to exercise options in word choice
- Use some abstract words and understand that these words differ from concrete things, places, or people
- Use verbs referring to cognition, communication, and emotions

---

Examples of Reading Standards (Kindergarten)

Standard 1: Print-Sound Code

Phonemic Awareness (Resnick & Tucker, 1999, p. 54)

Children leaving kindergarten are expected to do the following:

- Produce rhyming words and recognize pairs of rhyming words
- Isolate initial consonants in single-syllable words (e.g., /t/ is the first sound in *top*)
- When a single-syllable word is pronounced (e.g., *cat*), identify the onset (/c/) and rime (-at) and begin to fully separate the sounds (c/-/a/-/t/) by saying each sound aloud
- Blend onsets (/c/) and rimes (-at) to form words (*cat*) and begin to blend separately spoken phonemes to make a meaningful one-syllable word (e.g., when the teacher says a word slowly, stretching it out as "mmm—ahhh—mmm," children say that the word being stretched out is *mom*).

Table 4-1. New Standards for Listening, Speaking, Reading, and Writing[1] (*Continued*)

Standard 2: Getting the Meaning

Self-Monitoring and Self Correcting Strategies (Resnick & Tucker, 1999, p. 60)

Children leaving kindergarten are expected to self-monitor and self-correct when necessary to determine the following:

- They are looking at the correct page.
- The word they are saying is the one to which they are pointing.
- What they read makes sense.

Children should also monitor a story they hear read aloud and be able to do the following:

- Ask why a character would do that
- Say they don't understand something
- Say the character "is scared because…" or "did that because…"

Examples of Writing Standards (Kindergarten)

Standard 1: Writing Purposes and Resulting Genre

Producing and Responding to Literature (Resnick & Tucker, 1999, p. 82)

Children leaving kindergarten are expected to do the following:

- Reenact and retell stories (borrow and burrow into stories, poems, plays, and songs)
- Create their own stories, poems, plays, and songs
- Use literacy forms and language (e.g., if they produce a poem, students should write with some poetic language, perhaps even using poetic devices such as imagery and repetition)

Standard 2: Language Use and Conventions

Vocabulary and Word Choice (Resnick & Tucker, 1999, p. 88)

By the end of kindergarten children are expected to use their own language to produce writing in which they do the following:

- Use words in their writing that they use in their conversation, usually represented phonetically

By the end of kindergarten children are expected to use more of author language to produce writing in which they do the following:

- Use in their writing some words they like from the books read to them
- Make choices about which words to use on the basis of whether they accurately convey the child's meaning

[1]To properly gain the full knowledge available in the New Standards, this information must be considered in the context of the CDs of cases and practical and theoretical information included in the full documents.

These documents provide expectations for what children can do, but, more important, they provide a context for how adults can access and integrate the information to inform teaching practices. For example, in *Starting Out Right,* practical and theoretical knowledge is used to inform and contextualize child expectations; in the Resnick and Tucker books, CDs of case studies and background information are included, so that practical and theoretical information is connected. All three of these documents were developed by a reputable group of experts.

Administrators and supervisors should ensure that all teachers have access to and responsibility for instructing children using child outcomes grounded in current research and theory. Professional development should therefore be aligned with such standards based on current research and best practices (Committee on Teacher Education, in press).

To use child outcomes effectively for instruction, teachers need to understand Pre-K and kindergarten children's development of literacy and reading in particular. They need to know, for example, that although a few children seem to learn to read without instruction, for most children it is not easy. Pre-K and kindergarten teachers have important early literacy instruction to provide (Neuman & Roskos, 1993; International Reading Association & National Association for the Education of Young Children, 1998). Effective Pre-K and kindergarten teachers know how to teach young children to do the following:

1. See how print functions, that "it is the print that tells people what to say when they are reading" (Ballenger, 1999, p. 43)

2. See that written language has certain characteristics (e.g., it is a symbol system that has identifiable letters, that English starts at the top of the page and goes to the bottom, that it goes from left to right)

3. Produce personally meaningful writing (e.g., journal writing and scaffolding writing)

4. Develop their sensitivity to the individual sounds in words (e.g., rhymes, alliteration, letter sounds)

5. Explore books (e.g., setting up environments with easy access to books and other print material)

6. Be proficient oral language users (e.g., use conversation and shared reading for children to build vocabulary, knowledge of narrative, and listening comprehension)

Preventing Reading Difficulties in Young Children (Snow et al., 1998) identifies courses of study, such as psychology of reading, pedagogy of reading, linguistics, and psycholinguistics studies (p. 285), that are necessary to have the knowledge and teaching skills to provide children the opportunity to perform as expected based on the New Standards.

Effective teachers of Pre-K and kindergarten children must also possess knowledge of language systems and reading processes in order to support literacy development (Committee on Teacher Education, in press; Moats, 2000; Strickland, Snow, Griffin, Burns, & McNamara, 2002). This knowledge is a necessary—but by itself insufficient—component of successful child outcomes. In addition, teachers at this level must possess an understanding of the under-lying cognitive proficiencies that make literacy possible and of the role of play in advancing those proficiencies.

Bodrova and Leong (1996) remind us that access to high-quality play is essential to the development of literacy in young children. They identify how play underlies three major developmental ac-complishments for children at this age level: (a) *imagination*, which supports children's development of complex ideas; (b) *symbolic func-tioning*, in which the use of objects, actions, words, and people to stand for something else prepares the way for more conventional literacy; and (c) *the integration of emotions and thinking*, in which children's behavior is no longer simply reactive but comes to in-clude memory and reflection upon experiences and ideas. Pre-K and kindergarten children also need experiences in which they consciously access their memories, develop self-regulation (pur-poseful control over their own behaviors), and access materials for writing.

Saracho (2001) identifies numerous aspects of effective instruc-tion at the kindergarten level. To foster learning in children, kin-dergarten teachers must be capable of monitoring, facilitating, interacting, inquiring, extending play, discussing, and decision making. Of course, many of these capabilities are not fully realized by the end of a preservice program; only sustained inservice pro-fessional development combined with reflective teaching experi-ences solidify these skills. Effective use of assessment is central to these effective instructional practices (Shepard, 2000). Of particu-lar importance is the ability to use ongoing, in-class assessments related to child outcomes, assessments that help teachers to un-derstand child progress in literacy activities and toward child out-comes. Assessment information should inform instructional decision making. An effective teacher at this level is able to match the content (skills) that children need to achieve a literacy goal with effective instruction that is attuned to individual children's levels of competence. An understanding of scaffolding is introduced in preservice programs and increased through professional development. Scaffolding children's learning requires usable knowledge of the content of early language and literacy, including language systems previously mentioned (phonological processes, word and sentence structure, lexical development, pragmatic development, and orthography). Consider, for example, the three children that Mary, Kathy, and Beth discussed in the opening vignette. Each needs different emphases in content and pedagogy to achieve literacy goals.

Telling Does Not Equal Understanding

For adults to learn to be effective literacy instructors, they need to participate in professional development opportunities in which they are engaged in inquiry about their own practice. This can take place through a number of activities, such as case studies of young learners and teacher-learners' implementation of effective literacy strategies. To illustrate this point we present one example of enactment, analysis, assessment, and reflection taking place in implementing effective teaching strategies. This instructional strategy, scaffolded writing (Bodrova & Leong, 1996), along with others used in professional development, would be tied to the knowledge of oral and written language needed by all teachers (Fillmore & Snow, 2000; Moats, 1994), the relationship between this knowledge and standards in listening, speaking, reading, and writing (Resnick & Tucker, 1999, 2001), classroom instruction and materials, and assessment.

Scaffolded writing is a technique developed to support and investigate early writing. Teachers guide children as they learn to write a message that has meaning and consequence for the child. Using a complex teaching procedure, teachers provide social scaffolds and instructional tools so that young children are able to make line-word and letter-sound connections. As children take on more of this process as their own, teacher scaffolds are withdrawn. Positive child outcomes include phonemic and print awareness, letter knowledge, sound-symbol correspondence, and concepts of writing. The language and literacy knowledge applied in enacting this instructional strategy includes phonological awareness (rhyming, blending, segmenting), print awareness, and alphabetic knowledge. Teachers learn pedagogical strategies such as scaffolding and also learn how to use child outcome measures to assess the child's progress, engaging in continual data collection and assessment.

Figure 4-1 illustrates how teachers have used reflective methods to implement scaffolded writing with young children. After learning the procedure, enacting it, and assessing and analyzing each child's behavior, they share their methods and findings in their professional development course. Teacher-learners (a) share their knowledge of language and literacy content; (b) share the data they collect with one another; (c) discuss the implications of these data

The teachers who implemented scaffolded writing began by collecting performance data on their young children's early writing; identifying, for example, what they produced in terms of conventional writing (e.g., left to right, top to bottom) and what they produced that indicated that they knew something about sounds in words (e.g., there are more letters in a long word than in a short word—one child wrote "A" for "go" and "AANANJ" for housekeeping; another used the phonetic spelling "KMPTR" for "computer.") The teachers collected these baseline data until they had a stable picture of each child's performance. Next, teachers began using an appropriate scaffolding strategy in their instruction, with continual data collection. Informed by the child's performance, and with support from the professional development instructor, the teachers moved to the next step in the instructional procedure. These graphs show two children's performance. The first child is a child with a specific language impairment who is receiving special education services, and the second is a child in Head Start who speaks English as a second language.

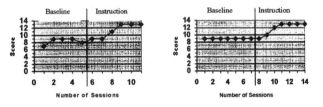

Both children began the instruction with an understanding of a number of important concepts about early writing. For example, they wrote from left to right and used conventional letters during baseline (one child's writing of "train" looked like the first writing sample below). After instruction, their writing took on the use of some consonant sounds in the words they were spelling ("I want to play computer" is reflected in the second writing sample.)

Figure 4-1.   Reflective Teaching of Scaffolded Writing

for how to appropriately scaffold their students' learning; and (d) examine the trends in the data and jointly identify what those trends suggest about the efficacy of the instruction and how it could be modified to enhance its effectiveness with different children.

A Lifelong Learning Process

To support literacy development in Pre-K and kindergarten children, teacher knowledge of language systems, reading, and instruction should also be seen as a developmental process (Committee on Teacher Education, in press). Consider the three teachers mentioned in our vignette.

Preservice phase. In the vignette, Mary refers to her teacher preparation program, in which she learned knowledge of literacy-related content and instructional methods. She learned about child development—and especially language systems—from a developmental perspective. Research-based knowledge was made explicit; she was taught both to analyze and to synthesize relevant information. Throughout her training, she was encouraged to answer direct questions related to observing children, planning instruction, and making instructional decisions. Her internships (practica) were valuable sources of learning as well as opportunities for her to raise questions and comments about what she learned in her classes. As she approached graduation, her coursework and assignments were directed so she could function independently within a classroom.

Beginning teacher. Mary is a beginning teacher. At this point in her career she knows that even though she had a good preservice program, no amount of preservice training can completely prepare anyone to teach Pre-K and kindergarten children. She has a good grounding in child development and language systems, can apply this information in a standard fashion, and can implement careful assessment, thoughtful curriculum, and generally effective classroom management practices. Like other beginning teachers, she is also prepared to learn from experience without seriously compromising her knowledge of research-based principles. It is to be expected that beginning teachers will need ongoing support in the form of mentoring, instructional leadership, and effective professional development experiences. In particular, beginning teachers need to "unload" some of the stresses associated with teaching and to build their capacity to plan and implement effective instruction. In particular, beginning teachers will likely need assistance with a wide variety of individual "cases" of children. This assistance is what Beth and Kathy, more senior teachers, are providing for her.

Teachers at this level should be capable of implementing a variety of practices to support literacy while still developing their understanding of language systems, reading, and instructional methods.

Experienced teacher. Beth and Kathy are both accomplished, effective teachers even with a classroom of diverse children. They need to be supported to consolidate their practice and to continue to incorporate new knowledge. This level of adaptive knowledge enables teachers to critically think through instructional and behavioral situations and to develop a set of problem-solving skills that have been proven in the classroom over time. Teachers at this level can be expected to develop their own insights into research-based principles, to function effectively with less supervision and support, and to offer counsel and advice to other teachers. At the same time, teachers at this level need (and deserve) opportunities to reflect upon their practices and to receive support from others at critical periods. Teachers at this level should be capable of implementing a strong set of practices to support literacy, using published curricula and/or local and state standards as guidelines, not prescriptions, for their practice.

Master teacher. Although Beth and Kathy are effective teachers in their own classes, at this point in their careers they are working toward being master teachers. Providing mentoring to Mary as a beginning teacher is part of this process in which they are learning how to articulate their knowledge of content and instruction. They are developing the skills to carefully observe other teachers and to provide feedback and suggestions that are of immediate benefit to the mentee. In addition, master teachers are a resource for selecting curriculum and suggesting adaptations, providing input into professional development offerings, and communicating their knowledge by teaching preservice courses.

Conclusion

Children need access to Pre-K and kindergarten environments that provide appropriate levels of support for their emerging literacy skills. This entails much more than the daily application of lessons that teachers don't have the knowledge base to understand. Teachers need usable access to the complex knowledge base on language and literacy. Pre-K and kindergarten children need teachers who plan and implement instruction that meets standards and builds upon children's prior knowledge and motivation to learn. As Mary is learning, effective instruction takes time: Individual children's strengths and needs must be considered. The ability levels of the three children in the vignette present a challenge for any teacher. Effective instruction requires the knowledgeable integration of research-based principles, standards, and instructional methods and techniques that bring everything together.

Instruction must be able to include a wide range of opportunities for children, including rich conceptual experiences that promote vocabulary; development of listening comprehension skills; sensitivity to the sounds of language; and a sense of story, among others (Snow et al., 1998). At the kindergarten level, the ability to recognize potential reading difficulties should also be part of the teacher's skills. In addition, young learners must be nurtured so that a lifelong appreciation for reading can be sustained.

Given the complexity of Pre-K and kindergarten children's literacy development, professional development opportunities should be designed to promote effective age-appropriate practices—focusing on what is known about early literacy and how adults can best support children's development. In addition, professional development ought to encourage adults to enact, assess, analyze, and reflect upon the principles and practices that are termed appropriate for Pre-K and kindergarten children. As Mary is learning, even a good teacher preparation program cannot provide all of the knowledge that one needs to become an effective teacher. Preservice programs *can* provide a good grounding in research-based evidence for effective instruction as well as the basis for reflective practices. However, it is through ongoing and high-quality professional development opportunities that new teachers can develop into good teachers, and good teachers can develop a mastery of their profession. Children require and deserve teaching that is guided by research-based standards and thoughtful reflection upon practices. In turn, teachers require and deserve professional development opportunities that support their continued learning and improvement—including personally directed inquiry—throughout their careers.

References

Ballenger, C. (1999). *Teaching other people's children: Literacy and learning in a bilingual classroom.* New York: Teachers College Press.

Bodrova, E., & Leong, D. J. (1996). *Tools of the mind: The Vygotskian approach to early childhood education.* Columbus, OH: Merrill.

Burns, M. S., Griffin, P., & Snow, C. (1999). *Starting out right: A guide to promoting children's reading success.* Washington, DC: National Academy Press.

Committee on Teacher Education. Teaching children to read well: A career of commitment to knowledge in action (in press). National Academy of Education.

Fillmore, L. W., & Snow, C. E. (2000). *What teachers need to know about language.* Washington, DC: Center for Applied Linguistics.

International Reading Association & National Association for the Education of Young Children (1998). Overview of learning to read and write: Developmentally appropriate practices for young children [On-line]. Available: http://www.naeyc.org/resources/position_statements/psread0.html

Mason, J. M., & Sinha, S. (1993). Emerging literacy in the early childhood years: Applying a Vygotskian model of learning and development. In B. Spodek (Ed.), *Handbook of research on the education of young children* (pp. 137–150). New York: Macmillan.

Moats, L. C. (1994). The missing foundation in teacher education: Knowledge of the structure of spoken and written language. *Annals of Dyslexia, 44,* 81–101.

Moats, L. C. (2000). *Speech to print: Language essentials for teachers.* Baltimore: Brookes.

National Institute of Child Health and Human Development (NICHHD). (2000). *Report of the National Reading Panel. Teaching children to read: An evidence-based assessment of the scientific research literature on reading and its implications for reading instruction.* (NIH Publication No. 00-4769). Washington, D.C.: U.S. Government Printing Office.

Neuman, S. B., & Roskos, K. (1993). Access to print for children of poverty: Differential effects of adult mediation and literacy-enriched play settings on environmental and functional print tasks. *American Educational Research Journal, 30,* 95–122.

Resnick, L. B., & Tucker, M. S. (1999). *Reading and writing grade by grade: New standards.* Washington, DC: National Center on Education and the Economy.

Resnick, L. B., & Tucker, M. S. (2001). *Speaking and listening for preschool through third grade: New standards.* Washington, DC: National Center on Education and the Economy.

Saracho, O. N. (2001). Teachers' perceptions of their roles in promoting literacy in the context of play in a Spanish-speaking kindergarten. *International Journal of Early Childhood, 33* (2), 18–31.

Shepard, L. A. (2000). The role of assessment in a learning culture. *Educational Researcher, 29* (7), 4–14.

Snow, C. E., Burns, M. S., & Griffin, P. (Eds.) (1998). *Preventing reading difficulties in young children: A Report of the National Research Council.* Washington, DC: National Academy Press.

Strickland, D. S., Snow, C. E., Griffin, P., Burns, M. S., & McNamara, P. (2002). *Preparing our teachers: Opportunities for better reading instruction.* Washington, DC: Joseph Henry Press.

Chapter 5

Professional Development for K–3 Teachers: Content and Process

Janice A. Dole and Jean Osborn

Key Ideas

✓ Educators need to attend to content and process as they plan effective professional development for teachers.

✓ Primary-grade teachers benefit from a deep understanding of theory and practice in the five components of reading: phonemic awareness, phonics, fluency, vocabulary, and comprehension.

✓ Primary-grade teachers benefit from professional development that includes demonstrations and guided practice with feedback through in-class coaching.

For

• Professional development providers

• Administrators, curriculum coordinators, teacher educators

I learned how to become a teacher by trial and error. After a few years of teaching, I got the hang of it, and I felt comfortable in the classroom. Of course, as a second-grade teacher, reading was the most important part of what I did, but it was the hardest for me to learn. Those first few years, I held on to that basal teacher's manual like it was a bible. But you know, I never really got it. I went through the motions, but I never understood what I was doing. I went to graduate school to learn more about how to teach reading. The professors and the readings helped, but it was when I had to tutor a child one-on-one that things finally began to make sense for me.

I was required to tutor a first-grader, Joshua, twice a week as a part of a class on assessment and intervention. I had to give Joshua a series of informal assessments to figure out where he was in phonemic awareness, phonics, fluency, and comprehension. Then I had to make up an instructional sequence of activities to teach him the skills he was missing.

That's when it all came together and began to make sense to me. Somehow, working with a class of 25 students, I was never able to see the whole reading process. But when I worked with Joshua I began to see how the different parts fit together. It was like a click for me. Everything I had learned and read about came together for me. That was when I felt like I understood the reading process and how children learn to read. I know I am a much better second-grade teacher now. I get it.

It is likely that this teacher's experience of tutoring a child was just one of many professional development experiences in her career. However, this particular experience was a culminating one for her in that she was able to see the big picture and how all the pieces fit together in that large picture. How can we best prepare primary-grade teachers to see this big picture so that they will have the knowledge, skills, and confidence that will enable them to help their students meet the high literacy standards required by our society? Of critical importance is that all teachers possess up-to-date and research-based knowledge about the reading process, about how children learn to read, and about beginning reading instruction.

In this section, we outline the essential content of a program of professional development for primary-grade teachers as well as the process of how best to involve teachers in programs of professional development. In our discussion, we include the importance of teachers being able to evaluate the instruction and practice materials provided by the published programs of reading instruction they use in their classrooms, programs that are often referred to as core reading programs or basal reading programs.

Professional Development for K–3 Teachers: The Content

What do primary-grade teachers need to know and be able to do to effectively teach reading in kindergarten, first, second, and third grades? We propose three broad categories of knowledge that these teachers need to have: theory and practice, classroom organization, and assessment.

Theory and Practice

Teachers need to know about both theory and practice. They need deep knowledge of the research on the reading process and on how children learn to read. They need to know about the research-based instructional practices that efficiently and effectively support student learning. Teachers also need to know how to look for the sequence of instruction, as well as how to evaluate the quality of instruction and practice, in the core reading programs they use in their classrooms. The *Report of the National Reading Panel* (NICHHD, 2000) identifies five critical components of reading instruction that are verified by rigorous research: phonemic awareness, phonics, fluency, vocabulary, and comprehension. These components are described below.

Phonemic Awareness Instruction

Phonemic awareness instruction assists children in the ability to notice, think about, and work with the individual sounds in spoken words. Teachers need to know when phonemic awareness can be developed, how it can be taught most effectively, and how to use word games and manipulatives to support this learning. They need to be able to evaluate the extent to which their core reading programs provide explicit, systematic, and carefully sequenced instruction in phonemic awareness. They need to know how much time to spend on phonemic awareness instruction and how to group their students for this instruction.

Phonics Instruction

Phonics instruction teaches the relationships between the letters of written language and the individual sounds of spoken language. Research-based phonics instruction involves the explicit teaching of letter-sound relationships in a clearly defined sequence. Teachers need to evaluate the extent to which their core reading programs contain explicit and systematic phonics instruction. The major sound-to-spelling relationships of consonants and vowels should be specified in the sequence of instruction. In addition, teachers need to know how to evaluate the quantity and quality of student practice materials that their core reading programs provide. The books these programs provide for students to read should include stories and other texts that contain a large number of words that the students can decode by using their newly learned sound and letter relationships. Core programs of reading instruction should also include suggestions for students to use their newly learned letter-sound relationships to spell words as they write their own stories.

Fluency Practice

Fluency practice improves students' ability to read a text accurately and quickly. It is not enough that students can automatically recognize words that they read aloud on isolated word lists. They need to be able to read sentences, paragraphs, and stories on their grade level, pronouncing almost all the words correctly, and reading with enough speed and expression so that their reading sounds like oral language. Teachers need to evaluate the extent to which their core reading programs provide effective instructional strategies to support fluent reading as well as passages to be used for repeated oral reading practice with assistance from the teacher, another adult, or peers.

Vocabulary Instruction

Vocabulary instruction involves assisting students in learning the words, both spoken and written, that they must know to communicate effectively and to understand what they read. Children learn vocabulary indirectly through engaging in daily oral language, listening to adults read aloud, and reading extensively on their own. However, children can and should be taught vocabulary directly as well. Teachers need to know how to evaluate the specific word instruction in their core reading programs. They need to examine the extent to which important words are taught before reading, the extent to which active word learning is promoted in programs, and the extent to which important words are repeated in different contexts. They also need to examine and evaluate the specific word learning strategies that appear in the program, and the practice associated with these strategies.

Comprehension Instruction

Comprehension instruction involves helping students to understand the meaning of the stories and other texts they read in and out of school. More than 30 years of research has shown that instruction in comprehension can help students to understand what they read, remember what they read, and communicate to others about what they read. Teachers need to evaluate the quality of the comprehension instruction in their core reading programs. In particular, they need to determine the extent to which the program helps students to become active and purposeful readers. The program can accomplish these goals through the explicit teaching of strategies such as monitoring comprehension, generating questions, recognizing story structure, and summarizing. Teachers will want to look for programs that include modeling, direct explanation, guided practice, and feedback as comprehension strategy instruction is presented.

Primary-grade teachers can learn to place these five critical components of reading instruction—phonemic awareness, phonics, fluency, vocabulary, and comprehension—into a framework that guides their instructional decisions about what to teach, when, and how. This framework can help teachers as they evaluate and select activities in their basal reading programs. For example, phonics instruction that is readily connected to spelling and writing instruction can also support the learning of both phonics and spelling. With an eye toward the connection among phonics, spelling, and writing, teachers can select activities and skills that reinforce one another.

In addition, the framework can be used to assist teachers as they incorporate other important aspects of reading instruction into their reading program. For example, teachers will want to use high-quality literature as part of their reading program. They will want to read aloud to students every day. Basal programs may make suggestions about other literature resources for teachers to use with their students. Teachers will also want to incorporate writing into their phonics and comprehension instruction. Again, they can select activities from the teacher's manual that incorporate writing into the reading framework. These aspects of reading are critically important, and although they are not mentioned specifically in the National Reading Panel report, they should be included as part of a sensible, comprehensive reading program.

Classroom Organization

Knowledge of how to schedule and organize classroom instruction is essential. Our own experiences suggest that if teachers do not learn how to set up their classrooms appropriately, their knowledge of research-based reading instruction cannot be used effectively. Teachers are often stymied by the procedural aspects of organizing a classroom and scheduling instructional events, sometimes so much that the important knowledge they have about how to instruct their students remains unused. We have been in classrooms of teachers with advanced degrees in reading who know about research-based instructional practices but who fail to implement them because they do not know how to change their current classroom organization.

For professional development to be effective, teachers must be helped with developing new organizational structures and routines in their classrooms. For example, when teachers decide to reorganize their classrooms so that their students spend more time working on fluency, how will they do it? When and where will fluency practice take place? How will the students be organized? Similarly, when teachers decide to spend more time on direct instruction of vocabulary, when and how will this be accomplished? How will this instruction be coordinated with the rest of the reading program? As teachers become critical evaluators of their core reading programs, they should examine these programs for their grouping suggestions. Do these programs suggest organizational routines that will help teachers to restructure their classrooms for different kinds of instruction?

Assessment

Teachers often enter classrooms with insufficient knowledge about the assessment and instructional cycle and how to use that cycle to move students through the instructional program. They may use their core reading programs ineffectively, teaching all students all lessons without an awareness of which students already know what they are being taught and which students need more explicit instruction and/or more practice. Several researchers have shown assessment to be a critical element of reading instruction, especially at the lower grade levels (e.g., Good, Simmons, & Kame'enui, 2001). Citing the phrase "Catch them before they fall," Torgesen (1998) has shown how to use assessment to prevent reading failure. Catching children before they fall behind in reading depends on the wise and efficient use of informal assessments. These assessments provide ongoing feedback to teachers about which students are making adequate progress and which students require immediate attention and help *before* they fall behind. Teachers should examine their core reading programs to see the extent to which specific but informal assessments are provided for them to use with their students. Teachers should learn how to use these assessments to evaluate students' progress in all of the critical components of reading instruction, as a basis for providing some students with extra instruction and practice and as a guide for moving all students through the curriculum so that they make continual progress.

Professional Development for K–3 Teachers: The Process

It is our experience that, regardless of how much professional development teachers have had and how thorough their core reading program is, many teachers have to rethink their existing conceptions about the teaching of reading. Research suggests that the process of professional development is a difficult one, in part because many teachers may have to go through a change process to fully implement new instructional strategies and methods (Hawley & Valli, 1999).

We use an example of a third-grade teacher to demonstrate how difficult teacher change in classrooms can be. Suppose this teacher had been teaching for seven years. She always used a basal reading program as the foundation of her reading instruction, but she had her own way of choosing certain instructional procedures from the program. For example, she taught all of her reading lessons using whole-group instruction. She selected certain skills that she thought were important from the teacher's manual and skipped others. She typically taught all the phonics skills because she believed that phonics was the most important part of reading, and she routinely skipped the writing activities because she always thought that her students "did not have enough vocabulary" to write.

Imagine the difficult time this teacher would have in changing her instruction based on the research-based reading instruction supported by the National Reading Panel (NICHHD, 2000). This third-grade teacher would have to rethink her view of the reading process and how she taught reading on a daily basis. She would have to rethink her view of phonics instruction, using it not for everyone but only for those in her class who needed it. She would have to revisit the idea of small-group instruction, particularly for her struggling readers who needed phonics instruction as well as fluency practice in some easier texts. She would have to rethink her views of her children's abilities to write because writing is, among other things, a good way to practice the spelling-sound system. Given the complexity of most instructional days, these changes would likely appear to be overwhelming for this teacher.

What types of professional development are most likely to help this third-grade teacher adopt new and different instructional strategies and procedures for teaching reading in the primary classrooms? A large body of research suggests that the traditional service delivery model, typically a "one-shot" workshop, is largely ineffective in improving teachers' classroom instruction (Fullan, 1991; Sparks, 1995). In contrast, other research points to the need teachers have for ongoing assistance and support as they work to implement new instructional strategies in their classrooms (Guskey, 1995; Hodges, 1996). Joyce and Showers (1995) found that teachers are far more likely to implement new instructional strategies when they have or do the following:

1. *Theoretical knowledge.*   Teachers gain an understanding of why small-group instruction and grade-level text are important in helping students learn to read.

2. *Demonstration.*   Teachers have the opportunity to observe classrooms in which mentor teachers show how they organize their classes for small-group work, and then model the activities they use with their students in these small groups.

3. *Practice.*   With the help of a mentor teacher, teachers reorganize their schedules and then practice small-group instruction with their students.

4. *Feedback and In-Class Coaching.*   Mentor teachers observe teachers working in small groups with their students and provide help and feedback.

In their studies of teacher change, Joyce and Showers found that the last step, feedback and in-class coaching—when added to the other three steps—caused the largest increase in teacher use of new instructional strategies in their classrooms. In other words, after teachers knew the theory supporting an instructional practice, had seen a demonstration of the practice, and had an opportunity to practice the instruction, then feedback and in-class coaching increased the chances that teachers would take ownership of the instructional strategies and make them part of their repertoire of daily instructional practices in their classrooms.

Conclusion

Primary-grade teachers will need extensive professional development if we expect them to help children meet the high demands of literacy today. The daily task of teaching primary-grade children to read is a very complex one, involving instantaneous organizational and instructional decisions, even with solid reading materials from which to work and a teacher's thorough and thoughtful planning. Necessary parts of professional development include assisting teachers in knowing the latest theory and research about the five components of reading, observing model lessons by mentor teachers and others, and practicing in their own classrooms with support from mentor teachers. Without all of these elements of professional development, teachers will not have the amount of support they need to effectively improve their instruction to meet the high level of literacy we expect in our society today.

References

Fullan, M. G. (1991). *The new meaning of educational change*. New York: Teachers College Press.

Good, R. H., Simmons, D. C., & Kame'enui, E. J. (2001). The importance and decision-making utility of a continuum of fluency-based indicators of foundational reading skills for third-grade high-stakes outcomes. *Scientific Studies of Reading, 5,* 257–288.

Guskey, T. R. (1995). Professional development in education: In search of an optimal mix. In T. R. Guskey & M. Huberman (Eds.), *Professional development in education: New paradigms and practices.* New York: Teachers College Press.

Hawley, W. D., & Valli, L. (1999). The essentials of effective professional development: A new consensus. In L. Darling-Hammond & G. Sykes (Eds.), *Teaching as the learning profession* (pp. 127–150). San Francisco: Jossey-Bass.

Hodges, H. L. B. (1996). Using research to inform practice in urban schools: Ten key strategies to success. *Educational Policy, 10,* 223–252.

Joyce, B., & Showers, B. (1995). *Student achievement through staff development.* White Plains, NY: Longman.

National Institute of Child Health and Human Development (NICHHD). (2000). *Report of the National Reading Panel. Teaching children to read: An evidence-based assessment of the scientific research literature on reading and its implications for reading instruction.* (NIH Publication No. 00-4769). Washington, D.C.: U.S. Government Printing Office.

Sparks, D. (1995). A paradigm shift in staff development. *ERIC Review, 3,* 24.

Torgesen, J. K. (1998). Catch them before they fall. *American Educator, 22* (1, 2), 32–39.

Chapter 6

Fostering Literacy at the Later Elementary Grades: What Teachers Need to Know and Be Able to Do

Kathy Ganske and Joanne K. Monroe

Key Ideas

✓ The knowledge and skills that teachers need for helping children to fulfill their potential cannot be achieved in the short time that professors have with preservice teachers.

✓ If we want all students to receive the education they deserve, it is imperative that professional development be part of the fabric of the school and that a menu of professional development opportunities be available at each school.

✓ To ensure that this happens, it is the job of the instructional leader of the school to recognize and understand classroom expertise, to keep current on instructional research and theory, and to know how to orchestrate meaningful opportunities for teachers to collaborate and grow.

For

• K–12 teachers

• K–12 administrators

In this chapter we address some of the issues that intermediate-grade teachers must consider in delivering quality reading instruction: the learners, content and instruction, assessment, and classroom management. We suggest professional development that can help teachers to improve their practice in each of these areas. We begin with a statement from fourth-grade teacher Jean Anderson, who describes the professional development experience she has found most effective:

> Reading and writing were always favorite subjects of mine. So, when I began as a fourth grade teacher I was excited to share my enthusiasm with my students. In my college methods courses I had learned many activities to engage readers and writers and was eager to put them into practice. However, I soon began to question whether I was really teaching students to understand text and become writers. They read and they wrote, and the activities were fun, but I felt that students were really not reaching the heart of reading or writing.

> This reflection led me to seek answers. The main source of help for what drives my instruction today was professional text. I became familiar with many texts through district book studies. The book studies consisted of groups of colleagues striving to grow as professionals by seeking answers to questions through professional reading, sharing experiences, and giving advice. It was inspiring to be able to chat with other professionals and realize I was not the only one struggling with issues such as differentiation, reading comprehension, and writing workshop. By listening to others make meaning of the texts we read, I came to a greater understanding of the true meaning of literacy.

> However, my real growth as a teacher occurred when I set about bringing these texts into action in my classroom. The process reinforced my beliefs of what real reading and writing should be and taught me how to approach my students with new techniques and understandings. I was able to pass on to them the sense of empowerment I felt through the knowledge I had gained from reading and discussion. In doing this, the learning community I had fostered from the beginning became even stronger as the readers and writers in my classroom began using talk and problem solving to help each other. I realized that the community was the real foundation of literacy instruction. As I attuned to the needs of individual students, I began to motivate all learners, because success at any level sparked sharing, which excited others and created a domino effect of learning.

> My graduate studies, my involvement in my district's professional development committee, my attendance and participation in conferences and workshops, and my engagement in action research all contribute to my increasing ability to make effective instructional

decisions for my students. However, my ongoing involvement in reading and discussing professional literature with my colleagues continues to provide my most rewarding professional development.

Learners in the Intermediate Grades

As students move from the primary grades into the intermediate grades of later elementary school, mounting concerns over high-stakes testing and the need to "cover everything" sometimes lead to classrooms that are less personal and more curriculum-driven. This is not the case for teachers like Jean Anderson, whose effective, well-managed classroom displays a strong sense of community and a high regard for doing, knowing, and learning. Mutual respect, shared responsibility, and a pride of belonging are readily apparent in classrooms like Jean's. Students understand what they are to do and feel empowered and supported to confront challenges. Teachers know that in order to provide the kind of high-quality content and instruction that will enable all students to achieve, they must understand their students' particular needs and plan responsive instruction.

Differences among students tend to become more pronounced through the intermediate grades. Added to the diversity of students' linguistic, cultural, and economic backgrounds may be differences stemming from personal interests (such as a desire to be accepted), gender, and previous years of schooling, which may have fostered confidence and motivation or, inadvertently, failure and discouragement. Teachers in grades 3 through 6 can and must respond to these differences (Tomlinson, 1999). Those who do so will vary instructional formats to meet various learning needs, match readers to texts and instruction to readers, provide choice, encourage ownership of learning, and ensure opportunities for peer interaction.

By tailoring materials and instruction to their students, teachers encourage everyone to be an active and successful learner. In order to provide students with books they can read (with 90% or greater accuracy) and to assist them in learning to maximize their understanding as they read, teachers must come to know students' reading behaviors and reading preferences. Children in the intermediate grades are motivated by choice; therefore, teachers should ensure that students have access to books they want to read, a situation that is often not the case, especially for reluctant readers (Worthy, Moorman, & Turner, 1999). Besides being motivational, choice enables students to support their reading by drawing on areas of strength—their interests and knowledge—ingredients that may be crucial to the success of those who struggle with literacy.

To accommodate the diverse range of reading abilities and inter-ests found in the intermediate grades, it is essential that classroom libraries be well stocked with a wide variety of texts.

Being able to interact with peers is also important to intermediate-grade students. Wise teachers turn these social needs to worth-while purposes by planning activities that involve work with peers: collaborative projects, small-group discussions, and partner activi-ties. When carefully planned and appropriate, activities like these can increase motivation and learning as well as foster positive peer relations (NICHHD, 2000).

Content and Instruction

Sophisticated readers employ many strategies independently and spontaneously throughout their reading. For example, they rely on prior knowledge and prediction to make connections and set pur-poses before they read, they reread and think strategically while reading to maintain meaning, and they apply graphic organizers and note-taking tools to refer back to the text after reading. Most students in the intermediate grades require instruction to develop and gain control of strategies needed for comprehension as well as to enhance their word knowledge and oral reading fluency. The comprehension skills and strategies identified in the current litera-ture provide a guide to what must be taught at these grade levels. For example, according to the report of the National Reading Panel (NICHHD, 2000), students need to learn to do the following:

1. Monitor for comprehension

2. Focus and discuss reading

3. Use graphic organizers, active listening, mental imagery and mnemonic strategies, and prior knowledge to improve memory and comprehension

4. Coordinate multiple strategies

5. Self-question and answer questions

6. Use story structure

7. Summarize

8. Develop vocabulary

In addition to being knowledgeable of their students and of what to teach, teachers must know how to effectively help their students to learn comprehension strategies like those above, and they must realize that it is not just a matter of assigning and questioning

(Durkin, 1978–79). Teaching students to comprehend requires carefully scaffolded instruction that moves from explanation to demonstration, then to guided practice, and finally to opportunities for students to independently apply what they have learned. Once completed, the cycle begins anew with a fresh focus. Such explicit teaching of comprehension is critical beyond the primary grades, where comprehension of narrative and expository text takes on an increasingly significant role throughout the content areas.

Teachers must also be familiar with a large and varied body of literature appropriate to the intermediate-grade learner so they can teach and recommend appropriate texts to their students throughout the scaffolding cycle. Read-alouds enable teachers to expose students to a wide range of genres, low-frequency vocabulary, and fluent oral reading. The integration of think-aloud teaching strategies (Davey, 1983; Keene & Zimmermann, 1997), which often feature picture books with read alouds, make it possible for intermediate-grade teachers to demonstrate what good readers do to monitor their understanding and to show how they resolve confusions when comprehension breaks down. Sometimes the purpose of the think-aloud is to alert students to special features associated with expository text like headings, graphics, and captions, and to demonstrate ways to use these features to facilitate understanding. Other demonstration lessons might focus on modeling journal writing or specific reading responses, note-taking in preparation for report writing, and summarizing. Teachers must be aware of their own strategic reading and thinking in order to explain and demonstrate comprehension strategies for their students, and many teachers need professional development to gain this awareness.

Guided practice for reading can be arranged through various instructional formats, including the whole class, small groups, and one-to-one. The small-group option enables teachers to differentiate instruction while supporting several students at a time. During small-group guided-reading instruction, strategies and skills are taught in a timely manner, and all students engage in guided practice with texts that have just the right amount of challenge, those at their instructional level. The teacher plays an active role in helping students to learn to monitor and adjust their reading for understanding. Literature circles also involve small groups, but the support afforded by them is somewhat different. This instructional approach addresses students' needs for choice and social interaction; the motivation and collaboration that result will assist students in reading strategically while teachers observe and intervene as necessary (Strickland, Ganske, & Monroe, 2002). Other types of small-group teaching and guided practice may be necessary to accommodate students who require modified instruction, materials, or evaluation.

At times students may engage in guided practice with a partner. For example, multiple readings of the same text that help students to develop fluency (Rasinski, 1990) can be effectively managed in pairs. This format affords a number of benefits, especially when students are asked to switch partners for each reading. Readers gain a fresh audience and a purpose for repeating the reading and profit from the feedback of a number of listeners. Listeners are exposed to new stories and information and have opportunities to articulate their own criteria for reading fluency through the feedback they provide.

After students have had the benefit of sufficient explanation, demonstration, and supported practice, they need time and occasions to apply their understandings through silent reading of self-selected and assigned texts, thereby completing the cycle of scaffolded instruction.

The scaffolding techniques that are effective for teaching comprehension and fluency are also valuable for vocabulary study, including the skills of rereading, dictionary and context use, morphemic analysis, structural analysis or decoding, and other word study. Teachers should bear in mind that although most students in the intermediate grades are likely to be well on their way to becoming skilled readers, some are not. Novice readers still need to learn basic spelling patterns to enable them to read and write efficiently (Ganske, 2000).

Teachers who effectively scaffold their instruction acquire this ability through professional development that includes professional reading and discussion (e.g., the book studies described by Jean Anderson at the beginning of this chapter) or through workshops that feature a facilitator who demonstrates the techniques. Videos of expert teachers using these techniques and peer coaching (Robbins, 1991) can also help teachers to improve their reading instruction.

Assessment

Understanding Learners

To provide students with "just right" books and instruction, it is imperative that teachers understand their students as individuals and as learners. In addition to data that may be available from district, state, or national testing, teachers in the intermediate grades need to be familiar with informal measures and methods that can supply them with ongoing information about their students. Interest inventories, reading surveys, peer interviews, conversations about reading preferences, and autobiography writing are often planned as beginning-of-the-year activities so that teachers can get to know their students. In some schools students write end-of-the-year letters to their next year's teacher ("Dear Fourth-Grade Teacher") describing their strengths, weaknesses, and interests. Regardless of the means, it is critical for teachers to discover their students' interests and capitalize on them to foster motivation and confidence.

Various techniques can be used to gather information about the specific reading behaviors of a child and to estimate the child's reading level. Running records (Clay, 1993) and informal reading inventories (IRIs) are particularly useful; however, both require practice for teachers to gain competence. When learning one of these procedures, most teachers find it beneficial to first observe the process and then to tape-record their practice efforts so they can relisten to the session and check for accuracy in scoring. Being able to receive feedback from an experienced colleague about the analysis of miscues is beneficial, too. Teachers can also gain valuable insights about their students' comprehension, fluency, and pattern-sound knowledge from measures like written or oral retellings, checklists, and spelling inventories. Intermediate-grade teachers must learn to use the assessment data they gather to plan and improve instruction. Professional development in this area may take the form of action research. Action research that includes follow-up assessment can help teachers to determine the effectiveness of instructional change (Sagor, 2000).

Evaluating Performance

Teachers need to be knowledgeable of various ways to evaluate student performance, including alternatives to the traditional paper-and-pencil test. When the latter approach is used, teachers should be sure that what they are testing is what they have taught and that students know how to respond to the types of questions being asked. For example, if students are expected to demonstrate their understanding of informational and narrative text through multiple-choice and open-ended responses (as, for example, the National Assessment of Educational Progress requires), they need experiences that teach them how to approach these tasks.

Various alternatives, including teacher observation, rubrics, and student self-evaluations can supplement more traditional forms of assessment. Observing students at work in various instructional formats provides teachers with ongoing information about the students' performance and involvement so they can intervene immediately when necessary; it is an essential part of the assessment process. Teachers need to develop an efficient and effective system for taking and maintaining anecdotal records of their observations so that the notes can be used to inform instruction. Teachers also need to know how to design and use rubrics. These scoring guides can assist teachers with assessing projects, oral and written reading responses, fluency, and other reading-related tasks. Although it takes time, and sometimes peer support, for teachers to become efficient in their use, rubrics allow teachers to evaluate objectively and consistently and thereby simplify the process of evaluation. Rubrics also let students know from the start what the expectations are and help them to recognize strengths and weaknesses in their products. Students in the intermediate grades can be taught to reflect on their progress over time, such as with response writing, and helped to identify areas for improvement. Self-evaluation and goal setting encourage students to take responsibility for their learning.

Classroom Management

In most intermediate-grade classrooms, time for teaching and practicing reading is limited. Successful teachers are well prepared, and they know how to manage time, materials, and student behavior to maximize students' learning. They establish classroom routines and monitor their effectiveness, making changes as necessary; transition times require specific procedures to ensure a smooth change from one activity to another with minimal disruption of the teaching time. Posting a schedule and using organizing tools, such as a work board, can help teachers and students pace their work and anticipate transition times. Labeled baskets or folders for filing finished work, including homework, can expedite the process of verifying that assignments due are complete. Materials needed for reading instruction or independent work should be readily available to students and able to be easily stored by them after use. The more students know about the procedures in their classroom, the more likely they are to consistently follow them.

In addition to establishing routines and procedures that encourage students to manage their own behavior in responsible ways, it is critical for intermediate-grade teachers to carefully plan interesting and meaningful reading work for various instructional formats. Small-group instruction allows for the use of appropriately leveled texts and/or differentiated tasks that promote active student involvement rather than frustration or boredom, which often lead to off-task behavior. When the teacher meets with a small group while the rest of the class works independently or in small teams, students working without the teacher need tasks that are appropriately challenging and absorbing. Response writing, purposeful re-reading, and hands-on word study are examples of activities that can engage and maintain each student's interest. If a cooperative learning structure is used, all students must have clearly defined responsibilities to ensure accountability for everyone. Because students work at different paces, teachers need to plan and explain to students their alternatives once the assigned tasks are completed, such as reading a self-selected book.

Students in the intermediate grades respond to teachers' expectations of their behavior when the expectations are clearly articulated and respectful of students' need to have a voice in their learning and behavior. Setting procedures for moving about and entering or exiting the room—to sharpen a pencil, collect or return materials needed for class work, or join or leave a small group—is helpful to the long-term maintenance of student behavior. Immediately reminding students who veer from expected procedures helps to reinforce appropriate behavior.

The establishment of an effective classroom management system is an important part of any school district's mentoring of its new and novice teachers. It often falls to teacher colleagues who work as mentors to direct and encourage new teachers in the classroom management element of their professional development; theirs should be a proactive rather than reactive approach. For all teachers who require assistance with classroom management, resources such as descriptions of exemplary classroom practices (Danielson, 1996) are helpful. The most effective professional development in these situations may be classroom observations of teachers whose management systems are effective. These may be followed by conversations with colleagues and/or supervisors to determine specific goals for changing current practice and setting standards that will be used to determine whether the goals have been met. If classroom observations are difficult or uncomfortable to arrange, videotapes of effectively managed classrooms can be substituted.

Conclusion

Teachers who create and manage classrooms that work for intermediate-grade students attend to myriad details. In addition to organizing the environment in which students will learn, they plan the content of their instruction and the ways they will deliver it and assess their students' learning. Some teachers begin their careers knowing how to orchestrate classrooms that function effectively for their students. Most teachers, however, require experience and professional development throughout their years of teaching to develop and maintain the knowledge and sensitivity required of exemplary teachers.

References

Clay, M. (1993). *An observation survey of early literacy achievement.* Portsmouth, NH: Heinemann.

Danielson, C. (1996). *Enhancing professional practice: A framework for teaching.* Alexandria, VA: ASCD.

Davey, B. (1983). Think-aloud: Modeling the cognitive processes of reading comprehension. *Journal of Reading, 27,* 44–47.

Durkin, D. (1978–79). What classroom observations reveal about reading comprehension instruction. *Reading Research Quarterly, 14,* 481–533.

Ganske, K. (2000). *Word journeys: Assessment-guided phonics, spelling, and vocabulary instruction.* New York: Guilford Press.

Keene, E. O., & Zimmermann, S. (1997). *Mosaic of thought: Teaching comprehension in a reader's workshop.* Portsmouth, NH: Heinemann.

National Institute of Child Health and Human Development (NICHHD). (2000). *Report of the National Reading Panel. Teaching children to read: An evidence-based assessment of the scientific research literature on reading and its implications for reading instruction.* (NIH Publication No. 00-4769). Washington, D.C.: U.S. Government Printing Office.

Rasinski, T. (1990). Effects of repeated reading and listening-while-reading on reading fluency. *Journal of Educational Research, 83,* 147–150.

Robbins, P. (1991). *How to plan and implement a peer coaching program.* Alexandria, VA: ASCD.

Sagor, R. (2000). *Guiding school improvement with action research.* Alexandria, VA: ASCD.

Strickland, D. S., Ganske, K., & Monroe, J.K. (2002). *Supporting struggling readers and writers: Strategies for classroom intervention 3–6.* Portland, ME: Stenhouse.

Tomlinson, C. A. (1999). *The differentiated classroom: Responding to the needs of all learners.* Alexandria, VA: ASCD.

Worthy, J., Moorman, M., & Turner, M. (1999). What Johnny likes to read is hard to find in schools. *Reading Research Quarterly, 34,* 12–27.

Professional Development Content for Reading Educators at the Middle and High School Levels

. . . .

Donna E. Alvermann and Allison Nealy

Key Ideas

✓ The focus of this chapter is on the content of professional development for reading educators at the middle and high school levels.

✓ A learning specialist discusses her collaboration with social studies and science middle school teachers.

✓ A university professor examines some assumptions underlying the reading profession's knowledge base and invites a reexamination of what constitutes the content of professional development for reading educators.

For

• Teachers, teacher educators, and administrators responsible for secondary (middle and high school) and special education

---

Professional development courses for reading educators often emphasize process over content, and understandably so. At the undergraduate level, prospective teachers are often more concerned about classroom management issues than about the content they will teach, believing (understandably) that unless they have good classroom control, students will not attend to content. At the graduate level, teachers in reading education courses are often encouraged to update their teaching strategies, rethink classroom routines, and delve deeper into the pedagogies they practice. Content, when it is taught in reading education courses, is usually embedded in curriculum issues, or it is the vehicle through which strategies and skills are presented and practiced.

In this chapter, the emphasis is reversed. Here we focus on the content of professional development for reading educators at the middle and high school levels, and only secondarily do we consider the processes. We begin with Allison's description of how her collaboration as a learning specialist with social studies and science middle school teachers allows her to examine some of her own assumptions underlying the tension between teaching content and process. After that, Donna examines some assumptions underlying the reading profession's knowledge base and invites a reexamination of what constitutes the content of professional development for reading educators.

Allison

I am fortunate that my multifaceted role enables me to see students and teachers from several angles. First and most important, I am a teacher—not just one particular kind of teacher, but a teacher who has the opportunity to work with students across ability levels, grade levels, and content areas. You see, by definition I am an eighth-grade, special education teacher. I serve students with mild disabilities such as learning disabilities, emotional-behavior disorders, and intellectual disabilities. In addition to direct services for these students, I collaborate with science and social studies teachers in my school. Collaboration, or co-teaching, as many call it, involves two teachers—the content specialist and the learning specialist—mutually providing instruction. I have been afforded the opportunity to act as the learning specialist for several classes that serve general education students.

Layered onto my identity as a teacher is the role of doctoral student in the field of reading education. I began my program several years ago thinking that I would learn the "tricks" to improve reading comprehension skills. I saw my coursework through my special education lens, not bothering to consider the possibility that students other than the ones with disabilities were struggling in reading. That was one of many lessons learned in my career as a teacher of adolescents. Upon entering my first collaboration class, I was shocked to find general education students struggling with comprehension of the textbook. I remember thinking to myself, "This can't be! These are *regular* education kids!" I began speaking with content area teachers across grade levels. My second lesson learned was that these content area teachers were adamant that they were not reading teachers. What were they to do, they asked me, with students who could not access the curriculum? After all, they weren't reading teachers.

I pondered this question for many months. As a resource teacher, I had inaccurately assumed that the only students who struggled in reading were receiving assistance through resource, tutoring, or student support services. My role as a collaborator, in my mind, became fuzzy. Do I forsake teaching the content for assisting with comprehension? Then one day I heard the statement "We are all reading teachers." I initially heard it from our principal in regard to a recent initiative requiring all middle school teachers to receive 50 hours in reading instruction. Then, not long after that, I heard it again, this time at the university. I thought to myself, "This expression must certainly mean something."

As I continued to toss around the notion of "every teacher a reading teacher," I was assigned several practicum students and a student teacher from the special education department at the university. I was excited to share my new discoveries that students outside our special education world actually had difficulties with reading. The college students were initially intimidated by the idea of collaboration, but they were relieved to find students in the classroom who demonstrated learning characteristics and needs similar to the ones they were trained to teach. By watching the children, the college students, and myself that first year of collaboration, I learned that students are more alike than they are different. Despite differences due to disability, gender, race, and personal background, all students need assistance in improving content area reading, and it is my job as a teacher and supervisor of student teachers to provide that assistance. After all, we *are* all reading teachers.

Donna

Allison's discovery that students other than those with disabilities were struggling to comprehend their reading assignments in social studies and science surprised her. Yet any of us who have been "regular" education teachers know from experience that all readers struggle at some point with certain texts in certain contexts. It is the rare individual, indeed, who has never met a text that did not prove too challenging a read, at least initially. What distinguishes that kind of reader from the reader Allison was accustomed to teaching in her role as special educator is a whole set of assumptions underlying how students come to be viewed as struggling, at least as portrayed in the professional literature.

This literature covers a broad spectrum and varies in specificity according to the perceived reasons behind the struggle. Researchers focusing on individuals with clinically diagnosed reading disabilities (e.g., Shaywitz et al., 2000) tend to see in their data a cognitive or neurological basis for the struggle. Researchers studying second-language reading (e.g., Bernhardt, 2000; Garcia, 2000), on the other hand, consider the social, cultural, motivational, and linguistic factors that may account in part for the struggle and that vary according to the population of English language learners being studied. Clearly, there are different points of view on what contributes to a reader's struggle to comprehend, including those advanced by education anthropologists McDermott and Varenne (1995), who suggest that society at large produces the conditions necessary for some individuals to succeed, others to struggle, and still others to fail outright.

Adolescents with a history of reading difficulties present particular challenges to content area teachers. Because they read so infrequently, these youth typically will not have acquired the requisite background knowledge and specialized vocabulary needed for comprehending most school science texts. Some teachers understandably become frustrated when this occurs and resort to what Finn (1999) calls a "domesticating" education. That is, they expect less of these students in exchange for the students' good will and reasonable effort in completing content area assignments that typically require little, if any, reading. Or, unwilling to give up, they may pursue what is commonly known as the search for a "silver bullet"—a so-called best practice that will enable them to reach all their students in an effective yet manageable way.

One of the difficulties associated with the latter approach, however, is that professional development experts do not always agree on what constitutes "best practice" in teaching youth to read texts of various types (e.g., print, visual, symbolic, digital). At a time when literacies are changing quickly and in complex ways to meet the demands of new communication technologies, a one-size-fits-all model of reading seems inadequate to the task. In fact, one can increasingly observe in U.S. teacher education circles a growing number of literacy educators who are critical of a one-size-fits-all model of reading. This is particularly the case for individuals whose work is focused on reconceptualizing the literacies in adolescents' lives (e.g., Alvermann, Hinchman, Moore, Phelps, & Waff, 1998; Bean & Readence, 2002; Moje, Young, Readence, & Moore, 2000). Building on the work of Gee (1996), Lankshear, Gee, Knobel, and Searle (1997), and numerous others whose writings question an autonomous, one-size-fits-all model of reading, professional development experts at the middle and high school level are coming to understand why some students' literacy development is every bit as dependent upon access to certain socioeconomic and cultural resources as it is to skills instruction. In effect, the very content of professional development for reading educators is coming under investigation.

Feeding into this need to examine and question what we once comfortably assumed was an adequate knowledge base for reading teacher education is the work on adolescents' multiple literacies. For example, it is becoming clear that credence must be given to the literacies that adolescents use outside school (Alvermann, 2002; Hull & Schultz, 2001, 2002; Moje et al., 2000), while at the same time fully acknowledging that there is much blurring and overlapping between those literacies and what are commonly referred to as school literacies. At the high school level, particularly, there is considerable debate over what counts (or should count) as literate behavior among adolescents.

More often than not, professional development experts who have engaged in this debate have differences of opinion as to whether school literacy—what Street (1995) refers to as Literacy with a capital L—should reign ascendant over the multiliteracies that youth use in their everyday worlds outside school (e.g., surfing the Web, e-mailing, instant-messaging). The tendency to assume that school literacy (with its emphasis on printed texts) should be privileged over adolescents' other literacies (visual, digital, and symbolic) is being questioned more and more. Why this is the case and what it might mean for the content of professional development is explored next within the context of new literacies for new times.

Rethinking the Content of Professional Development

Literacy is on the verge of reinventing itself, and with this reinvention will come implications for the content of professional development for reading educators at the middle and high school levels. Allan Luke and John Elkins, former editors of the *Journal of Adolescent & Adult Literacy*, noted in their first issue of the journal more than five years ago that the potential for such reinvention is reflected in the way that "texts and literate practices of everyday life are changing at an unprecedented and disorienting pace" (Luke & Elkins, 1998, p. 4). Attributing these changes largely to new communication technologies and to the complex multiliteracies that such technologies entail, Luke and Elkins went on to characterize the era in which we are living as new times. It is a time of major shifts in cultural practices, economic systems, and social institutions on a global scale—a time when literacy educators around the world are speculating about the ways in which these changes will alter people's conceptions of reading and writing.

It is also a time in which scholars are becoming critical of a view of youth culture that treats adolescents as incomplete adults (Amit-Talai & Wulff, 1995; Lesko, 2001). Rather than view them as "not-yet" adults and thus less competent and less knowledgeable than their elders, there is growing support among professional development experts for viewing adolescents as people who know things that have to do with their particular situations and the particular places and spaces they occupy. This situated perspective on youth culture argues as well for exploring how people (adolescents and adults alike) act provisionally at particular times, given particular circumstances within various contexts (Morgan, 1997). Similar to those scholars who write about the blurred relationships between adolescents and adults as they engage in multiple forms of literacy within and against the backdrop of a digital world, we believe that how such relationships develop, change, or sustain themselves over time have implications for how the content of professional development for reading educators must change to keep pace with what is being learned about adolescents and their literacies in new times. Armed with this kind of knowledge, professional development experts are less likely to make inappropriate assumptions about what content is salient and what is not.

Finally, in light of the changes that we perceive will come from rethinking the current knowledge base for the professional development of reading educators, we return to the notion of collaboration that Allison introduced earlier. We see value in rethinking the very content of collaboration—for example, who is included, why, and how participants across different age groups might interact. Collaborations need not, for example, be largely teacher-conceived and teacher-driven. They can also go on among students as they learn to take greater responsibility for their own learning in what Wade and Moje (2000) describe as the participatory classroom.

Participatory approaches to literacy instruction are no less concerned with content mastery than is the more traditional teacher-centered transmission approach. However, rather than emphasize the teacher's responsibility for transmitting facts and concepts, participatory approaches can support adolescents' academic literacy development by incorporating classroom structures that promote peer interaction (e.g., peer-led literature discussion groups, reading and writing workshops) and interactions with more knowledgeable others (e.g., scaffolded instruction, in which a teacher supports students' learning and then gradually withdraws that support as students show they are capable of assuming more responsibility for their own learning).

In transmission classrooms, texts (like teachers) are viewed as dispensers of knowledge, whereas in participatory classrooms, students use texts as *tools* for learning and constructing new knowledge. Researchers who have studied participatory approaches to reading instruction point to the authenticity of student-constructed texts, especially when compared to texts that serve as repositories of information in the transmission model (Wade & Moje, 2000). However, in actual classroom practice, it is rarely the case that one can draw lines separating the two approaches as cleanly as is possible on paper. As Pearson (1999) has noted, teaching approaches that seem contradictory on the surface often support one another. This seems also to be the case in the literature that Moore (1996) reviewed on the contexts for literacy at the middle and high school levels. In that literature, teachers' knowledge and beliefs about the goals that should drive literacy instruction, the availability of resources, and classroom participation structures influenced how a particular approach was used. Thus, peer-led literature discussions enacted in one context did not necessarily resemble the same approach used in a different context. This has relevance for professional development purposes inasmuch as it would be inappropriate to assume that mandating so-called best practices would work or look the same in different school and classroom contexts. Nor would such mandating work for teachers who are accustomed, like Allison, to thinking through decisions they make about their own teaching, and particularly about the balance they will strike between teaching processes (skills) and teaching content.

References

Alvermann, D. E. (Ed.). (2002). *Adolescents and literacies in a digital world.* New York: Lang.

Alvermann, D. E., Hinchman, K. A., Moore, D. W., Phelps, S. F., & Waff, D. R. (Eds.). (1998). *Reconceptualizing the literacies in adolescents' lives.* Mahwah, NJ: Erlbaum.

Amit-Talai, V., & Wulff, H. (Eds.). (1995). *Youth cultures: A cross-cultural perspective.* New York: Routledge.

Bean, T. W., & Readence, J. E. (2002). Adolescent literacy: Charting a course for successful futures as lifelong learners. *Reading Research and Instruction, 41,* 203–210.

Bernhardt, E. B. (2000). Second-language reading as a case study of reading scholarship in the 20th century. In M. L. Kamil, P. B. Mosenthal, P. D. Pearson, & R. Barr (Eds.), *Handbook of reading research* (Vol. 3, pp. 791–811). Mahwah, NJ: Erlbaum.

Finn, P. J. (1999). *Literacy with an attitude: Educating working-class children in their own self-interest.* Albany, NY: State University of New York Press.

Garcia, G. E. (2000). Bilingual children's reading. In M. L. Kamil, P. B. Mosenthal, P. D. Pearson, & R. Barr (Eds.), *Handbook of reading research* (Vol. 3, pp. 813–834). Mahwah, NJ: Erlbaum.

Gee, J. P. (1996). *Social linguistics and literacies* (2nd ed.). London: Taylor & Francis.

Hull, G., & Schultz, K. (2001). Literacy and learning out of school: A review of theory and research. *Review of Educational Research, 71,* 575–611.

Hull, G., & Schultz, K. (Eds.). (2002). *School's out: Bridging out-of-school literacies with classroom practice.* New York: Teachers College Press.

Lankshear, C., Gee, J. P., Knobel, M., & Searle, C. (1997). *Changing literacies.* Buckingham, UK: Open University Press.

Lesko, N. (2001). *Act your age! A cultural construction of adolescence.* New York: Routledge.

Luke, A., & Elkins, J. (1998). Reinventing literacy in "New Times." *Journal of Adolescent & Adult Literacy, 42,* 4–7.

McDermott, R., & Varenne, H. (1995). Culture *as* disability. *Anthropology & Education Quarterly, 26,* 324–348.

Moje, E. B., Young, J. P., Readence, J. E., & Moore, D. W. (2000). Reinventing adolescent literacy for new times: Perennial and millennial issues. *Journal of Adolescent & Adult Literacies, 43*, 400–410.

Moore, D. W. (1996). Contexts for literacy in secondary schools. In D. J. Leu, C. K. Kinzer, & K. A. Hinchman (Eds.), *Literacies for the 21st century: Research and practice* (pp. 15–46). Chicago: National Reading Conference.

Morgan, W. (1997). *Critical literacy in the classroom: The art of the possible.* New York: Routledge.

Pearson, P. D. (1999). Foreword. In R. Schoenbach, C. Greenleaf, C. Cziko, & L. Hurwitz, *Reading for understanding* (pp. xi–xiii). San Francisco: Jossey-Bass.

Shaywitz, B. A., Pugh, K. R., Jenner, A. R., Fulbright, R. K., Fletcher, J. M., Gore, J. C., & Shaywitz, S. E. (2000). The neurobiology of reading and reading disability (dyslexia). In M. L. Kamil, P. B. Mosenthal, P. D. Pearson, & R. Barr (Eds.), *Handbook of reading research* (Vol. 3, pp. 229–249). Mahwah, NJ: Erlbaum.

Street, B. V. (1995). *Social literacies: Critical approaches to literacy in development, ethnography, and education.* New York: Longman.

Wade, S. E., & Moje, E. B. (2000). The role of text in classroom learning. In M. L. Kamil, P. B. Mosenthal, P. D. Pearson, & R. Barr (Eds.), *Handbook of reading research* (Vol. 3, pp. 609–627). Mahwah, NJ: Erlbaum.

Part *III*

Issues in Professional Development

Chapter 8

Building Capacity for the Responsive Teaching of Reading in the Academic Disciplines: Strategic Inquiry Designs for Middle and High School Teachers' Professional Development

Cynthia L. Greenleaf and Ruth Schoenbach

Key Ideas

✓ For all students to continue to develop as readers beyond the early grades, plentiful opportunities to read and to learn strategic approaches to reading, with the support and guidance of knowledgeable teachers, are necessary. Yet for many reasons, secondary teachers are reluctant to teach reading in their subject area classes.

✓ Those of us responsible for teachers' professional learning must design effective learning environments for teachers, providing strategic opportunities, tools, resources, and collaborations to assist teachers in developing key capacities necessary to "teach for understanding" in the complexity and diversity of modern classrooms.

✓ By engaging secondary teachers in a variety of inquiries into their own and their students' reading practices, we can assist teachers in constructing richer and more complex theories of reading, in seeing in new and more generous ways their students' capacities to read and learn, in drawing on and developing their own resources and knowledge as teachers of reading, and in transforming their classrooms into places where students develop new identities as capable, academic readers.

For

• Teacher educators
• Administrators, teachers, researchers

These kids just can't, or don't, or won't read.

I don't know anything about teaching reading.

Besides, teaching reading is not my job.

These and similar laments are likely to be familiar to anyone who has talked to middle or high school teachers about the ways their students' reading proficiencies affect their teaching goals or their expectations for student learning. Delivered with sighs of resignation or frustration, these words give voice to the theories that subject area teachers hold about their students' reading abilities and attitudes, about their own capabilities and knowledge to serve as reading mentors, and about the roles and responsibilities they hold as educators. Contributing to teachers' sense of futility, an expanding curriculum and increased public scrutiny in recent years have lodged teachers between the rock of standards and accountability and the hard place of students' actual preparation to read and learn in the subject areas. Given these pressures and teachers' beliefs about their own or their students' limitations, it isn't surprising that many teachers find ways to engage students in learning science, history, math, or even English without relying on students' reading of class texts.

We know that for students to continue to develop as readers beyond the early grades, they need plentiful opportunities to read and to learn strategic approaches to reading with the support and guidance of knowledgeable teachers (for a recent review of this research see Snow, 2002). Despite this knowledge, for decades reading educators have documented that little in the way of comprehension instruction actually occurs in intermediate or secondary classrooms (Durkin, 1978; Snow, 2002). For decades, middle and high school students' reading proficiencies have fallen far short of the mark for a democratic society that depends on a knowledgeable citizenry for increasingly complex dialogue, debate, and decision making (Donohue, Voelkl, Campbell, & Mazzeo, 1999; Mullis, et al., 1994). A considerable body of scholarship has documented secondary teachers' apparent resistance to teaching reading in the subject areas (Alvermann & Moore, 1991; Pajares, 1991; Richardson, 1990).

Our view, however, is that the teachers whose voices open this chapter are misreading the motivations and capacities of their students and underestimating what they themselves can accomplish in the classroom, based on their limited access to the literacy proficiencies that students exhibit outside school and on their own limited conceptions of reading and its relationship to disciplinary thinking. How can we help subject area teachers rethink their assumptions, engage students more deeply in reading, and help students draw on their out-of-school experiences to develop the advanced literacy required to be lifelong learners and participants in a democratic, information-based society? This is the complex problem we are addressing in our work with middle and high school teachers and teacher educators from our own region and around the country.

We have found that by engaging teachers in a variety of inquiries into their own and their students' reading practices, we can assist teachers in constructing richer and more complex theories of reading, in seeing in new and more generous ways their students' capacities to read and learn, and in drawing on and developing their own resources and knowledge as teachers of reading. We have seen teachers transform their classrooms into places where students develop new identities as capable, academic readers. In this chapter we will present a case for an inquiry-based approach to teacher learning that is strategically designed to transform teachers' classroom practices by building key teaching capacities and a deeply experiential knowledge of reading. In designing inquiries for professional development, our goal is to build generative knowledge for teachers—that is, knowledge that enables teachers to create, or generate from their deep understanding of reading, informed and helpful instructional responses to students' reading and thinking in the academic disciplines.

We will describe the professional development tools and approaches that we have been creating, implementing, and studying in collaboration with teacher colleagues, highlighting the key principles of theory and design upon which they are based. We will share the accumulating evidence that this way of working initiates powerful and ongoing teacher learning, changes in teaching practice, and positive literacy growth for students. Finally, based on the lessons we have learned and our experiences in this work, we will offer some recommendations for professional development practice.

A Program of Research and Professional Development

Since 1995, we and our colleagues in the Strategic Literacy Initiative have engaged in collaborative inquiry with various communities of middle and high school teachers to develop tools to assist them in becoming teachers of strategic reading in the context of their ongoing subject area teaching. These tools include an instructional framework, Reading Apprenticeship, which draws on the metaphor of apprenticeship to signal the talent and expertise that both teachers and their students bring to the work of reading, as well as the collaborative relationship that is at the heart of their learning together (Schoenbach, Greenleaf, Cziko, & Hurwitz, 1999, describes the Reading Apprenticeship framework and documents our progress in this work with teachers and students). Over the past eight years, with teacher partners we have developed case studies of students carrying out reading tasks, studies of teachers' work to implement Reading Apprenticeship approaches in various subject area classrooms, and videotapes of classroom literacy events and interactions that serve as resources for professional development. In response to the voices that opened this chapter, our work aims at helping teachers to understand that students bring many reading strengths to academic reading tasks, that teaching reading in their disciplines *is* part of teaching their disciplines, and that they can apprentice students to more powerful ways of working with class texts by drawing on what they know as more expert readers and on what students know as resourceful and strategic adolescents (Greenleaf, Schoenbach, Cziko, & Mueller, 2001).

For several years we have provided a yearlong series of professional development sessions for approximately 300 middle and high school teachers from our local region, as well as several national institutes for an additional 50 to 150 teacher leaders from other states and regions. Teachers who volunteer for this professional development come to the Strategic Literacy Initiative in cross-disciplinary school teams and meet in a learning network with several other school teams to develop cross-disciplinary and cross-site perspectives on reading instruction. To further develop teacher leadership capacity, we engage teachers who have completed their first year of professional development in a continuing professional development network, at which they work in both subject-specific groups and school teams to develop tools and resources to support the work of teacher colleagues. To bring resources and tools to the preparation of beginning teachers, we conduct a collaborative teacher education consortium for colleagues in preservice education. Our scope of work focuses broadly on designing and studying many ways of engaging communities of middle and high school teachers in inquiry modes of teaching and learning, in order to help teachers embrace and develop the work of apprenticing students to discipline-specific ways of reading.

Design Matters: The Research Base for Inquiry-Based Professional Development

The professional development approach of the Strategic Literacy Initiative derives from new conceptions of teaching that have emerged over the past 30 years as researchers have studied teachers' thinking and decision-making processes in the dynamic flow of teaching events and practices (Darling-Hammond & Sykes, 1999). In this research, variously carried out by cognitive scientists, learning theorists, and teachers themselves, teaching has been shown to be a highly complex undertaking. Teachers carry out curriculum or lesson plans in interaction with their students, who are themselves dynamically responding to teaching and learning opportunities. Through myriad and instantaneous appraisals of student responses to lessons, teachers make decisions and carry out instructional actions that shape students' opportunities to learn, evaluate students' performance and capabilities, and orchestrate students' interactions with one another and class materials, including texts.

Based on this understanding of teaching as interactive thinking and decision making, educators have increasingly begun to recognize the importance of teachers' abilities to understand the thinking and learning processes of their students. Defining teaching as a complex and responsive interaction with learners, David Cohen and Deborah Ball write that "'teaching' is what a teacher does, says, and thinks *with her learners, concerning materials and tasks, in a particular social organization of instruction, in environments, over time*" (Cohen & Ball, 2000, p. 5, emphasis added). To be effective, teachers need to acquire the capacity to listen to and interpret student thinking and learning processes.

This capacity is particularly important in teaching key domains like literacy, where the challenge of helping the diverse students in modern classrooms develop into proficient, academic readers offers a particularly clear view of the complexity of high-quality teaching. Reading has long been understood as a complex, interactive process of constructing meaning with text. In addition to a cognitive task, reading is an essentially social and communicative task. Yet students in U.S. schools come from a variety of economic, linguistic, cultural, and ethnic backgrounds, bringing significantly different experiences and expectations about how to initiate and sustain conversations, how to interact with teachers and peers, how to identify and solve different types of problems, and how to go about particular reading and writing tasks (Greenleaf, Hull, & Reilly,

1994; Lee, 1995). In addition, they have experiences with and proficiencies in home and community language and literacies that are generally not tapped for classroom learning (Alvermann, 2002; Jiménez, 2000; Kamil, Intrator, & Kim, 2000; Lee, 1995; Moje, Young, Readance, & Moore, 2000; Moll, 1992).

The variability of reading tasks and the proficiencies needed for successful performance of school literacy tasks adds to this complexity. Proficient reading of particular texts is influenced by the specific contexts and situations in which reading occurs as well as the social functions that it serves (Moje, Dillon, & O'Brien, 2000). All texts are also shaped by specific conventions and structures of language, and proficient reading of all texts therefore demands the knowledge of these conventions to navigate layers of meaning (Cope & Kalantzis, 1993). In addition, reading becomes increasingly specialized through one's school career, reflecting the broader literate, scientific, or historical conversations that characterize the academic disciplines (Applebee, 1996; Borasi & Seigel, 2000; Lemke, 1990; Wineburg, 1991).

Based on these understandings, literacy researchers have argued that for our diverse learners to successfully carry out academic reading tasks, teachers will need to make explicit the tacit reasoning processes, strategies, and discourse rules that shape successful readers' and writers' work (Delpit, 1995; Freedman, Flower, Hull, & Hayes, 1995; Pressley, 1998). To be effective, teachers must have a deep knowledge of the reading process and the demands that subject area texts place on readers. Furthermore, teachers must learn to tap the language and literacy proficiencies that their students display outside the classroom (Moje, Young, Readance, & Moore, 2000). Describing the kind of responsive teaching that is needed to help students grow as readers beyond the early grades, Alvermann et al. (in press) write, "This teaching involves interactive responses between teachers and students—a process where teachers actively listen as their students express what they know and how they know it, and where teachers help students when they are confused."

The Need to Build Teacher Capacity for Responsive Teaching

Given this conception of teaching as responsive and interactive, a consensus among educators has been growing as to what constitutes high-quality professional development (Guskey & Huberman,

1996; Sparks & Hirsch, 1997). Professional development is recognized as high quality if it engages teachers as learners over time, offers teachers the resources necessary to gain skill and knowledge, creates opportunities for teachers to reflect on their teaching and their students' learning, and recognizes (as well as builds) teachers' expertise. Inquiry methods are thought to be a particularly promising way to build teachers' understanding of the learning issues facing students in the classroom (Shulman, 1986). To effectively teach a variety of learners, many scholars of teaching argue that teachers should take a stance of inquiry toward their own teaching because such a stance offers a way of actively learning while teaching (Ball & Cohen, 1999). To these theorists, high-quality professional development engages teachers in inquiry modes of learning—"reading" students to know more about what they are thinking and learning, examining longstanding beliefs and assumptions about learning, and gaining a repertoire of teaching practice that enables teachers to anticipate the many likely responses students will have to particular assignments and classroom situations.

Yet traditional pedagogies of teacher professional development transmit ideas and conceptions stemming from research in reading to teachers in a delivery mode, focusing much of the professional development time on specific instructional techniques. These traditional pedagogies may build declarative knowledge, knowing *about* reading. However, remaining as they do on the outside of reading and merely referring to reading activity rather than taking place within or alongside reading activity, these traditional methods cannot build the kind of situated and generative understandings of the domain that can guide the moment-by-moment actions that teachers take in the classroom. Similarly, training focused on helping teachers to carry out instructional techniques alone does not, in its typical form, offer teachers practice in addressing the problems that are likely to come up in response to real students carrying out real reading tasks.

Similarly, because diversity is the norm in our communities, schools, and classrooms, it is necessary but not sufficient for teachers to know *about* particular cultural, linguistic, or socioeconomic groups of students. Teachers will also need to know *how* to tap into the resources that all students bring into the classroom, to learn from students how to best guide their learning (Cazden & Mehan, 1989; Lee, 1995). To help all students succeed with academic tasks, teachers must be able to help students from all backgrounds build from the familiar to the unfamiliar, from the known boundaries of their culturally shaped, everyday lives to the unknown terrain of broader academic and scientific and civic participation. To do this, teachers will need new conceptions of learners—specifically, conceptions of students as strategic and resourceful theory builders—as well as ways of learning from the students in their classrooms in order to guide students responsively toward more proficient, engaged, academic reading. To develop this generative conception of students and this kind of navigational capacity, middle and high school teachers need greater access to student thinking, supportive tools and procedures for inquiring into student thinking and reading, and guided practice conducting these inquiries and linking them to instructional decision making.

To develop a rich and generative repertoire of classroom practice, teachers also need access to experientially rich demonstrations of specific teaching approaches, with opportunities to make connections between these approaches and their own understandings of the domain, of student learning, and of their own teaching goals and approaches. They need access to one another through a professional dialogue about teaching and classroom lesson design that is linked to the broader enterprise of helping all students to develop as readers. This collaborative work in the professional development community sets a purpose and goal for individual teachers' investigation of and engagement in new practices. Teachers need encouragement to take risks and experiment in the classroom, to approach their own teaching practice and the teaching practice of their peers as an inquiry into instructional purposes, actions, and outcomes. To approach teaching as an inquiry, they need frequent opportunities to reflect on their classroom teaching with the collegial support of their peers and knowledgeable professional development facilitators.

We cannot mandate the kind of insightful and responsive teaching that researchers have described as effective, high-quality teaching for today's students; we can only invest in developing teachers' capacities to carry out the complex actions that such high-quality teaching demands. Also, given the many demands on teachers' time and attention, we have the obligation to work as strategically and effectively as possible in developing these capacities. To do so, those of us responsible for teacher professional learning must turn our collective attention to the task of designing effective learning environments for teachers. Such learning environments will provide strategic opportunities, tools, resources, and collaborations to assist teachers in developing the key capacities necessary for teaching for understanding in the complexity of modern classrooms.

The professional development approach we describe in this chapter is grounded in these understandings. Our inquiry methods are designed to assist teachers in developing generative knowledge of academic reading, insightful responses to students' thinking and reading, and an effective classroom repertoire of comprehension strategy instruction. In contrast to traditional training approaches, the strategic opportunities we give teachers to experience and inquire into reading and student thinking help teachers to build not only their knowledge *about* reading—the concepts and linguistic labels deriving from the work of reading researchers—but also the ability to anticipate problems that may occur and to draw on their own and their peers' know-how when approaching texts and literacy tasks with their diverse students.

We take teachers' and students' convictions about reading and the ways they approach reading tasks as a starting place for inquiry. Responding to "these kids can't, don't, or won't read," we ask, "What do we mean when we say 'these kids can't read?' What do we mean by 'reading?' What do students actually do when faced with the reading tasks they encounter in school? What experiences, knowledge, and resources do they bring to their reading? What do we do when we read challenging texts? What do we know and do as readers that we can use instructionally in the classroom? What are some instructional practices we can adopt or develop to build on students' strengths and draw on our own experience as readers to help students develop into strategic, independent readers of a variety of texts?"

These inquiries are supported by specific tools and protocols designed to situate and support teachers' thinking in its context of use—that is, in the complexities and challenges of reading academic materials and interpreting student responses to academic reading tasks. Through a variety of strategically designed inquiries, teachers practice the actual thinking, interpretive work, and instructional decision making that they must do in the classroom, thereby building critical capacities for teaching. Over time, teachers develop knowledge about reading and student learning that is deeply grounded in experience and that can be drawn upon in responding to students and texts in the dynamic activity of teaching. In the sections that follow, we describe the inquiry activities that we continue to design to build teachers' capacity to apprentice young people to the advanced literacies of the disciplines.

Inquiry Designs for Building Teachers' Generative Knowledge of Reading

This inquiry, which we call "capturing our reading processes," is one of many ways that we routinely engage teachers in reading challenging texts and in surfacing and sharing—and often developing—their knowledge and strategic capacities as readers. Imagine this scenario: A diverse group of urban middle and high school teachers is gathered around conference tables in interdisciplinary school teams, silently reading the first two paragraphs of *Father's Butterflies* by Vladimir Nabokov. We chose this fictional memoir of a Russian childhood steeped in the study and classification of butterflies to present English-speaking readers with particular challenges. Liberally sprinkled with Latin genus and species names as well as French, German, and Russian expressions, it demands that the reader engage any and all word and language analysis skills at his or her disposal. Moreover, Nabokov's densely layered sentences, with their embedded parenthetical remarks and dependent clauses, challenge the prose reading fluency and sentence-processing capacity of every English reader we've met. The topic *lepidopterology* (the study of butterflies), though familiar to some, is usually obscure enough to most of the teachers in the room to present them with background knowledge and conceptual challenges. In our years of using this text with teachers, they have variously experienced Nabokov's tone as comic, pedantic, obsessive, reflective, and arrogant. Entering this text can therefore present, for various readers, considerable affective challenges as well.

After reading the introductory paragraphs, the teachers are invited to write in response to the following questions: What did you do while you were reading to make sense of this text? Even if you were unaware of it at the time, what comprehension strategies did you use? What comprehension problems did you encounter? What comprehension problems still remain? The teachers write for several minutes but soon begin to talk in low voices to one another, intrigued with the reading experience they have just had. They want to know, "Did you understand this? Could you figure out what he's trying to get across?" At this point, the professional development facilitator asks for a few responses to the writing prompts in order to model an inquiry conversation aimed at getting readers to share not only *what* they did to make sense of *Father's Butterflies* but *why* they were moved to do so, *how* they carried these various strategies out, and the results of their strategic actions.

One reader offers, "I got to the end of the first sentence and realized I had no idea what I had read. I had to go back and reread it, taking out all the stuff in parentheses and all the parts of the sentence in between the commas. Then, once I got the core idea of the sentence, I could fill the detail back in." "Why did you omit those particular parts of the sentence?" the facilitator inquires. "Because I guess I know that what is in parentheses, or between commas, is usually detail or an illustration of an idea. I needed to find the heart of the sentence first, and all the detail was getting in the way." "That seems like important knowledge you bring to your reading. Did it help?" the facilitator presses. "Oh yeah. I got the idea, and I even got a sense of the rhythm of Nabokov's writing. That helped me as I went on with the piece."

After a few of these interactions, the facilitator encourages teachers to converse in small groups, sharing their problem-solving processes and probing more deeply into one another's reading. In each group, a recorder is charged with capturing the variety of approaches taken by the various readers on poster-size paper. Later the groups will share their work publicly, and a core set of strategies along with the variety of individual approaches to reading—the wonderful and particular knowledge and experiences, the sheer inventive strategic capacity of readers in the group—will surface, to everyone's interest and amazement. Teachers will turn to colleagues across the room with curiosity: "You mean you really saw that image when you were reading that passage? What brought that to mind?" "How did you know this was a memoir? What were the cues? How come I didn't see that?" "When you decided that Nabokov was trying to earn his emotionally distant father's attention, how did that affect you? Did you reread it from the beginning with that idea in mind?" "As a science teacher, did you find this easy to understand? You mean you really struggled as much as I did? Why?"

Frequently, problems of motivation and engagement emerge. Teachers will confess that they were tempted to put the text aside because they were not interested in it or because they found Nabokov's tone insulting. Alternatively, someone will find Nabokov's apparent arrogance a personal challenge and engage in a spirited debate with the text. Almost always, after a good deal of conversation focused on strategy use, a brave soul will reveal that he was worried that the others were reading the piece easily while he struggled with it, and he feared that his own lack of reading proficiency or knowledge would be exposed to his colleagues. Many heads will nod, revealing teachers' secret fears of exposure. The parallels to student reading experiences in school become a felt presence in the room.

We have adapted and designed a variety of inquiries to surface and analyze reading processes with various texts—routines for thinking aloud while reading, for talking to (interacting conversationally with) the text, for keeping dual- and triple-entry journals reflecting on reading processes as well as texts, for surfacing and analyzing the knowledge demands of texts, and for identifying the interpretive practices at play when readers steeped in various disciplines approach a text. (Many of these inquiry processes are described in chapter 9 of Schoenbach et al., 1999.) Over several sessions, teachers will have opportunities to carry out reading-process inquiries and analyses in subject area groups, working to surface the particular mental habits that an informed reader needs to develop in one's own discipline. In addition, teachers will often work across subject areas to identify the many ways that a skillful, academic reader needs to approach various reading tasks and materials. In the company of a naive reader of science from another subject area, for example, science teachers can begin to see the important role that only they can play in guiding students' science reading in more purposeful and strategic directions. These inquiries into challenging reading offer teachers practice in carrying out the very processes that they can and should promote in the classroom to support students' reading engagement and growth toward more proficient academic reading. These inquiry practices can also build key capacities for generative, responsive teaching of reading.

Building Richer Conceptions of Reading: Making the Invisible Visible (and Developing a Language for Talking About It)

As college graduates, most middle and high school teachers are proficient readers of many types of texts, even if they find particular texts challenging. However, many of these teachers believe that they cannot help students with reading because they are not reading specialists. Few middle and high school teachers see their own abilities to read subject area texts as a powerful resource for helping students to approach these texts independently, confidently, and successfully. Because most teachers have not thought much about the mental processes by which they make sense of texts in their fields, this knowledge—embedded in their own experiences as readers—is invisible and therefore unavailable to them and to their students. One very important reason, then, to engage teachers in collaborative inquiries into their own reading processes with challenging texts is that helping teachers to become more aware of the literacy proficiencies they bring to their subject area can open up powerful resources for students' learning in the classroom (Graves, 1990; Vacca, 2002). Working collaboratively with one another and with knowledgeable facilitators of these inquiries, teachers develop not only an awareness of their own reading processes but also a language for talking about their thinking and problem solving with others. They can draw on these resources to model their own strategic approaches to texts for their students, to name the reading strategies they see students using, and to facilitate students' acquisition of these strategies.

Building Empathy and Engagement: Acknowledging That All Readers Struggle and the Struggle Can Be Worthwhile

As busy adults and proficient readers, few middle or high school teachers regularly read texts that challenge and stretch their strategic capacities. Like many adults, they read in familiar genres and generally encounter ideas and concepts with which they are already familiar. Regular opportunities to grapple with challenging reading materials helps to build teachers' appreciation for the difficulties that students face as readers. When teachers feel insecure with their colleagues because they read at a slower pace or have less experience reading particular kinds of materials than others, they readily recall and empathize with the students in their own classrooms. They begin to see that reading presents students not only with cognitive challenges but also with social ones. Experiencing challenge, becoming "struggling readers" themselves as they read, and benefiting from the social resources they encounter as they inquire with colleagues over time, teachers begin to recognize the importance of creating social support for students' reading in their classrooms. They eagerly engage in conversations about how to turn students' comprehension problems into instructional assets for the whole class. They share ways that they can work to convince students that all readers struggle to construct meaning with challenging materials like their course texts. At the same time, teachers often experience the exuberance that comes along with tackling a difficult text or a new subject. They are intellectually stimulated and recall their own love of learning. They come to understand that challenging, academic reading unavoidably entails strategic problem solving and that effort spent rereading and marshaling strategic resources pays off in increased comprehension, a lesson they become eager to help their students learn. They become sensitive to the need to help adolescents save face and tolerate ambiguity while also engaging in the vigorous but stimulating work of reading and learning.

Building Support: Fostering the Metacognitive Conversation Among Students

For some time educators have known that students learn best when they have opportunities to talk about their ideas and collaborate with others (NICHHD, 2000; Snow, 2002). Researchers have demonstrated measurable effects on student achievement when teachers engage students in only a modest amount of increased classroom conversation (Alvermann et al., 2002; Applebee, 1996; Nystrand & Gamoran, 1991). Talk about *how* we read in subject areas has been linked to increases in students' reading achievement (Duffy et al., 1994; Fielding & Pearson, 1994). Even so, this kind of talk is rare in middle and high school classrooms. In the Reading Apprenticeship framework of adolescent literacy development, the metacognitive conversation is at the heart of the work that teachers and students do together as they engage in reading and inquiry; *how* we read and *why* we read accompany classroom conversations about *what* we read. In reading process inquiries in the professional development setting, teachers gain experience participating in metacognitive conversations in which they make their own thinking processes evident to others and also have access to the ways their colleagues think and solve comprehension problems with texts. Teachers can draw on this experience as they begin to promote and support metacognitive conversations in their own classrooms. As teachers learn to engage in reading-process analyses and metacognitive conversations in professional development sessions over time, they take increased responsibility for facilitating these inquiries with their colleagues. To further assist teachers in fostering metacognitive conversations in their own classrooms, we may ask them to pair up and practice how they might introduce and facilitate a reading-process inquiry with their students, using their course texts as reading materials during professional development sessions.

Inquiry Designs for Developing Teachers' Insight Into Student Learning

To help teachers develop insight into students' struggles with texts, we have designed a variety of inquiries into students' thinking and reading. These inquiries illuminate students' thinking during the process of reading and comprehending and give teachers practice interpreting and responding to students' attempts to make meaning with challenging texts. A key resource for these inquiries is a set of literacy learning cases, drawn from our early work with teachers to carry out detailed case studies of student readers and to characterize the resources and instructional needs these students brought to their reading. The student literacy learning case materials—video and text-based "close-ups" of ninth-grade students struggling with and making sense of various texts—give teachers a chance to hear individual students talking about their reading histories and habits and to see students reading a variety of academic and recreational texts and responding to an interviewer's questions about their reading.

These cases not only give teachers clarity into students' reading missteps and challenges but also offer a closer look at the strengths and theories about reading that students use to make sense of school texts and reading practices. They are based on our prior work to develop a set of literacy learning cases for teacher professional development as part of a research study of literacy learners in postsecondary settings (Greenleaf et al., 1994). Because these materials are focused on the student and on learning rather than on the teacher's perceptions of teaching events, they are formatted as intellectual puzzles rather than as narratives. Instead of offering a completed analysis of student reading, these case materials offer teachers selected data—excerpts of student's videotaped reading performances, transcripts from literacy history interviews, descriptions of classroom contexts, and teachers' reflections on the case study student—to analyze and interpret.

In many of the cases, teachers see students read expository texts, such as magazine articles about popular sports or music figures, that students have chosen for recreational reading. By analyzing the reading strategies and strengths that students bring to their recreational expository reading, teachers are able to generate ideas for building on these strengths to help students understand the expository texts assigned in school. Across the various cases, teachers have the opportunity to see that students approach and read different texts quite differently, that reading is shaped by many situational factors, and that students' reading of one text will not demonstrate the full range of reading strategies and skills they may actually have at their disposal. The case materials are designed to present contrasting views of students' reading performances in different circumstances. They are crafted with the aim of unsettling teachers' first impressions of students, driving them to look more deeply at how students are thinking and what resources they are bringing to reading tasks, and helping them to recognize what Rose (1989) has called "the incipient excellence" that characterizes many underperforming students in our classrooms.

One literacy learning case, for example, features Mario, a Nicaraguan immigrant, reading "True Love," a short story by Isaac Asimov, as well as an expository article from *Scholastic* magazine for youth on the NAFTA debates, which were occurring at the time of the 1996 presidential election, when Mario was interviewed. In a literacy history interview excerpted for the case, Mario talks about the reading he does outside school in his native language—poetry by Ruben Dario, which he discusses with a Nicaraguan friend, and expository texts about Nicaragua, which his father proudly provides and discusses with him. In this interview, Mario also worries aloud about being placed back into an ESL class after being in regular English because of the impact this may have on his future eligibility for college and the disappointment he fears his father may feel should he find out about Mario's ESL placement. As he reads the two school texts, Mario shows greater facility in both oral reading and interpretation with Azimov's short story than he does with the *Scholastic* article about NAFTA. In response to the interviewer's questions about any instruction he may have had with expository texts, Mario reveals that he has had virtually no opportunities to read in his world geography course or other social studies courses. Mario's unfamiliarity with English exposition and with the world knowledge that the NAFTA piece demands is palpable, along with his missing opportunities to learn to grapple with such texts. The world *seems to close in* around this young man, narrowing the opportunities he desires for himself. This case gives teachers the opportunity to elaborate their concepts about background knowledge and reading fluency, coming to understand how familiarity with specific text features influence their own and students' fluency with different types of text, and how students' opportunities to read in school have profound affects on their educational achievement and life chances.

In all of the literacy learning cases, diverse urban students share metacognitive insights into their thinking and reading processes. In our experience over the years of this work, teachers almost uniformly find this metacognitive talk intriguing. Many are surprised by the ninth-grade students' capacity to be reflective and want to begin tapping this potential resource in their own classrooms. In the process of interpreting students' reading performance and talk about reading, teachers express their own conceptions of reading and student ability. This provides an excellent opportunity to engage, challenge, and enrich teachers' theories, but only if we can create a professional conversation that is both supportive and rigorous. To support individual teachers in sharing and reflecting on these theories, to generate norms for collegial discussion, and to develop the habits of using evidence from the case data to support their claims and of exploring multiple possible interpretations of these data, we have developed a set of conversational routines, or protocols, for case inquiry.

Looking closely at an individual student's reading performance is unfamiliar territory for middle and high school teachers, who see 100 to 160 students per day in short class periods. These teachers need a variety of types of support to learn how to look productively at literacy learning case materials. First, if teachers are to appreciate the complexity of reading literacy and to be able to see in the case materials the student readers' strengths and accomplishments as well as what students need to learn, teachers must read the texts they will encounter in the case materials, reflecting on their reading processes and looking closely at the kinds of knowledge and strategic comprehension these texts demand of readers. This is critical; without teachers reading and closely analyzing the reading, the case inquiries stay at a very global and unproductive level. At the same time, carrying out what is essentially a reading task analysis gives teachers practice in viewing the text from the point of view of inexperienced learners and in seeing in it the possibilities for instruction.

Teachers also need practice perceiving the assets students bring to reading, breaking a well-ingrained if functional habit of perceiving only students' deficits. Taking an inquiry stance toward student performance in order to see how students are making sense of school tasks runs counter to a very strong, existing teacher schema for "reading" student performance, particularly in the context of professional development enterprises. Generally, teachers view student performance in such settings either as examples of learning problems or as models of instructional interventions, as either problems or their solutions. We try to break this framework.

Through a deliberate and facilitated process of making *observations* from the case data (evidence) and separating these observations from their possible *interpretations*, we help groups of teachers to surface, articulate, and explore their assumptions about the meaning of student reading performances. We develop this capacity further by asking teachers to identify the strengths these students bring to their reading in the case materials, explicitly focusing on recognizing students' assets as well as instructional needs and goals toward which teachers might productively work. Collaboratively, teachers work on designing classroom applications that build from students' strengths to meet their learning needs. In various ways, including role-playing, planning lessons, and writing reflections, we ask teachers to practice drawing insights from these cases and making connections between these individual student literacy cases and their own classrooms and students. These inquiries into individual students' reading performances build teachers' capacities to support the reading development of their students in a number of ways.

Developing More Generous Conceptions of Students: Accessing and Interpreting Diverse Students' Reading and Thinking Processes

In diverse urban classrooms, where teachers work with students from multiple cultural, linguistic, and socioeconomic backgrounds, teachers need to be able to respond in supportive and productive ways to students' very diverse conceptions of reading, subject matter, and learning. Apprenticing students into complex mental activities like discipline-based reading requires teachers to access student thinking and to have considerable insight into the competencies, misconceptions, and missteps that underlie students' literacy performances. To teach in response to students' thinking, teachers first need access to the ways in which students are making sense of their experiences in class, which is why the metacognitive conversation—with its various ways of routinely engaging teachers and students in talk about thinking and reading processes—is at the center of our instructional model. In addition, teachers need greater insight into students' thinking and reading processes and a deeper understanding of learning and conceptual change.

To foster this deepening of insight, we work in the literacy learning case inquiries to slow down, inform, and often interrupt teachers' automatic processes of evaluating students and making judgments about their capabilities with little consideration of the strengths and resources students bring to classrooms or of the difficulties that complex texts pose for student comprehension. Participation in these inquiry discussions provides the teachers with the experience and support to closely and critically "read" and explore the possible meanings of student performance on valued literacy tasks. We have seen that these inquiry processes help teachers to develop a more productive alternative to traditional ways of interpreting student reading and talk, basing claims on actual evidence from student performance, informed by teachers' own experiences and knowledge as readers. These are the very ways of interpreting literacy tasks, texts, and student performances that teachers need in the classroom to engage responsively in collaborative inquiry into reading with their students, to demystify academic reading and thinking processes, and to help their students to participate more skillfully in the academic literacies that are at the heart of schooling.

Developing Pedagogical Content Knowledge: Reasoning About Sources of Reading Difficulty and the Challenges That Subject Area Reading Poses for Students

Engaging teachers in experiencing and analyzing the reading processes, texts, and reading tasks through literacy learning case inquiries assists subject area teachers to teach reading in ways that are consonant with their disciplinary teaching. They begin to read their texts with the anticipation of the possible sources of student difficulty as well as the opportunities that these texts pose for student learning and reading development. Building this kind of understanding, which Lee Shulman (1986) called "pedagogical content knowledge," is an explicit goal of the case inquiry process. Teachers build pedagogical content knowledge about reading with inquiry into their own reading processes and with close attention to the demands that different kinds of texts make on them as readers. Close attention to the strengths and assets as well as the learning needs of the case study students then leads to a productive exploration of the ways in which promising classroom teaching approaches can build on student abilities to meet instructional needs. The case inquiry process and protocols resulting from this design work thus comprise a broad set of activities that link teachers' inquiry into their own reading processes, their inquiry into texts, and their inquiry into student reading processes to their ongoing classroom work.

Designing New Tools to Support Teachers in Accessing and Reasoning About Student Reading and Thinking Processes

As teachers' work in Reading Apprenticeship has developed over the past several years, we have designed other inquiry processes, in addition to the literacy learning cases, to offer teachers multiple opportunities to practice interpreting student thinking and reading and to further consolidate the links between these inquiries and their work in the classroom. In our professional development networks, as teachers begin to generate metacognitive conversations in their own classrooms, they routinely bring student work back to the professional development sessions to share with their colleagues. Inquiry questions support these opportunities to look closely at student work from the teachers' own classrooms. Like the literacy learning case inquiry process, opportunities to explore student work begin with teachers actually trying out the reading and thinking tasks assigned to students. They respond to prompts that focus their attention on the work that students have been asked to accomplish: What reading knowledge or strategies does the student need to accomplish this task? What content area knowledge or strategies does the student need to accomplish this task? What other knowledge or strategies does the student need, such as the ability to participate effectively in a small-group discussion, the ability to collaborate on a project, or the ability to provide feedback to another's work?

Based on their own experiences and insights into the demands of the tasks, teachers then explore the samples of student work. Some questions that guide this exploration and discussion are: What can we learn about the student's reading from this work sample? What knowledge, strategies, and schema is the student bringing to this task? What can we learn about the student's content area learning from this work sample? What knowledge, strategies, and schema in the content area is the student bringing to this task? What additional instructional support might students need in order to be more successful with this task? What will we need to do to apprentice students into important ways of thinking and doing discipline-based work? Finally, teachers are asked to reflect on their own learning from this opportunity to explore student work, expressing any new insights into student thinking and learning they may have gained and considering instructional implications for their work in the classroom. With supported opportunities to explore, interpret, and thereby develop insight into their own students' work with classroom texts, teachers continue to grow in their capacity to teach in response to student thinking.

Recently we have also begun to develop videos of classrooms where teachers are integrating Reading Apprenticeship approaches into their ongoing subject area teaching. To support a focus on student thinking and the metacognitive conversation, we are developing accompanying prompts and roles for teachers to take as they view these videotapes. Although there are many competing demands on teachers' attention in these classroom videos, we ask teachers to focus on two things: (a) What do you notice about students' reading or talk about reading? and (b) What do you notice about the supports for students' reading or talk about reading in this classroom? The videos offer many opportunities to see students engaged in reading or conversation. This way of viewing classroom videos underscores our focus on accessing, interpreting, and responding to student thinking as a way of supporting students' development as readers.

Inquiry Designs for Building Teachers' Capacity to Make Effective Use of Comprehension Strategy Instruction

There is ample evidence, given the long history of reading comprehension research, that students benefit from explicit instruction in comprehension strategies (Pressley, 1998; Vacca, 2002). Yet evidence is also accumulating that the social environment of the classroom—whether and to what extent teachers and students collaborate on comprehending course texts, rather than the type of comprehension strategy instruction that students are given, per se—mediates students' engagement with text and subsequent strategy use (Guthrie & Wigfield, 2000; Kucan & Beck, 1997; Moore, 1996; Rosenshine & Meister, 1994). Our work with teachers aims at helping them to develop a collaborative classroom environment in which metacognitive conversations about reading experiences can become routine and in which students have extensive opportunities to read with the support of the teacher and their peers. In such classrooms, instructional techniques for explicitly teaching comprehension strategies that have high leverage for developing students' conceptions and approaches to reading become valuable tools, for teachers and students alike.

Building Teachers' Capacity to Support and Deepen the Metacognitive Conversation

In the Reading Apprenticeship instructional model, metacognitive conversation is a means by which teachers gain access to students' thinking in the classroom, a means by which they can begin to intentionally draw on the knowledge and experiences that students are bringing to their understanding of classroom activities. This routine practice, in turn, helps students to gain access to the knowledge and thinking of their teachers and peers. They begin to see that the knowledge and strategic resources they develop outside the classroom have a valuable place in school learning (Jordan, Jensen, & Greenleaf, 2001). With our teacher colleagues, we have been developing and adapting tools that help teachers to routinely foster metacognitive conversations among their students, based on the reading process inquiries we experience together in the professional development setting.

One of the tools that helps teachers to take these inquiry processes into the classroom is recording and displaying—and over time updating, evaluating, and modifying—Reading Strategies

Charts based on "capturing the reading processes" of the members of the class (including the teacher) during reading tasks. Think-aloud bookmarks that offer sentence stems to prompt particular mental moves (Davey, 1983) support students as they practice thinking aloud while reading a section of a text, and teachers can alter these bookmarks over time to focus students' practice on new problem-solving strategies. Teacher colleagues have also developed various metacognitive prompts for reading logs and journals that accompany students' reading experiences (Schoenbach et al., 1999, p. 68). These prompts, along with material resources such as self-stick notes or photocopied excerpts, are important supports for teachers in developing students' mental engagement through other metacognitive routines like "talking to the text" (Jordan et al., 2001).

In professional development sessions, we make time for teachers to share the adaptive classroom routines they integrate into their work with subject area curriculum materials, focusing on routine ways of asking *how* members of the classroom community are making sense of these materials as well as *what* sense they are making. We encourage teachers to anticipate and plan the ways they will scaffold, sequence, and deepen these metacognitive routines over time in order to shape students' thinking while reading subject area texts in more productive and discipline-specific ways. In these professional communities, teachers engage in learning and further developing routine ways to share their own reading processes with their students and to both draw on and develop their students' resourceful problem solving with texts as part of their subject area teaching.

Building Teachers' Capacity to Integrate Comprehension Strategy Instruction Into Subject-Area Reading

In professional development sessions, we offer teachers many opportunities to develop firsthand experience using instructional techniques such as ReQuest (Manzo, 1969), Question-Answer Relationships (Raphael, 1982), Reciprocal Teaching (Palincsar & Brown, 1989), as well as strategies such as visualizing, summarizing, predicting, clarifying text meanings, and making connections (drawing on prior knowledge). We engage teachers in these strategic approaches as we read modern fiction and nonfiction materials together. Encountering these approaches to strategy instruction while working in groups to comprehend an essay from *Scientific American* or *Atlantic Monthly* gives teachers an opportunity to assess for themselves how these strategies work to support the group's learning. Teachers learn these strategic approaches in the very context in which they will need to apply them, while working collaboratively with other readers to construct meaning with texts.

In doing so, they deepen their knowledge about the nuances of strategy application and use. For example, by exploring the use of Question-Answer Relationships (QAR) with challenging texts, teachers discover that categorizing a question as one of Raphael's (1982) question types—"right there," "putting it together," "text and me," or "on my own"—can be difficult. In fact, whether a question can be labeled "text and me" depends on the reader's storehouse of knowledge and experience. Working through these issues as they read together allows teachers to stumble on and think through problems that emerge in the practice of strategy instruction. They gain confidence as well as firsthand knowledge of the processes involved.

As teachers gain experience with these strategies, we encourage them to exercise their professional judgment about how well particular strategies serve their instructional ends. Teachers may respond to this invitation by adapting question frames to focus on key ways of thinking in particular disciplines or by selecting particular strategies for their utility in helping students to acquire particular thinking habits. For example, visualizing structures, processes, and interactions is important to learning in many branches of science. Focusing students' attention on creating mental images, drawing structures or processes, or walking through an interaction between objects can have high payoffs in increased comprehension when carried out with science reading. Similarly, helping students to ask discipline-based questions—for instance, "Is there a pattern here?" when exploring a math problem or graph, or "From whose perspective is this written?" when exploring a history text or artifact—may help students into discipline-based ways of thinking better than more generic questions focusing on who, what, when, where, and why. From the beginning, then, as teachers practice using comprehension strategies to support their own reading in professional development sessions, we invite them to adaptively integrate these strategies into their subject area instruction.

Ultimately, these invitations to inquire into the nature of reading and reading processes, into students' thinking and theory making, and into specific instructional approaches help teachers to begin to approach their own teaching as inquiry. Cycles of implementation, reflection, and refinement of teaching occur as teachers try out new approaches in the classroom and return to discuss their experience with their colleagues and to engage in additional inquiries and learning experiences. As teachers create metacognitive conversations in their own classrooms, they bring their work back to professional development sessions to share. They are asked frequently to reflect on how things are going in their classrooms, to use evidence from their classrooms to gauge the quality of student reading and thinking, and to anticipate their next instructional steps. Teaching begins to resemble a cycle of inquiry as teachers innovate, reflect, and refine their practices. This type of long-term recursive learning is a key feature of high-quality professional development that enables teachers to continue to learn in and from their own teaching practice.

Evidence Linking Teacher Knowledge Growth, Classroom Change, and Student Achievement

> Instructional capacity is partly a function of what teachers know students are capable of doing and what teachers know they are professionally capable of doing with students.... Every student and curriculum is a bundle of possibilities, and teachers whose perceptions have been more finely honed to see those possibilities, and who know more about how to take advantage of them, will be more effective. (Cohen & Ball, 1999, pp. 7–8)

> Teaching takes place on the 'outside,' and learning mostly goes on 'inside.' So much professional development is focused on the outside, yet it needs to be focused on the inside. (Participant, National Institute for Reading Apprenticeship, September 2002)

We value the considerable intelligence and resourcefulness of the young people we serve, and we aim to empower these students to take on more powerful, participatory, literate identities in their various worlds of school, community, and work. Because of this mission, throughout our history as a project we have continually gathered evidence to measure the impact of our inquiry-based professional development practices on teachers' knowledge, their classroom practices, and their students' learning. In one multiyear study of subject area teachers who participated in a professional development network, we examined the impact of these inquiry methods on 29 participating teachers' knowledge growth and change (Greenleaf & Schoenbach, 2001). We carried out close case studies tracing the changing thinking, instructional planning, and classroom practice of eight of these teachers over a period of two years. Data included interviews with teachers at the beginning and end of each year; teachers' written reflections and evaluations; audio- and videotapes of teachers engaging in reading process analysis, text analysis, analysis of students' reading processes, and collegial conversations about teaching practice at professional development meetings; and, finally, classroom artifacts such as lesson plans, assignments, and student work. Growth in students' reading engagement and comprehension was measured through pre- and postsurveys and administration of a standardized test of reading comprehension at the beginning and end of the year.

In this study, we found that participating teachers became more aware of the complex ways in which they themselves made sense of a variety of texts, and they gained new appreciation for the reading difficulties that students may face. They also developed a language for talking about invisible comprehension practices, which are at times difficult to articulate. They came to understand, by reading in the company of colleagues who may approach texts very differently, that their own ways of reading are learned conventions that can and must be taught to students. In turn, these changes helped teachers to create classroom environments that were characterized by high student engagement and self-direction, high expectations for student performance, frequent collaboration between teachers and students, and high accountability on the part of both teachers and students for student learning. Moreover, this pedagogy was motivated from within by teachers who now understood what reading entails and what texts demand, and who had the means to assist students in gaining this kind of strategic knowledge for themselves.

Students in these classrooms came to see reading as an active and strategic process. Taken as a group, students in these urban classrooms, who were behind their peers nationally, gained substantially more than a year's expected growth on a standardized measure of reading comprehension (Greenleaf & Schoenbach, 2001). We continue to study the impact of our inquiry methods of professional development on teacher and student learning, and have recently undertaken studies of classroom teaching across the curriculum with teacher partners who are involved in ongoing professional development with us. We regularly report our findings in professional journals (Greenleaf et al., 2001) as well as on our Web site (www.wested.org/stratlit). These studies give us confidence that the inquiry learning we offer teachers develops a repository of experiences that informs and transforms teachers' classroom practices. This learning is generative; the experiences teachers have and the kinds of thinking teachers practice together in these inquiries continue to enrich their thinking and inform their practices in the classroom beyond the professional development setting and over time.

Toward the Responsive Teaching of Middle and High School Teachers: Recommendations for Strategic Professional Development Design

We recognize that teachers will need a great deal of preparation for the kind of responsive teaching we envision, not least of which will be deep academic preparation in their disciplines. We offer these strategic designs for inquiry-based professional development as one contribution to the capacity building that is needed for high-quality teaching in our nation's schools. Based on our experience, and drawing on the work of others who have contributed to our way of working, we can highlight some principles to guide the development of effective teacher professional development in reading. In addition to the qualities of effective professional development already recognized by the field—that it engages teachers as learners over time, offers teachers the resources necessary to gain skill and knowledge, creates opportunities for teachers to reflect on their teaching and their students' learning, and recognizes (as well as builds) teachers' expertise—we offer the following. Professional development that effectively builds teachers' capacity to teach reading in response to student thinking does the following:

1. Takes teachers' convictions (about themselves, the domain of reading, and students) and perceived needs (for quick solutions) as a starting point for inquiry

2. Draws on teachers' expertise and prior experiences to build new understandings and practices

3. Engages teachers strategically in new inquiry experiences from which they can draw in the dynamic of teaching

4. Engages teachers in rigorous reading and metacognitive conversations about reading within and across academic disciplines

5. Focuses teachers' attention on particular ways of thinking, reading, and interpreting student performance that contribute to high-quality, responsive teaching

6. Provides teachers with frequent practice in thinking in these new ways through multiple inquiry activities, all designed to build these important capacities

7. Provides teachers with practice in carrying out inquiry routines and instructional approaches with complex reading—that is, experience in doing the very things we promote for teaching students to become engaged and strategic readers

8. Offers teachers multiple ways to encounter the domain of subject area literacy, thereby helping them to build flexible and generative knowledge of strategic teaching and reading

9. Offers many points of connection to teachers' own classrooms through relevant and various classroom and student examples, including those from teachers' own experiences

10. Acknowledges teachers as decision makers and builds the capacity for professional judgment through cycles of experiential learning, classroom innovation, and inquiry

11. Models precisely those rich, collaborative, metacognitive, respectful, and reflective ways of learning that we envision for our nation's youth

There is increasing evidence that teacher quality matters for student learning and achievement (Darling-Hammond, 2000; Laczko-Kerr & Berliner, 2002). Our studies of inquiry-based professional development for middle and high school subject area teachers demonstrate that with the support of well-designed inquiry activities, teachers are able to make profound changes in their teaching practice. These changes in turn provide powerful new learning opportunities to students that make a difference in student achievement. Through this kind of generative professional development, teachers learn to closely and critically read both their curriculum materials and their students' performances to inform their professional judgment and instructional actions. They develop the means by which to weigh competing ideas about literacy and classroom methodologies and move beyond the eddying currents of debate and mandate to take warranted action in the classroom. They become designers as well as implementers, informed professionals rather than mere conduits for other people's designs and agendas. The ability to educate all children to their highest potential rests on this kind of professionalism. This, rather than training teachers to faithfully reproduce lessons and teaching strategies in the classroom, holds the promise to build the kind of world-class, responsive, and professional teaching force that we so badly need in our nation's schools.

References

Alvermann, D. (Ed.). (2002). *Adolescents and literacies in a digital world*. New York: Lang.

Alvermann, D., Boyd, F., Brozo, W., Hinchman, K., Moore, D., & Sturtevant, E. (in press). *Principled practices for a literate America: A framework for literacy and learning in the upper grades*. New York: Carnegie.

Alvermann, D., & Moore, D. (1991). Secondary school reading. In R. Barr, M. L. Kamil, P. Mosenthal, & P. D. Pearson (Eds.), *Handbook of reading research* (Vol. 2, pp. 951–983). New York: Longman.

Applebee, A. (1996). *Curriculum as conversation: Transforming traditions of teaching and learning*. Chicago: University of Chicago Press.

Ball, D., & Cohen, D. (1999). Developing practice, developing practitioners: Toward a practice-based theory of professional education. In L. Darling-Hammond & D. Sykes (Eds.), *Teaching as the learning profession: Handbook of policy and practice*. San Francisco: Jossey-Bass.

Borasi, R., & Seigel, M. (2000). *Reading counts*. New York: Teachers College Press.

Cazden, C., & Mehan, H. (1989) Principles from sociology and authropology. In M. Reynolds (Ed.), *Knowledge base for the beginning teacher* (pp. 47–58). Oxford: Pergamon Press.

Cohen, D., & Ball, D. (1999). *Instruction, capacity, and improvement* [On-line]. Available: http://www.sii.soe.umich.edu/links.html

Cohen, D., & Ball, D. (2000, April–May). *Instructional innovation: Reconsidering the story* [On-line]. Available: http://www.sii.soe.umich.edu/links.html

Cope, B., & Kalantzis, M. (1993). *The powers of literacy*. Pittsburgh, PA: University of Pittsburgh Press.

Darling-Hammond, L. (2000). Teacher quality and student achievement: A review of state policy evidence. *Education Policy Analysis Archives, 8* (1) [On-line]. Available: http://epaa.asu.eda/epaa/v8n1/

Darling-Hammond, L., & Sykes, G. (Eds.). (1999). *Teaching as the learning profession: Handbook of policy and practice*. San Francisco: Jossey-Bass.

Davey, B. (1983). Think-aloud—modeling the cognitive processes of reading comprehension. *Journal of Reading, 27*, 44–47.

Delpit, L. D. (1995). *Other people's children: Cultural conflict in the classroom*. New York: New Press.

Donahue, P. L., Voelkl, K. E., Campbell, J. R., & Mazzeo, J. (1999). *The NAEP 1998 reading report card for the nation and the states*. Washington, DC: National Center for Education Statistics.

Duffy, G., Roehler, L., Sivan, E., Rackliffe, G., Book, C., Meloth, M., Vavrus, L., Wesselman, R., Putnam, J., & Bassiri, D. (1994). Effects of explaining the reasoning associated with using reading strategies. *Reading Research Quarterly, 22,* 347–368.

Durkin, D. (1978). What classroom observations reveal about reading comprehension instruction. *Reading Research Quarterly, 14* (4), 481–533.

Fielding, L. G., & Pearson, D. P. (1994). Reading comprehension: What works. *Educational Leadership, 51,* 62–68.

Freedman, S. W., Flower, L., Hull, G., & Hayes, J. R. (1995). *Ten years of research: Achievements of the National Center for the Study of Writing and Literacy.* Berkeley, CA: National Center for the Study of Writing.

Graves, D. (1990). *Discover your own literacy.* Portsmouth, NH: Heinemann.

Greenleaf, C., Hull, G., & Reilly, B. (1994). Learning from our diverse students: Helping teachers rethink problematic teaching and learning situations. *Teaching and Teacher Education, 10,* 521–541.

Greenleaf, C., & Schoenbach, R. (2001) *Close readings: A study of key issues in the use of literacy learning cases for the professional development of secondary teachers.* Chicago: Spencer Foundation.

Greenleaf, C., Schoenbach, R., Cziko, C., & Mueller, F. (2001). Apprenticing adolescents to academic literacy. *Harvard Educational Review, 71* (1), 79–129.

Guskey, T. R., & Huberman, M. (1996). *Professional development in education: New paradigms and practices.* New York: Teachers College Press.

Guthrie, J., & Wigfield, A. (2000). Engagement and motivation in reading. In M. L. Kamil, P. G. Mosenthal, P. D. Pearson, & R. Barr (Eds.), *Handbook of reading research* (Vol. 3, pp. 403–422). Mahwah, NJ: Erlbaum.

Jiménez, R. T. (2000). Literacy and the identity development of Latina/o students. *American Educational Research Journal, 37* (4), 971–1000.

Jordan, M., Jensen, R., & Greenleaf, C. (2001). Amidst familial gatherings: Reading apprenticeship in a middle school English language development class. *Voices From the Middle, 8* (4), 15–24.

Kamil, M., Intrator, S., & Kim, H. (2000). The effects of other technologies on literacy and literacy learning. In M. L. Kamil, P. B. Mosenthal, P. D. Pearson, & R. Barr (Eds.), *Handbook of reading research* (Vol. 3, pp. 771–788). Mahwah, NJ: Erlbaum.

Kucan, L., & Beck, I. L. (1997). Thinking aloud and reading comprehension research: Inquiry, instruction, and social interaction. *Review of Educational Research, 67,* 271–299.

Laczko-Kerr, I., & Berliner, D. (2002). The effectiveness of 'Teach for America' and other under-certified teachers on student academic achievement: A case of harmful public policy. *The Education Policy Analysis Archives* [On-line], *10* (37). Available: http://epaa.asu.edu/epaa/v10n37/

Lee, C. (1995). A culturally based cognitive apprenticeship: Teaching African American high school students skills in literary interpretation. *Reading Research Quarterly, 30,* 608–630.

Lemke, J. L. (1990). *Talking science: Language, learning, and values.* Norwood, NJ: Ablex.

Manzo, A.V. (1969). The ReQuest procedure. *Journal of Reading, 13,* 123–126.

Moje, E. B., Dillon, D. R., & O'Brien, D. G. (2000). Re-examining the roles of the learner, the text, and the context in secondary literacy. *Journal of Educational Research, 93,* 165–180.

Moje, E. B., Young, J. P., Readence, J. E., & Moore, D. W. (2000). Reinventing adolescent literacy for new times: Perennial and millenial issues. *Journal of Adolescent and Adult Literacy, 43,* 400–410.

Moll, L. (1992). Literacy research in a community classroom: A socio-cultural approach. In B. R. Beach, J. L. Green, M. S. Kamil, & T. Shanahan (Eds.), *Multidisciplinary perspectives on literacy research* (pp. 211–244). Urbana, IL: National Council of Teachers of English.

Moore, D. (1996). Contexts for literacy in secondary schools. In D. J. Leu, C. K. Kinzer, & K. A. Hinchman (Eds.), *Literacies for the 21st Century: Research and practice* (pp. 15–46). Chicago: National Reading Conference.

Mullis, I. V., Dossey, A., Campbell, J. R., Gentile, C. A., O'Sullivan, C., & Latham, A. S. (1994). *NAEP 1992 trends in academic progress* (Report No. 23-TR01). Washington, DC: U.S. Government Printing Office.

National Institute of Child Health and Human Development (NICHHD). (2000). *Report of the National Reading Panel. Teaching children to read: An evidence-based assessment of the scientific research literature on reading and its implications for reading instruction.* (NIH Publication No. 00-4769). Washington, D.C.: U.S. Government Printing Office.

Nystrand, M., & Gamoran, A. (1991). Instructional discourse, student engagement, and literature achievement. *Research in the Teaching of English, 25,* 261–290.

Pajares, M. F. (1991). Teachers' beliefs and educational research: Cleaning up a messy construct. *Review of Educational Research, 62* (3), 307–332.

Palincsar, A. S., & Brown, A. L. (1989). Instruction for self-regulated reading. In L. B. Resnick & L. E. Klopfer (Eds.), *Toward the thinking curriculum: Current cognitive research* (pp. 19–39). Alexandria, VA: ASCD.

Pressley, M. (1998). *Reading instruction that works: The case for balanced teaching.* New York: Guilford Press.

Raphael, T. (1982). Question-answering strategies for children. *The Reading Teacher, 36,* 186–190.

Richardson, V. (1990). Significant and worthwhile change in teaching practice. *Educational Researcher, 19,* 10–19.

Rose, M. (1989). *Lives on the boundary*. New York: Penguin Books.

Rosenshine, B., & Meister, C. (1994). Reciprocal teaching: A review of the research. *Review of Educational Research, 64,* 479–530.

Schoenbach, R., Greenleaf, C., Cziko, C., & Hurwitz, L. (1999). *Reading for understanding: A guide to improving reading in middle and high school classrooms.* San Francisco: Jossey-Bass.

Shulman, L. (1986). Just in case: Reflections on learning from experience. In J. Colbert, P. Dresberg, & K. Trimble (Eds.), *The case for education: Contemporary approaches for using case methods.* Needham Heights, MA: Allyn & Bacon.

Snow, C. (2002). *Reading for understanding: Toward an R&D program in reading comprehension.* Santa Monica, CA: Rand Education.

Sparks, D., & Hirsh, S. (1997). *A new vision for staff development: Results-driven education, systems thinking, and constructivism.* Oxford, OH: National Staff Development Council.

Vacca, R. (2002). Making a difference in adolescents' lives: Visible and invisible aspects of content area reading. In A. E. Farstrup & S. J. Samuels (Eds.), *What research has to say about reading instruction* (3rd ed., pp. 184–204). Newark, DE: International Reading Association.

Wineburg, S. S. (1991). On the reading of historical texts: Notes on the breach between school and academy. *American Educational Research Journal, 28,* 495–519.

The work described in this chapter would not have been possible without the generous support of the Carnegie Corporation of New York, The William and Flora Hewlett Foundation, The Walter S. Johnson Foundation, The W. Clement & Jessie V. Stone Foundation, The Spencer and MacArthur Foundations' Program in Professional Development Research and Documentation, The Stuart Foundations, The Stupinski Family Fund, WestEd, and, of course, the many adolescents, teachers, schools, and districts in the Bay Area and around the country that contributed wisdom and meaning to our work. The statements made and the views expressed, however, are solely the responsibility of the authors.

Reengaging Youngsters With Reading Difficulties by Means of Innovative Professional Development

Susan Florio-Ruane, Taffy E. Raphael,
Kathy Highfield, and Jennifer Berne

Key Ideas

✓ The Teachers' Learning Collaborative (TLC), organized in 1996 as part of the Center for the Improvement of Early Reading Achievement (CIERA), involved literacy teachers in Michigan in collaborative, inquiry-based professional development of struggling young readers from school literacy by grade 3.

✓ The members of TLC designed and piloted a curriculum framework called Book Club *Plus.* This aimed to scaffold youngsters' reengagement in authentic and challenging literacy, both individually, at their instructional level, and as a community, with age-appropriate texts in small-group and whole-class peer-led literacy activities.

✓ As part of their own professional development, the TLC teachers used multiple methods of data collection and analysis to research the curriculum framework and found that the third graders who were initially working below grade level in TLC classrooms showed increased engagement when it was used and at least a year's growth in reading during a yearlong pilot.

For

• Teacher educators, literacy researchers
• Teachers, policy makers

Overview of the Project

In 1996, as part of the Center for the Improvement of Early Reading Achievement (CIERA), Taffy E. Raphael and Susan Florio-Ruane initiated a study of innovative professional development. The study was twofold: to investigate teachers' learning in inquiry and dialogue, and to orient that learning toward solving the teaching problem of reengaging low-achieving youngsters in classroom literacy learning. The CIERA project grew out of our previous work on dialogue, inquiry, and learning in book clubs for both youngsters and teachers (Florio-Ruane with deTar, 2001; McMahon, Raphael, Goatley, & Pardo, 1997; Raphael, Florio-Ruane, & Kehus, et al., 2001). We defined "engagement" as participation in a community of learners. We studied inquiry-oriented teacher development that was focused on bringing pupils with reading difficulties more fully into the classroom literacy learning community.

Crossing Borders to Study a Common Problem of Practice

We organized and studied, as participant observers, an informal professional development network called the Teachers' Learning Collaborative (TLC). TLC included teachers working and living in cities, suburbs, and rural communities in Michigan. Its members came from a broad range of economic, educational, and cultural backgrounds. They taught youngsters who were similarly diverse. TLC was diverse not only in its membership but also in its activities and their social contexts. TLC's agenda, learning activities, and interactions were emergent, teacher-directed, and inquiry-based. TLC crisscrossed many borders—conceptual, personal, professional, geographic, social, and cultural. The network opened space for changing roles, activities, and sites of contact as well as for leadership that was shared, negotiated, and shifting. TLC members utilized the following diverse methods of communication:

1. Whole network weekend retreats

2. Meetings of subsets of network members

3. Communication via e-mail and telephone

4. Visits to one another's classrooms

5. Sharing curricular materials, student work samples, and videotapes of teaching

6. Presentations at CIERA-sponsored conferences as well as at state and national professional conferences

7. Written reports, articles, and chapters

TLC challenged all of its members to "understand another's understanding" as part of teacher education. It further confronted members with a problem experienced by most teachers: how to foster engagement among students who, because of reading difficulties, may have become alienated from classroom literacy. The cross-site nature of the professional development network was significant for several reasons. First, it depended on communication among teachers from various districts and communities. Second, TLC became an innovative site for teacher learning by combining virtual, textual, and face-to-face communication. Third, by crisscrossing the most diverse and fastest-growing part of Michigan, TLC confronted, as part of professional development, problems of social inequality, economic immobility, and community isolation that have vexed our state for the past half century (Farley, Danziger, & Holzer, 2000).

Engagement As Learning

Engagement is a significant factor in learning because time spent in learning tasks is linked to mastery of skills. Yet whether in a classroom or professional development setting, goal-oriented learning does not occur merely because people are engaged. Engaging tasks are educative when they are linked in authentic and principled ways to explicit learning objectives. Thus, in both literacy education and professional development, educators are challenged to make principled decisions about what engagement means, how it relates to learning, and which activities might foster engaged learning.

Our work is grounded in the theory that all learning begins on the social plane. This means that although individuals are learners, their learning is fundamentally a social process that occurs within social contexts, activities, and interactions with others. Within this view of learning, engagement is socially created. It is, for the individual, authentic participation in a community's contexts, activities, and interactions. Engagement enables and sustains both the learning community and its individual members by means of participation in activities. Members of this learning community vary in knowledge and expertise, but newcomers are gradually socialized into membership (Cole, 1996).

In early literacy acquisition, for example, we can see very young children engaged in "proto-literacy," authentically participating in emergent ways in the everyday forms and functions of literacy in their families and other primary communities. More experienced others help beginners move closer to full, mature participation by a mix of modeling, normalizing and expanding, and instructing directly. This illustrates how engagement and learning depend on individuals as well as on the group. As such, the engagement that supports learning is reflected in the group's cultural practices as well as in the individual's interests and efforts.

The classroom is a special learning community whose cultural features reflect its public, explicit responsibility to inculcate and assess literacy in its members. Here the youngsters are gathered for the explicit purpose of learning about the forms, function, and features of the written language system. In the classroom, novices far outnumber experts. Activities are planned rather than spontaneous, and instruction is the primary means by which more experienced members teach beginners. Thus, classroom learning is typically a function of instruction and practice. Formal assessment of mastery occurs at socially agreed-upon points in the stream of development (e.g., grade level). In such assessments, learners are compared with themselves in a prior time, with one another, and with a standard definition of literacy learning appropriate to their grade.

Socially, classroom assessment serves as both "gatekeeping" and "identification" of learners. Measures of achievement not only contribute to a learner's identity in the community but also admit learners to increasingly complex, higher order literacy practices of the community. Thus, when a student fails to pass through achievement "gates," she is less able to participate fully in the core literate practices of the community even as she is instructed in them. We are familiar with the ways that "pulling students out" of the class for extra help or to group by ability for instruction tend to reinforce rather than redress the problem of outsider status for students not reading at grade level. Thus, paradoxically, the effort to help them reach mature membership and participation in a literate community functions to close them out: They do not learn the same content, they do not learn in the same social or physical spaces, they do not learn in the same kinds of activities, and they do not engage literacy in grade-appropriate or age-appropriate ways. Yet we also recognize that youngsters are not mystically swept up in mature literacy practices merely by inclusion in the classroom's reading and writing activities. The social aims and features of the classroom demand pedagogy and curriculum that expand and extend youngsters' literacy development by engaging all learners in the social construction of knowledge about complex literacy skills and practices (Newman, Griffin, & Cole, 1989).

Our prior research cited above studied two groups: youngsters learning to comprehend and interpret age-appropriate literature, and teachers (both beginning and novice) learning to read multicultural literature as it reveals aspects of the concept of "culture." In both cases, we found that a powerful mix of spontaneous participation, scaffolding understanding by peer-led inquiry, and self-directed reference to textual information seemed to foster participants' movement toward understanding. We were not so sure, however, if these processes would serve all participants equally well. Moreover, we did not identify features of a pedagogy or curricular framework that would address either the problem of struggle and disengagement or the question of how teachers might foster learning environments in which all participants have access to the complex concepts under study. TLC was a place to push our thinking by asking harder questions and solving this more complex problem of practice. We did this in a cycle of learning activities described below.

A Cycle of Learning Activities

In our research on learning in book clubs, the private activity of reading and writing and the public activity of dialogue worked together to support engagement, time on task, and the framing and solving of complex problems (Florio-Ruane & Raphael, 2001). From this research we distilled a general cycle of learning activities to guide the work of TLC. This cycle involves talk, text, and practical action to solve complex problems. It is grounded in a theory of the social mediation of learning and development first described by Soviet psychologist Lev Vygotsky. Gavelek and Raphael (1996) adapted this theory to literacy teaching, proposing a text-based cycle of public exchanges, private transformations, and the making public of those concepts in language, both oral and written. The model is interactive and iterative, assuming neither a simple distinction between private and public nor a neatly sequential causal relationship between the "coming together and going apart" of learners (Berne, 2001).

The following steps compose the activity cycle for engaged problem-solving:

- Frame a common problem
- Engage in authentic reading, writing, speaking, and listening to address it
- Take from these activities insights for action to solve the problem
- Investigate the adequacy of your solution to solve the common problem
- Share what is learned with others who have conducted similar inquiry
- Recycle the common problem with new insight and additional possible solution

We applied this theory to professional development in TLC, and TLC members also applied it to their classrooms. As a collective, TLC members researched learning in both settings with a variety of tools, including participant observation, interview, analysis of teachers and of pupils' written work, and formal and informal assessment. We asked the following research questions:

1. How does TLC's professional development model foster engagement and teacher learning?

2. How and in what ways does engagement in authentic practice in TLC transform teachers' classroom practice?

3. How do changes in practice foster struggling youngsters' reengagement with classroom literacy learning?

These are important questions about teacher learning and the relationship between teacher learning and classroom practice. They underlie the question of improving reading achievement among youngsters who, by failing to achieve at grade level, may become alienated from reading in the classroom community of learners by grade 3.

Our study was not designed to measure reading achievement over time and among large numbers of pupils. However, as we will describe later in this chapter, it was able to track changes in the literate practices of small groups of students as evidenced in case study, comparison of instruction in TLC and non-TLC classrooms, and context-sensitive as well as standardized tests. Below we describe each phase of the professional development model as TLC members enacted it. As we do this, we refer to the activity cycle just described. We close with evidence of teacher learning as it is reflected in pupil engagement and learning in TLC classrooms.

Framing a Common Problem and Solving It

Our common problem was reengaging youngsters who were not reading at grade level into authentic, educative participation in classroom literacy practices. Our attention to those who typically "fall through the cracks"—who are promoted, though lacking in grade-level skills—grew out of concern about three consequences for these children. First, youngsters are identified, and self-identify, as unsuccessful learners. Second, they may be isolated from meaningful literacy curriculum as they focus on remedial drill and practice of isolated skills. Third, their difficulties with reading and writing thwart engagement in learning activities across the content areas, sowing the seeds of alienation from school very early in their educational lives. Yet, since not all engaging activities are inherently instructive, teachers must craft, in educationally justifiable ways, the engaging activities and materials within the school learning community and provide within them systematic instructional support (Raphael, Florio-Ruane, & George, 2001). This applies in teaching all learners, but it is even more pressing with low achievers. For them, instruction cannot simply help to maintain their progress; it must help them cover ground in ways that make up for lost time.

Engage in Authentic Reading, Writing, Speaking, and Listening to Address the Common Problem

The members of TLC began their inquiry by analyzing what readers do, what challenges readers face, and the specific needs of diverse youngsters. Although we, as adults, thought of ourselves as successful readers, we recognized that we usually did not practice reading in the ways in which we ask youngsters to read. No longer students, we now rarely read to learn and for other purposes. When we do read, we are accustomed to reading silently and privately. We rarely read a text and discuss it with others. In short, we are inexperienced in reading and learning within a learning community, as well as in reading and talking about texts that were not of our own choosing and perhaps not within the sphere of our own background knowledge and experiences. For these reasons, we sought or created opportunities to participate in our own reading and study groups as a starting point. In so doing, we hoped to learn more about what we were asking our pupils to do and learn in our classrooms.

TLC members took part in several book clubs, each with a different focus. One focused on learning about culture by reading autobiographical literature. Another focused on creating and researching book clubs in our own classrooms. A third focused on reading reports of current research on improving literacy instruction. We kept logs to record our responses to the texts we read and discussed. We then analyzed our experience in terms of impact on our learning and sense of ourselves as readers and learners. We also reflected on what we could draw from our experiences to create a curricular framework for literacy instruction that would provide new and exciting challenges for all youngsters—those who were alienated from classroom reading as well as those who were fully engaged.

Take From These Activities Insights for Action to Solve the Problem

From these experiences, we learned to value the reading of diverse texts and the role of conversation in learning. We also learned about the power of theme and genre in fostering authentic participation. From our experience, we learned that autobiography and culture could be a powerful genre and theme for the pilot framework. Reading diverse life stories together moved us to think in new ways about ourselves, others who are different from us in culture and/or language, and the power of both oral and written language to help us make our way in the world.* Reading recent research on effective literacy instruction reminded us of the crucial role that instruction plays in literacy learning. We applied these insights in developing and piloting a curricular framework we called Book Club *Plus*.

The Book Club program designed by Raphael with her associates (McMahon et al., 1997) provided a strong conceptual base for our curricular framework. However, TLC members believed that we needed to modify Book Club significantly to meet new needs and solve new problems of practice. This was a point of major insight for participants in TLC. It evidenced a stance of inquiry rather than one of transmission of ideas from university "experts" to classroom teachers. In addition, by advancing the particular situation of engagement of low-achieving students, TLC asserted for itself that in an effective curricular framework, engagement is sustained action, often in difficult circumstances and within communities where that action is valued.

To sustain action and thereby support engagement requires skill, knowledge, and purpose. It also presumes a social context where

---

*We are grateful to our colleague Victoria Purcell-Gates for observing that this focus on personal identity and literacy echoes the work of Paolo Friere on literacy learning among disenfranchised adults.

the practice and application of skill and knowledge is purposeful. Our curricular framework would have to address engagement as both a personal and a social phenomenon. Central to engagement would be clear learning goals, activities appropriate to achieving those goals, a coherent and cohesive context that challenges but supports all learners to engage in those activities, and authentic forms of assessment of learning within that context.

Engagement is supported and sustained by competent use of the tools of the written and oral language system—and this requires authentic activities and texts as well as systematic instructional support and assessment. Such support and assessment, though necessary for all students, is essential to readers working below grade level. Thus, to solve the problem of exclusion of these low-achieving readers from more mature practices in the learning community, we reasoned that we would need to design a framework that transformed the learning community itself—its norms, activities, and curriculum. Thus the challenges facing us were twofold: how to instruct in ways that supported engagement in reading, and how to instruct in ways that accelerated students' movement toward grade-level reading achievement.

We have described the framework in articles published in journals, reports, and periodicals (see www.ciera.org). In brief, however, the framework, which we called Book Club *Plus,* integrated book clubs of age-appropriate texts with thematically related guided practice at the students' instructional level. All of this was woven into unit and yearly plans. The yearly theme, "Our Storied Lives," was taught in three multiweek units: Stories of Self, Stories of Family, and Stories of Culture. The thematic framework was designed to be adaptable by grade level, across a variety of school and classroom contexts, and in districts with or without mandated textbooks and tests. Its multimodal assessment system was also reflective of state and national curriculum standards and locally adaptable to grade level and school district standards.

Investigate the Adequacy of Your Solution to Solve the Common Problem

We developed a skeletal frame for "Our Storied Lives" and a pilot unit on Stories of Self. TLC decided that for purposes of piloting the units in the school year to come, some of the activities and components of the unit would be held in common and considered "core" to the Book Club *Plus* conceptual framework. Others, however, that had been successful in some classrooms during the pilot sites would be locally adapted and serve as potential extension activities. In this way, we could extend the group's understanding based on members' individual inquiries and invention in their own classrooms.

Network teachers conducted a pilot of the Book Club *Plus* curriculum across different districts (representing rural, suburban, and urban settings) and grade levels. This was a work in progress, an iterative process of drafting, teaching, revising, and teaching again. We used a combination of assessments—some that were required of all participating teachers (e.g., asking students to respond to a prompt, "Tell Me About Yourself," at the beginning and end of the school year), and others that individual teachers developed, growing out of their interests in a particular problem of practice.

Individual TLC members also identified their own questions for study. These typically reflected the local situations in which they were engaged and tended to fall into categories of exploring the content of the literacy curriculum (including its relationship to teaching other school subjects and the thorny issues related to assessment practices), classroom management and organization for effective literacy instruction, the role of technology in teaching and in our work within TLC, and professional development.

Amy Heitman, for example, taught in a school district in a rural area midway between Detroit and Flint. As a young teacher, classroom management was a focal concern of hers, and she believed that much of why Book Club could be effective in her classroom was attributed to the beginning-of-year routines that she establishes annually. Reengaging students in literacy by providing more peer-led activities was interesting and challenging to her, and she was interested in better understanding the context in which the Book Club *Plus* framework would be embedded. She therefore decided to focus on the social challenges and consequences of creating a new type of community of learners in the classroom. Her research provided insights into how to get started as a Book Club *Plus* classroom, and she readily shared this with others in the network who were also trying to reorganize their classrooms as part of piloting the Stories of Self unit.

Nina Hasty, in contrast, taught a large first- and second-grade class in inner-city Detroit. As she designed and assessed the pilot unit in her classroom, she moved from exclusive reliance on direct instruction by grade level to a blend of grade-level and ability-level activities including guided reading, writing workshops, direct instruction in phonics, and book clubs. The Stories of Self unit in Nina's classroom considered the class as a single community with a broad span of reading levels rather than two parallel classes in one room—first and second grade. Thematic content proved to be the thread with which she could join parts into a whole or, in her words, patches to patchwork. In her study she documented how to build flexibility into a seemingly inflexible basal-based reading program, a significant issue in many urban districts.

Because assessment is such a powerful gatekeeping force for all teachers and students of literacy, it was, not surprisingly, a central part of TLC members' inquiries. To think about assessment, we had to share our work with others and also research what others had already learned. For example, in thinking about assessment in TLC, we were drawn to the work of literacy researchers and teacher educators, Kathryn Au and Sheila Valencia (Au & Valencia, 1997). Each led a teacher collaborative working on the development of assessment portfolios aligning classroom literacy curriculum with state and district standards, identifying clear instructional goals, and making these goals visible to students, parents, and administrators. In addition to reading their reports, we invited Kathy to visit Michigan and share her experiences and the work of the Hawaii collaborative with us.

Learning about the Hawaii collaborative helped us to create our own vision of an assessment plan. By consensus, TLC members focused on aligning national, state, and district standards and benchmarks. Taking stock of the literacy benchmarks from state and local assessments, the TLC members transformed their language and content into student-friendly "I can" statements that would serve as the benchmarks in the Book Club *Plus* framework and its units (Au, 2002). Table 9-1 is an example of the "I can" statements we developed. It shows the standards for speaking and listening within peer-led discussions of autobiographical literature and illustrates their accessible language and activity-based nature. As such, these statements became handy tools for ongoing assessment by teachers, opportunities for pupils to catalogue their own work in self-assessment, evidence and illustration of learning to report to parents and administrators, and guides for planning curriculum and instruction.

While the TLC network included teachers across grade levels, we focused intensive data collection and analysis on grade 3—a watershed time in the curriculum and in the development of learners' school careers. The third-grade focus was an interesting twist on what we usually expect of practitioner research in that it involved numerous participants in TLC designing ways to collect and analyze data, and even helping with the collection of that data, in classrooms that were neither their own nor even the same grade level as their own. Yet by this work, TLC members were able to engage in cross-site study that heightened their awareness of other settings

Table 9-1. *"I Can"* **Statements for Book Club Study of Autobiographical Literature**

I Can...

Reading

I can retell a story in my own words.

I can make meaning when I read a variety of texts.

I can make connections between my own life and what I am reading.

I can make connections within and between texts. (*Texts* = broad definition)

I can figure out a theme from my reading.

Writing

I can write to communicate my ideas.

I can use writing for different purposes and audiences.

I can show "me" in my writing.

Discussion

I can contribute to a good book club discussion.

    (a) I can stay on topic when I talk.

    (b) I can share my feelings and ideas.

    (c) I can respect others' ideas and opinions.

    (d) I can build on others' ideas.

    (e) I can bring others into the discussion.

Evaluation

I can show and tell what I learned and how I learned it.

Culture

I can use artifacts to describe the following:

    (a) My own cultural heritage

    (b) Others' cultures

    (c) Similarities and differences across cultures

I can define culture and how it changes.

©Book Club *Plus,* 2000

and also of the nature and dynamics of their own classrooms as literacy learning environments.

Although we did not have the resources to do a quasi-experimental study, we decided to attempt a systematic comparison of classroom learning in Book Club *Plus* third-grade classrooms and in the classrooms of several "buddy" teachers—third-grade teachers who worked with TLC third-grade teachers but had not participated in the network and were not using the Book Club *Plus* framework. When possible, these classes were also matched for qualities such as percentage of free and reduced lunch, ethnic diversity, gender, and student needs.

We conducted a comparison of students in each of the "buddy" classrooms using the Metropolitan Achievement Tests and found that the students in the Book Club *Plus* classrooms performed at an equal level to those in the control classrooms. This is an interesting finding, as TLC teachers spent only half of their literacy instruction engaged in the traditional activities that these tests are designed to evaluate. The remaining time was spent in less often recommended activities related to student-led discussions and personal writing in response to reading.

In each of the TLC teachers' third-grade classrooms, we also assessed the growth of the students who had the most reading difficulty. We used the Qualitative Reading Inventory with three students who were performing at the lowest levels in their classroom on a range of reading tasks. The teachers gathered information at the beginning and end of the year. A pattern across classrooms was that all the students made at least a year's growth during that academic year, but even more encouraging, more than half of the students made more than a year's growth, and a few even achieved grade-level performance

We also examined all TLC third-grade students' work qualitatively for evidence of growth, especially in voice and engagement. For example, we studied third graders' reading logs for evidence of engagement. Rikki (pseudonym) was a student in TLC member Marianne George's multilingual third-grade suburban classroom. She struggled with reading and writing and had been in remedial programs since the end of first grade. Her writing samples (collected over time and during her Book Club *Plus* work) show her level of engagement as she becomes more agile in expressing herself in writing logs. The examples below illustrate both the way we assessed learning and changes in Rikki's engagement in the reading process as evidenced in her responsive writing.

One of Rikki's early reading log entries is written in response to a story about a young girl who, as a result of her parents' divorce, is sent to live with her grandparents on a farm that has a chicken coop. She believes that there is a monster inside the chicken coop, and the story evolves as she faces her fears, both literally—the monster in the chicken coop—and metaphorically, her family's changes. Rikki's entry is connected to her own life but shows little engagement with the text other than topical connection. She wrote as follows (NOTE: Her original spelling is preserved in both samples):

Me and the Book

When I was litel I
Owes was afad of
Sperts. But Im still afrad
Of sperts. I covered My
Self at night.

Her entry reflects her personal response to the book. It connects the fear that the story character has of the chicken coop monster with her earlier fears of spirits in the night. In contrast, by spring, in response to reading the book *Stone Fox*, Rikki created the following reading log entry, evidencing both personal response and thinking about her own thinking and the text (or metacognitive strategies):

I have a queshten on the end of chapter 3.

Was litel Willy in the race or was he pracising? Thats the reason I was getting comefused.

I like the book alot so far. I wonder what's going to happen next. This book is so exicting so far. it's like you are in the book. I'm getting comfused thogh.

Was litel Willy's granfather alive or dead? Because litel Willy is talking to his granfather.

Dous he have any parints arond?

dous litel Willy have any frenids?

Well I don't know!"

This entry is both longer and more substantive, with evidence of metacognitive awareness of her reading process. Rikki's use of questions is notable for her intent to engage her peers in a discussion of the ideas that she finds confusing and/or interesting. She uses questions to explore story events (e.g., whether he was in the race or just practicing) and story characters (the status of Willy's grandfather at this point in the story, whether or not Willy has friends) and she grounds her questions in her personal response to the story (that it is exciting and that it feels like she is in the story).

We traced engagement of the sort illustrated in the brief example of Rikki's work to teacher thought and action. Specifically, engagement is prompted and sustained in meaningful content and in a range of contexts that invite youngsters to participate with their texts and their peers through reading, writing of different formats and purposes, and talk within dyads, small groups, and whole-class settings. Within the heterogeneously grouped weekly Book Club, students saw why they were being taught about literacy. Within the ability-grouped weekly Literacy Block, they understood that the skills and strategies they were learning would support their access to the books they want to read and the writing they want to create. In both contexts, students saw themselves as active members of and participants in a literate community.

Share Your Learning and Learn From Others Who Have Conducted a Similar Inquiry

Members of TLC shared the progress that they made with their own research questions and experiences with the pilot unit. These peer interactions were helpful in building a common knowledge base that expanded as each person contributed their expertise to the group. Student-to-student interactions also took place between some participating classrooms. For example, Nina Hasty was preparing her class of first and second graders to participate in "fishbowl" as a way to learn how to discuss books. In fishbowl, students learn, with teacher support, the ways to have an educative book discussion. The norms for such a discussion, as well as the methods for organizing a class for fishbowl, were new to both Nina and her students. However, other members of TLC experienced with fishbowl designed ways to support and encourage Nina and her students as they learned how to talk about books in fishbowls. Amy Heitman and Kathy Highfield, for example, worked with Amy's class to develop a video that would teach Nina's students how to participate effectively in a "fishbowl" that helps teachers scaffold student discussions. Amy's students wrote the script, designed the set, chose parts to read and represent, and made a video that was used to model fishbowl.

Members of the TLC also shared what they learned with teachers from other communities in several ways. They made presentations at district workshops, to help their teaching peers learn about their progress with struggling readers, and at local, state, and national conferences. We also shared information with our peers through articles in research-based journals, articles, and book chapters that various subgroups wrote on struggling readers in general and on their own research inquiry. In many other ways, sharing what was learned was an important aspect of the TLC network. Members of the network guest-spoke at both Taffy's and Susan's university courses for graduate students. Some members also participated in a Book Club Web site and in various CIERA-sponsored conferences. Going public with our work on a regular basis not only helped to focus our own attention on the goals of struggling readers, it also helped us to share our learning with the broader literacy education community. This activity transformed our audiences, purposes, and the nature of our voices and texts, and it sustained effort through the sometimes difficult work of collaborative inquiry. We found that we were held accountable by other professionals as we received their peer review and constructively critical feedback. We also received encouragement and praise for our work. All of these added to our growing sense that the work of TLC was meaningful, educative, and worthy of our engagement.

Return to the Common Problem With New Insight and Additional Possible Solutions

A crucial aspect to the problem of practice approach is attention to using what was learned to help transform understandings about literacy instruction. The work of the TLC network changed our understanding of the aims of literacy education in classrooms. We moved from starting positions based on various categories and oppositions (e.g., "I have low readers and high readers in my class"; "Low and high-achieving readers must learn separately since they read at different levels and have different instructional needs"; "I never group by ability since this would limit what my low readers can learn"; "My low-achieving readers cannot do the grade level curriculum") to a more dynamic and integrative view of our responsibilities to all learners in charge, something we came to call "the dual commitments."

Based on our TLC inquiries, we asserted that there are two essential commitments that literacy instructors must make to their students. On the one hand, teachers must ensure that all students are taught literacy with materials that are appropriate for their instructional level. Here the commitment is to assess where students are and to provide instruction designed to help them achieve at least a year's growth in a year's time. On the other hand, all children, even those not yet reading at grade level, need continual opportunities to engage meaningfully with texts that have been written for their age group. This is important even if a reader cannot decode these texts independently. Here the commitment is to provide access to these texts, through listening centers, books on tape, buddy reading, and so forth, and to allow students to respond to and discuss these texts with same-age peers.

As we have described in this chapter, we integrated students' work in these two contexts by means of thematically related texts and small-group projects within the "Our Storied Lives" curriculum and the Book Club *Plus* instructional framework. With these changes in the literacy learning community, even readers not yet working at grade level were full participants in the classroom learning community. Students of all reading levels engaged in both age-appropriate peer-led activities and in teacher-led activities at their instructional levels. In addition, every student engaged in meaningful speaking, in listening and writing in response to text, and in peer-led and instructionally supported activities.

In TLC, we similarly worked within a learning community to explore problems of practice of local concern, and we also discovered how such work could contribute to the collective learning of a professional community. In many ways, the experiences of the teachers in TLC paralleled those of our students. The Book Club *Plus* framework blurred the borders between grade-level and non–grade-level readers for many of the social and conceptual aspects of reading comprehension and response to text. It also blurred the relationship between instruction in and use of skills and strategies as tools for authentic literacy. Blurring these borders accelerated the learning of readers by widening the circle of membership into the authentic practices of the literate classroom community while providing systematic instruction and assessment for all students, and especially for those who needed to make the greatest growth in the shortest period of time.

Similarly, teachers from such different communities, grades, and years of experience are traditionally held apart by few opportunities to discuss the issues of each other's teaching worlds or the compelling issues that affect all teachers. Like leveled reading groups, professional development had traditionally put teachers from like contexts together, thus hardening the isolation of their work. In TLC, the coming together of teachers whose contexts and daily experiences were so different mirrored the energy that arose from different-ability students working together. Teachers with different views and strengths brought various ideas to the table. This complication of implicit local knowledge spurred participants' reflection and learning.

Conclusion: Professional Development As Working Through Problems of Practice

Participation in any community of learners is part of the process by which each member grows and learns, and the community itself is both sustained and transformed (Cole, 1996). The community of teachers and teacher educators coming together in TLC held not only a shared commitment to inquiry and a common problem of practice, but each returned from network interactions to his or her classroom learning community. It is in the classroom setting that the public, social dialogues about knowledge in TLC were internalized, transformed, and made public again as teachers made their own local, situated efforts to inquire into student learning and try various possible solutions. This process can be thought of as one of application of learning, but it can also be thought of as the transformation of learning into the reconstruction of local knowledge, a kind of branching outward (in contrast to either the metaphor of implanting as in "dissemination" or increasing in size as in "upscaling"—both common in the lexicon of professional development and research and development work).

The model of professional development in TLC was an organic one in which participants, through the "common ground" of conversation and inquiry, worked through a cycle of "seasons" in the life of a problem: framing it, inquiring into its possible solution, documenting findings, and sharing them with others. The network was a "greenhouse for seedling ideas" that teachers took back to their own classrooms to "cultivate" in the particular contexts they afforded. Their knowledge was spread by the network's "branching out" to others, communicating about both what was learned and the social dynamics of that learning.

References

Au, K. H. (2002). Elementary program: Guiding change in a time of standards. In S. B. Wepner, D. S. Strickland, & J. T. Feeley (Eds.), *The administration and supervision of reading programs* (3rd ed., pp. 42–58). New York: Teachers College Press.

Au, K., & Valencia, S. (1997). The complexities of portfolio assessment. In D. Hansen & N. Burbules (Eds.), *Teaching and its predicaments* (pp. 123–144). Boulder: Westview.

Berne, J. (2001). *Connected teacher learning: An examination of a teacher learning network.* Unpublished doctoral dissertation, Michigan State University, East Lansing, MI.

Cole, M. (1996). *Cultural psychology: A once and future discipline.* Cambridge, MA: Harvard University Press.

Farley, R., Danziger, S., & Holzer, H. J. (2000). *Detroit divided.* New York: Russell Sage Foundation.

Florio-Ruane, S., with deTar, J. (2001). *Teacher education and the cultural imagination: Autobiography, conversation, and narrative.* Mahwah, NJ: Erlbaum.

Florio-Ruane, S., & Raphael, T. E. (2001). Reading lives: Creating and sustaining learning about culture and literacy in teacher study groups. In C. M. Clark (Ed.), *Talking shop: Authentic conversation and teacher learning* (pp. 64–81). New York: Teachers College Press.

Gavelek, J., & Raphael, T. E. (1996). Changing talk about text: New roles for teachers and students. *Language Arts, 73,* 24–34.

McMahon, S. I., Raphael, T. E., Goatley, V. J., & Pardo, L. S. (1997). *The Book Club connection: Literacy learning and classroom talk.* New York: Teachers College Press.

Newman, D., Griffin, P., & Cole, M. (1989). *The construction zone: Working for cognitive change in school.* Cambridge, UK: Cambridge University Press.

Raphael, T. E., Florio-Ruane, S., & George, M. (2001). Book Club *Plus:* A conceptual framework to organize literacy instruction. *Language Arts, 79* (1), 159–168.

Raphael, T. E., Florio-Ruane, S., Kehus, M., George, M., Hasty, N., & Highfield, K. (2001). Thinking for ourselves: Literacy learning in a diverse teacher inquiry network. *The Reading Teacher* [On-line], *54* (6), 506–507. Available: http://www.ciera.org, Report #00-07.

. . . .

The Center for the Improvement of Early Reading Achievement (CIERA) is funded by a contract with the U.S. Office of Educational Research and Improvement (OERI). This project was supported, in part, under the Educational Research and Development Centers Program, PR/Award Number R305R70004. The views expressed here are those of the authors and do not necessarily represent those of OERI or the United States government.

Susan Florio-Ruane and Taffy E. Raphael, co-principal investigators, are listed alphabetically as authors. They contributed equally to the leadership of this CIERA research project and shared equal responsibility for guiding and reporting it. The authors of this paper acknowledge the members of the Teachers' Learning Collaborative for their contributions to the ideas presented in this paper, especially Marianne George, Nina Hasty, and Amy Heitman.

Chapter 10

Professional Development in the Uses of Technology

Elizabeth S. Pang and Michael L. Kamil

Key Ideas

✓ Video technology is the most widely utilized technology for modeling effective teaching.

✓ There has been a sharp rise in research on Internet-based technologies in literacy teacher education.

✓ Future research should examine the connection between technology-based teacher education and student learning outcomes.

For

• Teacher educators, literacy researchers

• Teachers, policy makers

Literacy is an ever evolving concept, and changing definitions of literacy require modifications in how teachers approach literacy instruction in schools (Barr, Watts-Taffe, & Yokota, 2000). Among the topics that have emerged in recent years is the impact of technology on literacy. However, this is a complex, multifaceted issue for which there are no ready answers. An important trend is that computer technology has become the technology of choice as other established technologies, such as film, audio recordings, and video become incorporated into software or come under the control of computer hardware and software (Kamil & Lane, 1998). The development of computers has allowed for the inclusion of multimedia elements with conventional text. Because these multimedia elements effect change in how we perceive text, a broadening of the concept of literacy is required. The pervasiveness of computer and communication technology has made it imperative for teachers, teacher educators, and researchers concerned with literacy instruction to critically examine its impact on teaching and learning.

Trends in the Professional Development of Literacy Teachers

Research on the initial and continuing education of literacy teachers has received considerable attention in recent years. This reflects a larger public interest in teacher and teaching quality and its concomitant effect on student achievement. The report of the National Reading Panel (NICHHD, 2000), in its review and synthesis of the empirical research on literacy teacher education, concluded that appropriate teacher education does have positive effects on student achievement. However, much is still not known about the specific conditions under which this conclusion holds, such as the appropriate length of interventions, their intensity, and the amount of instructional and administrative support that teachers need. The issue of teacher quality and standards was reiterated by the U.S. Department of Education (2002), which called for rigorous standards in teacher education programs in its report, "Meeting the Highly Qualified Teachers Challenge: The Secretary's Annual Report on Teacher Quality."

In addition to the growing emphasis on teacher quality and standards, there is a definite shift in thinking toward more reflective practice in the professional preparation of teachers. Hoffman and Pearson (2000) point to the need to go beyond "training teachers" to "teaching teachers." They argue that the reality of teaching is one of constantly changing conditions with fairly abstract and even ambiguous learning outcomes. Hence, it is important to emphasize the internal process of change and reflection in teacher education, because teachers often change their beliefs prior to (or interactively with) changes in practice.

These are important trends in the field of literacy teacher education. However, the topic of technology and technology integration, which has gained in importance both in education and literacy research, is a relatively new but growing area of research in the professional development of reading educators. The advent of computer technology has considerably widened the scope for using technology in educational contexts. It has also opened up new possibilities and new or expanded conceptualizations of literacy such as visual literacy (Flood & Lapp, 1995; Reinking, 1995).

The use of traditional technologies, such as film, audio recordings and video, is not new to teacher education programs. However, the systematic study of such technologies, including more recent computer-based applications, with a view to prepare teachers to integrate technology in their classrooms and reading instruction, has not received a great deal of attention until recently. This is not surprising, given the traditional role that technology has played in classrooms as well as in teacher education programs.

Technology has traditionally played an adjunct role, such as delivering or presenting information, such as educational television and video recordings. In many preservice programs, video recordings have played an important role in presenting or re-creating situations and contexts as well as in modeling and simulation. Microteaching, where preservice teachers are videotaped in a simulated classroom for later viewing and analysis, is another instance of the traditional use of video technology in teacher education. In order to examine the trends in technology use and integration in literacy teacher education, we will review studies of prospective and practicing teachers that utilize technology either as a research tool, as data, or as curriculum.

Research on Technology and Literacy Teacher Education

As part of a wider review of the research on literacy teacher education, we conducted an extensive electronic search of literacy teacher education studies published in peer-review journals. This was supplemented by hand searches of the yearbooks of the College

Reading Association and National Reading Conference. We also examined published reviews of specific aspects of teacher education and included those studies that dealt with literacy. In total, we examined approximately 300 articles published between 1961 and 2001 on the initial and continuing education of literacy teachers. Of these, we found 56 articles that reported the use of technology. The studies that we examined included descriptive as well as experimental research reports. The descriptive studies provided a detailed examination of specific teacher education curricula as well as teachers' responses and insights, whereas the experimental research evaluated the effectiveness of particular instructional methods.

Among them we can distinguish two types of studies: (a) using technology in the professional development of prospective and practicing teachers, and (b) preparing teachers to integrate technology in literacy instruction. Most of the studies that we reviewed were of the first type. Many preservice programs demonstrate the importance of using technology in their teacher preparatory programs as a model for how teachers can and should make use of technology in instruction. However, there are currently relatively few studies that investigate the specific question of how literacy teachers are prepared to integrate technology in instruction, and still fewer address the question of how this might affect student learning or achievement.

Using Technology in the Preparation and Continuing Education of Reading Teachers

Technology is used in different ways and for different purposes in these studies. We identified three main uses of technology. The most common use of technology is to deliver content and model instructional methods. For instance, video recordings are often used to present instructional methods such as Directed Reading Activities (DRA) and Directed Reading and Thinking Activities (DRTA). Video recordings are also commonly used to model good teaching in authentic classroom settings. In addition, researchers use video and audio data as research tools to study teachers at work in classrooms. For instance, video and audio recordings may be used to compare experienced and inexperienced teachers to study prospective teachers' perceptions, or as a postintervention research tool to examine teachers' implementation of an instructional strategy.

One notable trend is the gradual transformation of technology use from content delivery and modeling or simulation to communication-based distance learning. This shift in focus is due to the rapid developments in computer and communication technologies, such as e-mail and hypermedia. Of the 56 studies we examined, 24 reported the use of non–computer-based technology such as audiotape, videotape, and film. Additionally, 10 studies utilized a combination of computer applications and video data (e.g., interactive compressed video and case-based instruction using videodisc and hypercard). The remaining 22 studies investigated the use of computer-based technology such as e-mail, discussion lists, and the World Wide Web.

Video Technology

The use of audio and video recordings to enhance preservice reading teacher education is particularly widespread, and many studies reported favorable findings. Thirty-four of the 56 studies we examined reported using some form of video, audio, or film recording. The early studies date back to the 1970s. In these early studies, videotapes were used to demonstrate specific methods, such as teaching word recognition skills (Tyre & Knight, 1972), as well as more general instructional approaches, such as teaching content area teachers about reading instruction (Dupuis, Askov, & Lee, 1979) and improving reading instruction for underachieving readers (Baker, 1977).

In the 1980s, audio and video technology was used by researchers to examine specific aspects of the learning process in order to improve teacher education. For instance, Allen, Freeman, and Lehman (1989) reported that the use of videotapes of exemplary teaching served as a catalyst for observation and reflection by both preservice and inservice teachers. In Hoover and Carroll's (1987) study, teachers evaluated their own reading instruction on videotape using a self-assessment procedure developed by the researchers. The analysis of pre- and postintervention data showed improvements in teaching behaviors. Streeter (1986) used video recordings of teachers for postcourse conferencing. In this study, teachers were given instruction on using techniques to convey enthusiasm, which led to increased levels of teacher enthusiasm. Students' perception that reading was difficult was also considerably reduced.

Throughout the 1990s, researchers continued to utilize video technology in teacher education programs. Of the 30 studies published between 1990 and 1999, 19 made use of video or video cum hypercard/hypermedia technology, 1 reported using audio data, and the remaining 10 utilized nonvideo computer technology. As a research tool, video data was useful for analyzing teachers' changing knowledge and practices (Button, 1992; Maimon, 1997). In particular, video-based case methodology was reported to be effective for contextualizing literacy instruction for preservice teachers, encouraging active construction of knowledge (Risko, McAllister, & Bigenho, 1993), meaning making (Copeland & Decker, 1996), and sustained thinking about complex cases (Risko, 1995). Increasingly, videotapes were being replaced by videodiscs, but more important, there was a gradual convergence between video and computer technology as video recordings became integrated into multimedia software and hardware configurations.

Computer Technology

The first research reports on using microcomputers (or personal computers) in reading teacher education appeared in the late 1980s. Doyle (1988) described an inservice workshop showing creative uses of computers for freewriting, brainstorming, and peer evaluation, whereas Balajthy (1988) reported on the evaluation of a preservice module that trained reading teachers in microcomputer applications. However, it is in more recent years that computer-based technology has come to be utilized and studied more extensively in literacy teacher education.

The 1990s saw a sharp rise in the number of studies using computer-based technology, such as multimedia (or hypermedia), e-mail, and discussion lists. Multimedia software enables digitized video images to be combined with sound and text. The term *hypermedia* is sometimes used to refer to multimedia applications because of the use of hyperlinks or electronic pathways for connecting various forms of text, graphics, and media. Multimedia and hypermedia typically incorporate software that enables on-demand or random access to video clips, audio data, text, and so forth. Access to data is no longer constrained by linear text or traditional videotape formats.

Hughes, Packard, and Pearson (1997) describe one such application, called Reading Classroom Explorer (RCE), which uses short video clips within a hypermedia system that integrates many different types of media including text, video, audio, and still pictures. In four exploratory case studies of student teachers' response to RCE, the researchers noted some common themes. There was generally a positive disposition towards the multimedia program. It was also adaptable to the needs, interests, and capacities of the participants, who varied in terms of both their background and their purpose for using the program.

In a related study, Hughes, Packard, and Pearson (2000a) compared the original VHS format of the videos (Anderson & Au, 1991) with the same video material that is digitized and incorporated in RCE as short video clips. The hypermedia system enabled users to quickly and easily revisit specific points in a video clip and facilitated cross-case analysis, but the VHS format was acknowledged to be easier to use. Each video case in VHS format was also longer and provided a fuller context compared to the shorter video clips in the hypermedia format. Clearly, there are both advantages and disadvantages to using traditional VHS formats compared to more novel formats such as hypermedia. The disadvantages of hypermedia may be short-term, as the cost of digitizing and storing large video files decreases. However, the task of designing and creating an appropriate hypermedia environment that facilitates teacher learning remains a challenge.

Stephens (1997) reports on a similar type of multimedia program called Literacy Education: Application and Practice (LEAP). This program utilizes video-based minicases on laserdisc and software that allows quick, random, and repeated access to the minicases. Both RCE and LEAP are grounded in cognitive flexibility theory (Spiro & Jehng, 1990), whereby cognitive flexibility refers to the ability to spontaneously restructure one's knowledge, in many ways, in adaptive response to radically changing situational demands. Stephens (1997) interpreted the richer post-LEAP discourse of the participating teachers (n = 29) to mean that the preservice teachers had a more lucid awareness of their own perspectives regarding their role as teachers, the role of their students, and the environment of their own future classrooms.

However, whether preservice teachers had truly adopted new perspectives as a result of learning through multimedia tools and how those perspectives will guide their performance as teachers and impact student learning remain as unanswered questions. The advantages of combining video-case methodology and cognitive flexibility hypertext have been quite well documented. The benefits for teacher education, especially at the preservice level, have also been explored in a number of studies. For instance, Kinzer and Risko (1998) found "increased class discussion (and correspondingly, less instructor talk), increased participation by a greater number of students, increased higher level questioning, and increased student-initiated questions and discussions" (p. 190).

The Internet and Communication-Based Technology

An important development is the pervasiveness of communication-based computer technology and the explosive growth of the Internet. With the advent of the Internet, even more possibilities exist for the delivery of video-based cases and hypermedia environments for both preservice and inservice teacher education. A web-based Reading Classroom Explorer (http://www.eliteracy.org/rce/) has been developed, and other educational service providers such as Teachscape (http://www.teachscape.com) also utilize Web-based video cases and multimedia to model exemplary literacy instruction. The advent of high-speed networks and faster computers has made it possible to deliver multimedia content in teacher professional development.

However, computer technology in professional development does not have to depend heavily on multimedia, which tends to demand considerable developmental effort and cost. E-mail is possibly the single most explosive use of technology in communication (Kamil & Lane, 1998). Of the 22 studies we examined that reported on the use of computer-based technology, 13—that is, more than half—investigated the effects of using e-mail or computer-mediated communication. Teachers learned about the technology as well as ways to use it to share ideas. For instance, Grisham (1997) found that online dialogue journals through e-mail among inservice teachers (n = 13) helped them to develop declarative knowledge (knowledge of Internet terminology), procedural knowledge (normal use of e-mail), and conditional knowledge (use of e-mail in other ways). The teachers ranged in age from 23 to 55 years old, and they had 1–26 years of teaching experience.

A key rationale for utilizing e-mail in literacy teacher education is to offer teachers a supportive environment in which to discuss ideas about literacy instruction and reflect on their teaching and learning experiences. Goetze, Walker, & Yellin (2000) found that teachers engaged in talk that supported their learning when communicating through e-mail in the context of a preservice program. Dodson (2000) reported that a combination of both face-to-face and computer-mediated communication enabled teachers to socially construct knowledge about literacy. Furthermore, e-mail communication in the context of a reading methods course between novice and experienced teachers facilitated better understanding of different philosophies of reading (Johnson, 1997).

A second rationale for using e-mail in teacher education is to connect teachers, especially those in preservice programs, with students. In a number of studies, preservice teachers communicate through e-mail with elementary (Johnson, 1996), middle school (Bowman & Edenfield, 2000; Traw, 1994; Van Valkenburgh & Sirpa, 2000), or high school students (Fey, 1997; Stallworth, 2001). In such a partnership, both prospective teachers and the students gained from the interaction, such as the fostering of a reciprocal and trusting relationship (Van Valkenburgh & Sirpa, 2000). E-mail correspondence also helped to support the learning of reluctant readers in combination with face-to-face tutoring, classroom visits, and technology-based activities (Bowman & Edenfield, 2000). However, in one study (Fey, 1997), it was found that the computer-mediated environment actually discouraged the active participation of female high school and college students (prospective teachers) because of tensions experienced in the initial technological problems encountered as well as the excessive participation of one male student.

Preparing Teachers to Integrate Technology in Reading and Literacy Instruction

Many of the studies we have reviewed so far subscribe to the view that making use of technology in teacher preparatory programs serves as a model for how teachers can make use of technology in instruction. Likewise, Preparing Tomorrow's Teachers for Technology (PT3), an initiative of the U.S. Department of Education, seeks to bring about a shift to "technology-infused teaching" within schools of education so as to transform the future classrooms of today's prospective teachers (see http://pt3.org/about/index.html). Although there are many types of technologies that impact literacy, it is computer and communication technology that currently dominates discussions about technology in education.

Many of the studies on using computer technology in teacher education described how teachers were taught to use the technology. Researchers also emphasized the importance of modeling for teachers how technology can be used to support literacy and learning (e.g., Johnson, 1996, 1997). However, the more specific question of preparing pre- and inservice teachers to integrate technology in literacy instruction and curriculum is less well investigated. It is a compelling issue, as pointed out by a number of researchers (Balajthy, 1996; Blanchard, 1994). We found only four studies that focused on this question.

Each study examined a very specific aspect of technology integration and literacy instruction: planning, creating instructional materials, teaching comprehension, and assessing literacy in at-risk learners. Richards (2001) explored how preservice teachers grappled with concerns in integrating print and computer technology and found that the planning of technology-infused literacy instruction posed a considerable challenge. Roberts and Hsu (2000) examined the effectiveness of using computers to create writing prompts by comparing the overall quality of handmade prompts with those made with computers. There was no significant difference in quality, but 85% of the teachers expressed a preference for using the computer to create prompts.

Bahr, Kinzer, and Rieth (1991) investigated the effects of training teachers (n = 5) to integrate prediscussion questioning techniques with computer software to teach comprehension to mildly handicapped high school students. This did not result in significant differences in students' comprehension scores, but placing the students in homogeneous groups did have an effect on achievement. Finally, Duckworth and Taylor (1995) described how a portfolio planning guide and hypermedia technology can be used by elementary and special education majors to assess literacy in at-risk students. These are promising directions, but clearly much more research is needed in this area.

Emerging Themes

Some common themes have emerged in the review we have undertaken of the studies on literacy and technology in teacher education. These themes reflect some of the most fundamental issues and concerns in literacy teacher education.

Connecting Theory and Practice

One of the great challenges in preparing literacy teachers is to provide a coherent and meaningful learning experience that is grounded in theory and truly reflective of classroom practice. Most teacher education programs combine coursework with field experiences, such as classroom observations, tutoring, or internships. Although this is intended to help preservice teachers connect theory with instructional practice, student teachers often find that coursework is devoid of context, whereas field experiences may not match what is being taught in academic coursework. One of the most promising areas that has emerged from the literature is the use of video-based case methodology to contextualize literacy instruction for both pre- and inservice teachers.

Video cases, as compared with print-based cases, enable teachers to observe literacy instruction and learning in actual classroom settings. Video cases also have the advantage of enabling teachers to observe teaching without the constraints of time and place, unlike real classroom observations. With the addition of hypermedia technology, video cases can be electronically linked and integrated with course readings. Multiple video cases can also be accessed, analyzed, and revisited with ease in hypermedia environments (Kinzer & Risko, 1998; Hughes, Packard, & Pearson, 2000b). The Internet offers further possibilities for the delivery of multimedia cases to support teacher education.

Modeling

Teaching is generally acknowledged to be an ill-structured domain, requiring the application of conceptually complex knowledge to diverse and unpredictable situations (Hughes et al., 2000b). Modeling enables teachers to observe the complexity inherent in literacy learning and instruction. From videotaped demonstrations of DRTA, to "behind-the-one-way-glass" observations in Reading Recovery teacher development (see Pinnell, 1987), to case-based multimedia, modeling remains one of the most powerful tools in teacher professional development. Technology clearly plays an important role in providing multiple ways to model instructional approaches in teacher education.

Reflective Practice

Reflection plays an important role in the internal process of change, which in turn affects behavior (see Roskos, Risko, & Vukelich, 2000, for a review of reflection studies in literacy). Studies of computer-mediated communication in teacher education show the potential for encouraging reflection and dialogue among both prospective and practicing teachers. Because discussion and dialogue are critically important in teacher education, technology can play a role in facilitating communication and, ultimately, the creation of a learning community (Anderson & Lee, 1995; Grisham, 1997).

Directions for Research on Literacy, Technology, and Professional Development

The 56 studies that we have examined constitute a relatively small body of research. This is not surprising because in education, the adoption and implementation of technology tends to lag behind other fields (Blanchard, 1999; Singer, Dreher, & Kamil, 1982). Furthermore, there are still many gaps in our knowledge about technology and literacy. Clearly, there needs to be a systematic research agenda to study the basic questions. For instance, how do we define literacy (or literacies) in today's technologically infused world? (See Kamil & Lane, 1998, for a discussion of research directions in literacy and technology.)

We can draw only tentative conclusions from the studies we have examined. Many interesting questions have been raised, but only a few have been systematically investigated. First, we know that teachers do learn how to use technology, although there are initial difficulties to be overcome. There have been positive reports of teachers' responses, reactions, and interactions with technology in the course of their professional education. Second, we know what researchers are focusing on from the emerging themes we discussed earlier. Technology is important in the work of teacher educators, not just in developing teachers' knowledge and skills but also in encouraging reflection and building communities of practice. Researchers are also exploring ways of using technology to study the world of teachers and learners through, for example, video recordings and, increasingly, on-line discussions. Third, we can conclude that we know far more about the use of technology in preservice literacy education than we do for inservice education. There are far more studies of preservice teachers than of practicing teachers in the area of literacy, technology, and professional development. The National Reading Panel report (NICHHD, 2000) found that there were no experimental studies of preservice teachers that examined student performances related to reading. Despite the larger number of preservice studies in the area of technology, we still need answers to the questions about the effects of such preparation on the students.

The more difficult questions remain to be answered. There are only a few studies examining technology integration and literacy instruction in teacher education. Indeed, the more fundamental question is: What do we teach teachers about literacy and technology?

Clearly, it is important for teachers both to learn how to use the technology and to experience it in their own learning. This is currently what many preservice programs seek to do. Beyond that, what we know about literacy and technology is still limited; hence, it is difficult to say what teacher education for literacy instruction with technology should look like. For instance, we know quite a bit about writing but much less about reading in relation to technology, such as reading of hypertext and viewing of multimedia (Kamil & Lane, 1998). Kamil, Kim, and Lane (in press) have conducted an analysis of the research on multimedia documents, demonstrating that there are, at least, a few guidelines. What is needed is a research program to see whether the inclusion of these guidelines in teacher education or professional development programs, for example, will improve students' ability to process multimedia information. Although we will find some amelioration of the problem as more students and teachers grow up with computers, it is a critical area to study. Leaving learning in these increasingly important areas to chance is not truly a desirable option. Future research should examine systematically what constitutes literacy in technology-infused teaching and learning.

Another issue that needs to be addressed in future research is that professional development must continue long enough for teachers to see progress in their students and themselves (Pinnell, 1987). In many of the studies we reviewed, it is not clear how effective the professional development course has been. For instance: What specific changes in teachers' beliefs, attitudes, or behaviors took place? Were they sustained over time? Did they have an impact on students' learning? It is often said that instructional change for teachers happens slowly. If this is the case, how do we support teacher learning over time? With the advent of advanced communication technologies and high-speed networks, will on-line support be able to sustain change in teacher behavior? These are critical questions that should guide future research.

The above discussion is an initial attempt to characterize a field that is still grappling with important basic questions. Many issues in technology, literacy, and teacher education remain as rich areas for further research and investigation.

References*

Allen, V. G., Freeman, E. B., & Lehman, B. A. (1989). A literacy education model for preservice teachers: Translating observation and reflection into exemplary practice. In S. McCormick & J. Zutell (Eds.), *Cognitive and social perspectives for literacy research and instruction* (pp. 473–480). Chicago: National Reading Conference.

Anderson, J., & Lee, A. (1995). Literacy teachers learning a new literacy: A study of the use of electronic mail in a reading education class. *Reading Research and Instruction, 34* (3), 222–238.

Anderson, R. C., & Au, K. H. (1991). *Teaching reading: Strategies from successful classrooms* [Videotapes]. Urbana, IL: University of Illinois, Center for the Study of Reading.

Anderson, V. (1992). A teacher development project in transactional strategy instruction for teachers of severely reading-disabled adolescents. *Teaching and Teacher Education, 8* (4), 391–403.

Bahr, C., Kinzer, C. K., & Rieth, H. (1991). An analysis of the effects of teacher training and student grouping on reading comprehension skills among mildly handicapped high school students using computer-assisted instruction. *Journal of Special Education Technology, 11* (3), 136–154.

Baker, J. E. (1977). Application of the in-service training/classroom consultation model to reading instruction. *Ontario Psychologist, 9* (4), 57–62.

Balajthy, E. (1988). Evaluation of a preservice training module in microcomputer applications for the teaching of reading. *Computers in the Schools, 5* (1–2), 113–128.

Balajthy, E. (1996). Changing themes for preparing teachers to use computers and multimedia for literacy learning. In E. G. Sturtevant & W. M. Linek (Eds.), *Growing Literacy* (pp. 247–255). Harrisonburg, VA: College Reading Association.

Barr, R., Watts-Taffe, S., & Yokota, J. (2000). Preparing teachers to teach literacy: Rethinking preservice literacy education. *Journal of Literacy Research, 32* (4), 463–470.

Blanchard, J. (1994). Teacher education and the integration of technology: A reading and language arts perspective. *Journal of Information Technology for Teacher Education, 3* (2), 187–198.

Blanchard, J. (1999). Technology, communication, and literacy: Critical issues. *Educational Computing in the Schools: Technology, Communication, and Literacy, 15* (1), 1–4.

---

*This is a blended list that includes both the studies reviewed and the studies cited in the paper.

Bos, C. S., Mather, N., Narr, R. F., & Babur, N. (1999). Interactive, collaborative professional development in early literacy instruction: Supporting the balancing act. *Learning Disabilities Research and Practice, 14* (4), 227–238.

Bowman, C., & Edenfield, R. (2000). Becoming better together through collaboration and technology. *English Journal, 90* (2), 112–119.

Button, K. (1992). Factors that enhance effective instruction: A single subject case study of changes in the knowledge base and practice of a kindergarten teacher. In C. K. Kinzer & D. J. Leu (Eds.), *Literacy research, theory, and practice: Views from many perspectives* (pp. 483–490). Chicago: National Reading Conference.

Copeland, W. D., & Decker, D. L. (1996). Video cases and the development of meaning making in preservice teachers. *Teaching and Teacher Education, 12* (5), 467–481.

Dodson, M. M. (2000). Monologic and dialogic conversations: How preservice teachers socially construct knowledge through oral and computer-mediated classroom discourse. In T. Shanahan & F. V. Rodriguez-Brown (Eds.), *49th yearbook of the National Reading Conference* (pp. 137–152). Chicago: National Reading Conference.

Doyle, C. (1988). Creative applications of computer assisted reading and writing instruction. *Journal of Reading, 32* (3), 236–239.

Duckworth, S., & Taylor, R. (1995). Creating and assessing literacy in at-risk students through hypermedia portfolios. *Reading Improvement, 32* (1), 26–31.

Dupuis, M. M., Askov, E. N., & Lee, J. W. (1979). Changing attitudes toward content area reading: The content area reading project. *Journal of Educational Research, 73* (2), 65–74.

Fey, M. H. (1997). Literate behavior in a cross-age computer-mediated discussion: A question of empowerment. In C. K. Kinzer, K. A. Hinchman, & D. J. Leu (Eds.), *Inquiries in literacy theory and practice* (pp. 507–518). Chicago: National Reading Conference.

Flood, J., & Lapp, D. (1995). Broadening the lens: Toward an expanded conceptualization of literacy. In K. A. Hinchman, D. J. Leu, & C. K. Kinzer (Eds.), *Perspectives on literacy research and practice* (pp. 1–16). Chicago: National Reading Conference.

Foegen, A., Espin, C. A., Allinder, R. M., & Markell, M. A. (2001). Translating research into practice: Preservice teachers' beliefs about curriculum-based measurement. *Journal of Special Education, 34* (4), 226–236.

Goetze, S. K., Walker, B. J., & Yellin, D. (2000). Preservice teachers' conceptual development using computer mediated communication in language arts classes. In P. Linder, W. M. Linek, E. G. Sturtevant, & J. R. Dugan (Eds.), *Literacy at a new horizon* (pp. 298–310). Readyville, TN: College Reading Association.

Grisham, D. L. (1997). Electronic literacy learning: Teachers' on-line dialogue journals. In C. K. Kinzer, K. A. Hinchman & D. J. Leu (Eds.), *Inquiries in literacy theory and practice* (pp. 465–473). Chicago: National Reading Conference.

Hedrick, W. B., McGee, P., & Mittag, K. (2000). Preservice teacher learning through one-on-one tutoring: Reporting perceptions through e-mail. *Teaching and Teacher Education, 16* (1), 47–63.

Hoffman, J., & Pearson, P. D. (2000). Reading teacher education in the next millennium: What your grandmother's teacher didn't know that your granddaughter's teacher should. *Reading Research Quarterly, 35* (1), 28–44.

Hoover, N. L., & Carroll, R. G. (1987). Self-assessment of classroom instruction: An effective approach to inservice education. *Teaching and Teacher Education, 3* (3), 179–191.

Hughes, J. E., Packard, B. W., & Pearson, P. D. (1997). Reading classroom explorer: Visiting classrooms via hypermedia. In C. K. Kinzer, K. A. Hinchman, & D. J. Leu (Eds.), *Inquiries in literacy theory and practice* (pp. 494–506). Chicago: National Reading Conference.

Hughes, J. E., Packard, B. W., & Pearson, P. D. (2000a). Preservice teachers' perceptions of using hypermedia and video to examine the nature of literacy instruction. *Journal of Literacy Research, 32* (4), 599–629.

Hughes, J. E., Packard, B. W., & Pearson, P. D. (2000b). The role of hypermedia cases on preservice teachers' views of reading instruction. *Action in Teacher Education, 22* (2A), 24–38.

Johnson, D. (1996). "We're helping them to be good teachers": Using electronic dialoguing to connect theory and practice in preservice teacher education. *Journal of Computing in Childhood Education, 7* (1–2), 3–11.

Johnson, D. (1997). Extending the educational community: Using electronic dialoguing to connect theory and practice in preservice teacher education. *Journal of Technology and Teacher Education, 5* (2–3), 163–170.

Johnstone, J. R. (1990). A comparison of ratings of student performance by supervising teachers, reading specialists, and preservice teachers. In N. D. Padak, T. V. Rasinski, & J. Logan (Eds.), *Challenges in Reading* (pp. 37–42). Provo, UT: College Reading Association.

Kamil, M. L., Kim, H. S., & Lane, D. (in press). Electronic Text. In J. Hoffman & D. Schallert (Eds.), *The texts in the primary grade classrooms*. Ann Arbor, MI: Center for Instruction in Early Literacy Acquisition.

Kamil, M. L., & Lane, D. (1998). Researching the relation between technology and literacy: An agenda for the 21st century. In D. Reinking, M. McKenna, L. Labbo, & R. Kieffer (Eds.), *Handbook of literacy and technology: Transformations in a post-typographic world* (pp. 323–341). Mahwah, NJ: Erlbaum.

Kinzer, C. K., & Risko, V. J. (1998). Multimedia and enhanced learning: Transforming preservice education. In D. Reinking, M. McKenna, L. Labbo, & R. Kieffer (Eds.), *Handbook of literacy and technology: Transformations in a post-typographic world* (pp. 185–202). Mahwah, NJ: Erlbaum.

Klesius, J. P., Searls, E. F., & Zielonka, P. (1990). A comparison of two methods of direct instruction of preservice teachers. *Journal of Teacher Education, 41* (4), 34–44.

Magliaro, S., & Borko, H. (1985). The reading instruction of student teachers and experienced teachers: A social organizational perspective. In J. A. Niles & R. V. Lalik (Eds.), *Issues in literacy: A research perspective* (pp. 272–279). Rochester, NY: National Reading Conference.

Maimon, L. F. (1997). Reducing resistance to content area literacy courses. In W. M. Linek & E. G. Sturtevant (Eds.), *Exploring literacy* (pp. 267–281). Platteville, WI: College Reading Association.

Moore, S. J., & Lalik, R. V. (1992). Circles within circles: The uses of storytelling within a seminar for preservice reading teachers. In C. K. Kinzer & D. J. Leu (Eds.), *Literacy research, theory, and practice: Views from many perspectives* (pp. 323–330). Chicago: National Reading Conference.

National Institute of Child Health and Human Development (NICHHD). (2000). *Report of the National Reading Panel. Teaching children to read: An evidence-based assessment of the scientific research literature on reading and its implications for reading instruction.* (NIH Publication No. 00-4769). Washington, D.C.: U.S. Government Printing Office.

Nierstheimer, S. L., Hopkins, C. J., Dillon, D. R., & Schmitt, M. C. (2000). Preservice teachers' shifting beliefs about struggling literacy learners. *Reading Research and Instruction, 40* (1), 1–16.

Oropallo, K., & Gomez, S. (1996). Using reflective portfolios in preservice teacher education programs. In E. G. Sturtevant & W. M. Linek (Eds.), *Growing literacy* (pp. 120–132). Harrisonburg, VA: College Reading Association.

Pinnell, G. S. (1987). Helping teachers see how readers read: Staff development through observation. *Theory into Practice, 26* (1), 51–58.

Porter, T., & Foster, S. K. (1998). From a distance: Training teachers with technology. *T.H.E. Journal, 26* (2), 69–72.

Reid, E. R. (1997). Exemplary Center for Reading Instruction (ECRI). *Behavior & Social Issues, 7* (1), 19–24.

Reinking, D. (1995). Reading and writing with computers: Literacy research in a post-typographic world. In K. Hinchman, D. Leu, & C. Kinzer (Eds.), *Perspectives on literacy research and practice* (pp. 17–33). Chicago: National Reading Conference.

Richards, J. (2001). "I did not plan ahead": Preservice teachers' concerns integrating print-based literacy lessons with computer technology. In J. V. Hoffman, D. L. Schallert, C. M. Fairbanks, J. Worthy, & B. Maloch (Eds.), *50th yearbook of the National Reading Conference* (pp. 507–518). Chicago: National Reading Conference.

Risko, V. J. (1995). Using videodisc-based cases to promote preservice teachers' problem solving and mental model building. In W. M. Linek & E. G. Sturtevant (Eds.), *Generations of literacy* (pp. 173–187). Harrisonburg, VA: College Reading Association.

Risko, V. J., McAllister, D., & Bigenho, F. (1993). Value-added benefits for reforming a remedial reading methodology course with videodisc and hypercard technology. In T. V. Rasinski & N. D. Padak (Eds.), *Inquiries in literacy learning and instruction* (pp. 179–190). Pittsburg, KS: College Reading Association.

Risko, V. J., McAllister, D., Peter, J., & Bigenho, F. (1994). Using technology in support of preservice teachers' generative learning. In E. G. Sturtevant & W. M. Linek (Eds.), *Pathways for literacy* (pp. 155–168). Pittsburg, KS: College Reading Association.

Risko, V. J., Peter, J. A., & McAllister, D. (1996). Conceptual changes: Preservice teachers' pathways to providing literacy instruction. In E. G. Sturtevant & W. M. Linek (Eds.), *Growing literacy* (pp. 104–119). Harrisonburg, VA: College Reading Association.

Risko, V. J., Yount, D., & Towell, J. (1991). Video-based CASE analysis to enhance teacher preparation. In T. V. Rasinski, N. D. Padak, & J. Logan (Eds.), *Reading is knowledge* (pp. 87–96). Pittsburg, KS: College Reading Association.

Roberts, E., Doheny, C., & Harkins, D. (2000). Literacy on-line: Learning about authentic assessments via the web. In P. Linder, W. M. Linek, E. G. Sturtevant, & J. R. Dugan (Eds.), *Literacy at a new horizon* (pp. 286–297). Readyville, TN: College Reading Association.

Roberts, S. K., & Hsu, Y.S. (2000). The tools of teacher education: Preservice teachers' use of technology to create instructional materials. *Journal of Technology and Teacher Education, 8* (2), 133–152.

Roskos, K., Boehlen, S., & Walker, B. J. (2000). Learning the art of instructional conversation: The influence of self-assessment on teachers' instructional discourse in a reading clinic. *Elementary School Journal, 100* (3), 229–252.

Roskos, K., Risko, V., & Vukelich, C. (2000). Preparing reflective teachers of reading: A critical review of reflection studies in literacy pedagogy. In T. Shanahan & F. V. Rodriguez-Brown (Eds.), *49th Yearbook of the National Reading Conference* (pp. 109–121). Chicago: National Reading Conference.

Roskos, K., & Walker, B. (1997). Analytic categories for practitioners' assessment of instructional discourse in literacy teaching: Observation in the reading clinic setting. In W. M. Linek & E. G. Sturtevant (Eds.), *Exploring literacy* (pp. 143–159). Platteville, WI: College Reading Association.

Scott, J. M., & Ballard, K. D. (1983). Training parents and teachers in remedial reading procedures for children with learning difficulties. *Educational Psychology, 3* (1), 15–30.

Singer, H., Dreher, M., & Kamil, M. L. (1982). Computer literacy. In A. Berger & H. A. Robinson (Eds.), *Secondary school reading: What research reveals for classroom practice* (pp. 173–192). Urbana, IL: National Council for Research on English.

Spiro, R., & Jehng, J. (1990). Cognitive flexibility and hypertext: Theory and technology for the linear and nonlinear multidimensional traversal of complex subject matter. In D. Nix & R. Spiro (Eds.), *Cognition, education, and multimedia: Exploring ideas in high technology* (pp. 163–205). Hillsdale, NJ: Erlbaum.

Stallworth, B. J. (2001). Using e-mail to facilitate dialogue between high school students and preservice English methods students. In J. V. Hoffman, D. L. Schallert, C. M. Fairbanks, J. Worthy, & B. Maloch (Eds.), *50th yearbook of the National Reading Conference* (pp. 572–583). Chicago: National Reading Conference.

Stephens, L. C. (1997). How video-cases helped preservice teachers begin to situate themselves philosophically. In C. K. Kinzer, K. A. Hinchman, & D. J. Leu (Eds.), *Inquiries in literacy theory and practice* (pp. 483–493). Chicago: National Reading Conference.

Streeter, B. B. (1986). The effects of training experienced teachers in enthusiasm on students' attitudes toward reading. *Reading Psychology, 7* (4), 249–259.

Trathen, W., & Moorman, G. (2001). Using e-mail to create pedagogical dialogue in teacher education. *Reading Research and Instruction, 40* (3), 203–224.

Traw, R. (1994). School/University collaboration via e-mail: A unique approach to teaching reading and language arts. *TechTrends, 39* (2), 28–31.

Tyre, B. B., & Knight, D. W. (1972). Teaching word recognition skills to preservice teachers: An analysis of three procedures. *Southern Journal of Educational Research, 6* (3), 113–122.

U.S. Department of Education. (2002). *Meeting the highly qualified teachers challenge: The secretary's annual report on teacher quality.* Washington, DC: Author.

Van Valkenburgh, N., & Sirpa, G. (2000). Mentoring in the information age: A study of telementor functions between preservice teachers and middle school students. In P. Linder, W. M. Linek, E. G. Sturtevant, & J. R. Dugan (Eds.), *Literacy at a new horizon* (pp. 271–285). Readyville, TN: College Reading Association.

Welch, M. (2000). Descriptive analysis of team teaching in two elementary classrooms: A formative experimental approach. *Remedial and Special Education, 21* (6), 366–376.

Wells, D. (1990). Literature study groups in a university methods class. In N. D. Padak, T. V. Rasinski, & J. Logan (Eds.), *Challenges in reading* (pp. 31–36). Provo, UT: College Reading Association.

Wham, M. A. (1993). The relationship between undergraduate coursework and beliefs about reading instruction. *Journal of Research and Development in Education, 27* (1), 9–17.

Chapter 11

Reflective Inquiry As a Tool for Professional Development

Gay Su Pinnell and Emily M. Rodgers

Key Ideas

✓ We describe a multifaceted model of professional development that provides opportunities for reflective inquiry in three different contexts: collaboratively with a group of teachers, individually with a coach, and independently.

✓ Effective reflective inquiry requires opportunities for collaborative problem solving with peers with a focus on children's behavior as evidence of learning.

✓ Professional development initiatives must be complex—nested within a comprehensive school reform effort that brings classroom teachers and literacy specialists together for further learning.

For

- Teacher educators and graduate classes with a focus on teacher education

- Researchers and those engaged in the professional development of teachers

Reflection literally means "mirror image," an apt metaphor for the process of looking closely at one's own work. For a number of years, we have worked alongside teachers who were willing to intensively examine their own teaching and that of others. As Rodgers (1999) suggested, we call this process *reflective inquiry*, because it requires not only looking closely, or reflecting upon, but also making deliberate inquiries about teaching practices and decisions. An element of inquiry or investigation is always present, whatever the instructional setting.

In this chapter we will discuss and describe a multifaceted reflective inquiry model of professional development that we have researched and developed in both classroom and tutorial settings. We have found that looking at reflective inquiry across these teaching contexts provides important insights into the kind of thinking that teachers must take on to improve their teaching, which is the goal of all professional development.

Within each setting we will draw from our research and experience with professional development for classroom teachers and for teachers of young struggling readers. The classroom teachers are part of Literacy Collaborative, a comprehensive school development project that implements research-based literacy practices in classrooms through ongoing professional development.

Capacity is built in each school by providing a school-based teacher educator who continues to teach children in language arts and literacy and is released for a half day to coach teachers. The school-based teacher educator, called a "literacy coordinator," also provides on-site inservice sessions, works closely with administrators, and oversees implementation and research. Each school not only works to improve classroom instruction but also provides early intervention, in the form of Reading Recovery tutoring, for first graders who are having extreme difficulty learning to read and write. The goal of professional development is to enable teachers to analyze and learn from their own work with children. Results are measured in terms of student achievement.

The tutors of struggling readers are Reading Recovery teachers who work one-to-one with the lowest-performing first-grade students in their schools. They teach daily 30-minute Reading Recovery lessons for half of the day and then work with small groups, classrooms, or, in some cases, as staff developers for the other half of the day. More than one million children have been served by Reading Recovery since its implementation in the United States 18 years ago. Results are measured annually in terms of student progress on literacy measures (Gomez-Bellange, 2001). Other researchers have documented the maintenance of student gains over time

(Jaggar, 1997) and the reduction in the number of students referred to special education or learning disabilities services (Lyons, 1994).

Reading Recovery teachers take part in a yearlong plan of professional development during their training year, and in subsequent years they attend six sessions with other teachers every year that they remain in the role of Reading Recovery teacher. A core feature of the professional development experience, both in the training year and after, is the experience of teaching behind a one-way mirror while colleagues on the other side of the mirror view the lesson and discuss the teaching. A specially trained staff developer, called a teacher leader, guides the teachers' observations and analyses of what the child is able to do and needs to learn how to do next. After the two lessons taught behind the glass, all teachers, including those who taught, analyze in greater depth the issues about teaching and learning that arose during the lessons.

Documenting Professional Development

In our work we have used many ways of evaluating professional development. We collect extensive feedback from the teachers and staff developers who are involved, and their responses indicate that reflective inquiry has a profound effect on their thinking (e.g., Rodgers, Fullerton, & DeFord, 2001). We have also closely observed in systematic ways the changes in teacher behavior that result from professional development. The bottom line, however, is student achievement. As Darling-Hammond (1997) claims, "A large body of research has revealed that teacher training is the critical factor in making a difference in students' learning" (p. 20).

In both the classroom and the tutorial settings that we describe, we have observed an upward trend in student achievement. Although we cannot directly attribute this student success specifically to reflective inquiry, it is reported by teachers to be a critical component of their long-term development of skill and by staff developers as an important and necessary factor in school improvement.

The Significance of Reflective Inquiry

Teaching and learning require complex thinking. Even in highly prescribed literacy programs that provide "scripts," teaching is not simply a matter of following directions. To be effective, teachers must observe students closely and make constant adjustments to their teaching to support learning.

In recent years, constructivist theories have been applied to help us better understand the adult learning that must take place if teachers are to constantly improve their work to meet the demands for higher literacy achievement. A key principle in constructivist theory is the critical role that reflection plays in the learning process. Schon (1983) demonstrates that self-reflection is central to clarifying one's understanding and making sense. He suggests that the key to adults' growth and development is the ability to reflect on their learning, to adapt behavior based on that reflection, and to develop a theoretical framework and set of understandings based on one's experience.

Reflective teaching is not a passive endeavor. Zeichner and Liston (1996), borrowing from Dewey, defined reflective teaching as "an active desire to listen to more sides than one, to give full attention to alternative possibilities, and to recognize the possibility of error ... and to take pains to seek out conflicting evidence" (p. 10). Likewise, Sprinthall, Reiman, and Thies-Sprinthall, (1996) describe reflective teaching as an "active, persistent, and careful consideration of any belief" (p. 688).

In both definitions, reflection is described as an active process in which the teacher considers more than one explanation or possibility. An effective model of professional development should provide opportunities for teachers to reflect on their practice, to think about what is working and why, and to consider what is not working and why not.

Teachers can work independently to be reflective about their teaching practices, but we also know that a coach can be instrumental in bringing about change. The coach supports and leads the teacher's reflections, helping the teachers to listen to each other and consider alternative views.

Our professional development model of reflective inquiry, for classroom teachers and tutors, includes all of these elements. Reflection is a key element, with an emphasis on inquiry. We provide opportunities for teachers to engage in reflective inquiry in three contexts: with a group of teachers, with a coach, and independently. These contexts represent a continuum from more to less staff development support, but they are not fixed states because all three ways of learning must be available to both novice and experienced teachers. Because we assume that learning is complex and support for teaching analysis will always be helpful, this professional development model makes provision for all three contexts for reflective inquiry.

In the next section, we discuss the three kinds of reflective inquiry that classroom teachers (Literacy Collaborative) and one-to-one tutors (Reading Recovery teachers) engage in throughout a school year. These are as follows:

1. Collaborative reflection, in which reflective inquiry is supported by colleagues and a staff developer. Teachers use live examples or videotapes of teaching to reflect together on their teaching practices.

2. Coached reflection, the kind of inquiry that takes place in schools as coaches work individually with teachers to support their inquiry into their own specific lessons, which have just been observed.

3. Independent reflection, in which a teacher is able to independently reflect on teaching decisions and practices.

Although the goal for this model of professional development is independent reflective inquiry, we never remove the support provided by collaborative or coached reflection. In Table 11-1 we outline these three contexts in both the classroom and tutorial settings.

Table 11-1. Contexts for Reflective Inquiry

	Collaborative Reflection	Coached Reflection	Independent Reflection
	Teachers work together in collegial groups to view and analyze examples of teaching.	Teachers are supported by a coach who observes lessons and then provides feedback as well as support for self-reflection.	Teachers reflect on their own teaching in an independent way, perhaps supported by videotapes.
Professional Development for Classroom Teachers	• Analyze and discuss videotapes of classroom teaching • Observe and discuss classroom visits • Observe small-group lessons through a one-way mirror.	• Analyze and reflect on classroom teaching with the support of a coach who has observed lessons	• Analyze and reflect while teaching (reflection in action) in order to adjust teaching decision to the needs of children in the class • Analyze and reflect after teaching to build an effective decision-making process that will continually improve teaching

(Continued on next page)

Table 11-1.   Contexts for Reflective Inquiry *(Continued)*

	Collaborative Reflection	Coached Reflection	Independent Reflection
Professional Development for Reading Recovery Teachers	• Analyze and discuss video-tapes of individual lessons • Make "colleague visits" to observe one-to-one lessons and discuss • Observe individual lessons through a one-way mirror.	• Analyze and reflect on individual lessons with one child or a series of children with the support of a coach who has observed the teaching	• Analyze and reflect while teaching (reflection in action) in order to adjust teaching decision to the needs of the child being tutored • Analyze and reflect after teaching to build a theory of teaching and learning, with particular application to struggling readers

Although these contexts move from highly supported situations to independence, help is always there for teachers as they analyze and reflect on their instruction. There are some parallels between the professional development for classroom teaching and the tutorial (e.g., support and coaching for teachers, self-analysis using videotape and other tools, and accountability in terms of looking at student learning). The focus for each group of teachers is different, however. First, they are using quite different instructional techniques. While they assess and take individuals into account, classroom teachers look broadly across groups of children to make instructional decisions that consider a spectrum of achievement, and they also analyze the complexities of whole-group and small-group instruction as their primary instructional contexts. Tutors analyze individual children in great detail and trace minute changes in behavior over time. They reflect on teaching interactions with one child so that they can work most efficiently, teaching what the child needs to know next about reading strategies. In both settings, however, teachers benefit from reflective inquiry.

Next we discuss the three contexts: collaborative reflection, coached reflection, and independent reflection.

Collaborative Reflection

The goal of collaborative reflection is to build group understanding of behavioral phenomenon and theoretical ideas. We see collaborative reflection going on in several different group configurations, including the following:

1. Teachers often work in small groups to view videotapes of their own teaching, which they then discuss.

2. Teachers view one of their group members or another teacher working with a group or a single child behind a one-way mirror.

3. A small group of teachers observe teaching in a classroom or tutoring room (called "colleague visits"). After observing a lesson, they discuss the teaching moves and children's responses.

Collaborative reflection supports teachers' thinking. In our work we have found that ideas build upon ideas. Others' perspectives help you "tease out" ideas and take them further. Each person has the responsibility to take others' questions and comments as invitations to help the group achieve better understanding. It means that someone has to hold his or her own agenda in abeyance while the group pursues a chain of reasoning (Lyons, 1993) that will contribute to learning in general. The features of collaborative inquiry must be present for it to work well. We will illustrate this concept with two examples, each from a different teaching setting.

Collaborative Reflection on Classroom Teaching

A group of first- and second-grade teachers are being introduced to an instructional practice, guided reading, which involves teaching a small group of children who are similar in their reading behaviors and reading levels. The structure of guided reading is as follows:

- Introducing the text
- Reading the text
- Discussing the meaning
- Teaching for processing strategies
- Extending meaning
- Working with words

The teacher selects and introduces a text that will be just a little more challenging than books that children can read independently. Each child reads the text independently while the teacher observes and interacts with individuals. After reading, they discuss the meaning of the text and the teacher will do some explicit teaching designed to enable students to learn more about reading strategies. That may be followed by extension through writing and/or working with words for one or two minutes.

Ann, the literacy coordinator, knew that as a group the teachers had some familiarity with the structure of guided reading lessons, but only one had actually implemented the practice in her classroom. Rather than focusing on the details of "how you do it," she chose to help the group consider the goals of guided reading—that is, what the teacher did to support children's learning. After looking briefly at the steps in guided reading, the group viewed a short videotape of a guided reading lesson. Erik, a second-grade teacher, was introducing a simple mystery book, *Cam Jansen and the Mystery of the Circus Clown* by David Adler, to a group of six. A transcript of his introduction follows:

> *Erik:* I think most of you have read a Cam Jansen book, haven't you?
>
> *Students:* [*nod, except for Samantha*]
>
> *E:* Who can tell Samantha what might be happening in this story?
>
> *Joseph:* She has a mind like a camera.
>
> *Andrea:* She solves mysteries.
>
> *Marjeta:* ...with her friend, Eric.
>
> *Roberto:* She has a photographic memory.
>
> *E:* Wait a minute—what do you mean by a photographic memory?
>
> *Roberto:* She just goes "click," and she remembers everything for, like, 10 hours.
>
> *E:* So Cam Jansen is very good at remembering things. She just looks at something and it's like she's taking a picture of it. So that's why she says, "click" and that's why they call her...
>
> *Joseph:* Cam.
>
> *E:* Yes, it's short for *camera*, although that is not her real name. Have any of you been to the circus?
>
> *Marjeta:* Yes, there are clowns and I don't like the clowns. They just run around.
>
> *Roberto:* There are lots of people and there are clowns and people.
>
> *E:* I see most of you know what a circus is. Well, in this story, Cam and her friend Eric go to the circus with Cam's Aunt Molly. Aunt Molly travels a lot and sometimes she gets things mixed up. Look at page 3. She says, I went to Milwaukee, or maybe it was Mexico, or Minnesota. Put your finger on Milwaukee. Say that word.
>
> *Students:* Milwaukee.
>
> *E:* Now put your finger on Mexico. I think you know that word. And now, Minnesota. Aunt Molly talks about all those places and they all

begin with M. At a circus you sometimes see acrobats. Do you know what acrobats are?

Joseph: They walk across a rope [*mimics a tightrope walker*].

E: Sometimes there are tightrope walkers who walk across ropes, but these acrobats do somersaults and fly through the air on trapezes and turn flips. They are part of a troop. The troop is a group of acrobats, and this troop is called the Elkans Troupe. Find those words on page 6. They are all members of a family called *Elkans* and they are a troop of acrobats who do tricks.

Erik goes on to explain that in the first three chapters, the readers will find out what the mystery is. He assigns them the first three chapters to read, then to determine what the mystery is and write a prediction of what will happen next.

After the introduction, Ann stopped the tape and asked teachers to describe as specifically as possible what they saw the teacher doing to help students read the book. Some comments are presented in the following partial transcript of the discussion, along with labels indicating their identification of teacher behaviors:

Teacher 1: He helped them use their background knowledge. [*Accessing prior knowledge*]

Teacher 2: Some of them had read other Cam Jansen books, but some hadn't. He asked them if they had read Cam Jansen books and then had them tell each other about them. [*Connecting to other texts*]

Teacher 3: He's working on the genre because he gave them the assignment to think what the mystery is. That's the structure of this kind of book. You have to know what the problem is and then use clues to guess how it will come out—to solve the problem. [*Special characteristics of a genre*]

Teacher 1: These are series books, too, so if they can read one, then they can read more and they will be easier. [*Special characteristics of a genre*]

Teacher 3: He is teaching vocabulary—like "troop" and the long place names. Those are hard and sometimes kids just won't even go on because they think they can't read those names. [*Vocabulary development*]

Teacher 2: There were other hard words in those chapters. I would have covered more of them so that they wouldn't trip up the readers. [*Vocabulary development*]

Ann: Possibly, he was thinking that children could solve those words with the strategies they currently had. What could happen if he pretaught all the words? [*Supporting independent problem solving*]

Teacher 3: He could take away the chance for the kids to decode them and do the work. Plus, the introduction might be really long and too tedious. [*Supporting independent problem solving*]

Teacher 1: He didn't just tell them; they found the words in the chapter. I wonder why he didn't write them on the board. [*Keeping the pace going*]

Teacher 2: Probably they just needed a little help and it was better to do it right in the book—locate the words in context. [*Supporting decoding while reading for meaning*]

Teacher 4: He's getting them to think about the characters so that remembering what they are like will help them understand it and solve the mystery. [*Thinking about character, plot, and text structure*]

Teacher 2: The concepts are being made more available to them and he also gave them something to do when they finished. [*Keeping the pace going*]

In a very short time, the group had identified the key teaching moves that would enable these readers to successfully process this text with understanding, as was evident in samples of oral reading, their discussion after reading, and their writing. Overall, this one lesson provided teachers with a good (not perfect) example and much rich discussion. Together, they reconstructed the lesson, drawing out factors related to comprehension and noticing the interactive nature of the text introduction and discussion. They observed and discussed Erik doing some very specific teaching for fluency and phrasing as he pointed out punctuation marks and had children demonstrate noticing and using them. Colleagues helped to expand one another's thinking as they addressed the issues.

Collaborative Reflection on One-to-One Tutoring

Collaborative reflection forms a cornerstone of professional development for Reading Recovery teachers. As described earlier, trained Reading Recovery teachers meet six times a year to view and discuss live demonstrations of Reading Recovery lessons. These demonstrations provide shared examples that ground each professional development session in real teaching, not abstract examples. Teachers challenge one another's hypotheses about teaching and learning in general, and in particular about the children they have just seen taught behind the mirror. The challenges are not empty ones; teachers are guided to observe the lessons closely and provide evidence for their theories. They are also guided by the teacher leader to build on one another's contributions to the discussion, in a genuine, collaborative "puzzling out" manner, using inquiry as a tool to expand group understandings, similar to the way described by Lindfors (1999, p. 23).

In the example below, the Reading Recovery teachers are engaged in a discussion after seeing each of two colleagues teach a lesson behind a one-way mirror. Earlier, while the teachers viewed the lesson from the other side of the mirror, they talked about each child's strategic reading activity and hypothesized about what each child needed to learn how to do next. Sometimes they questioned the value of a teaching decision, especially if it seemed that the teacher was working on something the child could already do, or if the teacher was expecting the child to try something beyond present capabilities. After the teaching sessions, the teachers gathered to reflect on the lessons they had seen together and to continue their analysis. We pick up the discussion just as the teacher leader is bringing closure to a conversation about the first student taught behind the mirror. The teacher leader shifts the conversation to the second lesson that they saw, when Latisha taught Tara. In this exchange, Barb questions Latisha's theory that Tara needs to learn how to reread to problem solve.

Coach: We saw that Jamie is working hard to keep things easy for the student to learn, keeping it simple, just teaching a few words at a time and making sure the student really learns them. Some item knowledge like that is certainly important, along with some strategies. Latisha, what are you working on with Tara?

Latisha: I would like to see Tara continue to go back and reread like she did today when I taught her behind the mirror, but do it on easier text. That's a strategy, isn't it?

Barb: But she also needs to monitor—she has to notice the mistake first, or why would she reread? I didn't see her do that today.

Latisha: Well, I think she's monitoring. She monitored today when she read *said* instead of *shouted*. She stopped reading and looked at me, so I think she noticed that she wasn't right. So now I'd like to see her go back and find a place to try to reread again and keep meaning going.

Coach: So noticing is strategic, but what about rereading—is that a strategy?

Barb: The student could be searching for more information when they go back, so rereading could be strategic.

Coach: So we've said that monitoring and searching for more information are both strategies. When a student monitors and it's something that you have been teaching her how to do, it's a good idea to praise the good strategic activity. You could say, "Good for you, you noticed that wasn't *said*." That will point up the good strategic activity.

Latisha: Yes, I never thought of that. Lots of time I don't say anything to the child when they've noticed an error even though that was something I was really working hard to teach the student to do.

The teachers' collaborative inquiry, grounded in their reflections on the lessons they have seen, extends their understandings about strategic activities while reading. They challenge each other about whether or not the student notices errors while reading, pointing out the futility of teaching a student to reread if she doesn't even notice that she has made a mistake, and they take up Latisha's invitation to sort out strategies. In sum, by listening carefully to one another, they help each other to sort out confusions and, as a group, take their analysis further than if they were working individually.

Coached Reflection

Coaching provides an individual consultant to assist teachers in reflective inquiry. Coaching is most effective when it assists teachers in performing their own analyses. Actually, coaching changes over time, as teachers become more expert in any given instructional practice, because they take over more of the process (Figure 11-1).

High Support

- Demonstration
- Review of procedures
- Specific suggestions
- Solving management issues
- Explicit feedback
- Direction

Less Support

- Questioning
- Collaborative problem solving
- Experimentation
- Goal setting
- Explicit feedback
- Debate

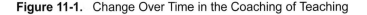

Figure 11-1. Change Over Time in the Coaching of Teaching

At first, the coach may demonstrate and/or tell the teacher the particular procedures involved in the instructional approach. The tone of the coaching is "just trust me for a moment and try this." As shown in Figure 11-1, once the teacher has implemented the practice, there is more opportunity to reflect on the process and go deeper into the kinds of adjustments required for powerful teaching. The coach's support is not necessarily less, but it is different because the two individuals are able to enter into collaborative problem solving about the practice. This evolution may take a short or longer time, depending on the complexity of the practice and how new it is to the teacher; but over time, with coaching, taking on new learning in this supported way will be quicker for teachers. We will present two examples from coaching situations.

Coached Reflection on Classroom Teaching

Ann was working with Heidi, a fifth-grade teacher who was learning about guided reading. Before the observation, Ann had a brief conference with Heidi to give her some information about what she would see. This preconference is valuable to the classroom coach because it provides insight into the teacher's thinking.

> *Literacy coach:* Tell me a little about what I am going to see.
>
> *Teacher:* I'm going to introduce a nonfiction book called *Five Brave Explorers* by Wade Hudson. The interesting thing about this book is that all five characters are African American, and these kids can relate to them but might not have heard of them, so I really think I need to do a lot in the introduction. It's a level P.
>
> *Literacy coach:* That is an interesting book. Why did you select it for these students?
>
> *Teacher:* Well, I thought they needed to learn about African American explorers and they would be interested in it and it's about their level. Actually I learned a lot from just reading it myself.
>
> *Literacy coach:* What do you think this text will demand of them, to read it with accuracy and comprehension?
>
> *Teacher:* I'd have to think about that. [*Looks through the book.*] They have to notice maps and see how that fits with their reading. There are also photographs. Oh, there are different periods of history, so they have to think about that. Come to think of it, being an explorer is kind of abstract, so they need to know how the stories of these guys are related with that concept. They have to notice the dates, too, and they don't have a lot of background to understand that.

In this preconference, Ann learned that Heidi had made a good text selection and had carefully prepared for the session. Her focus, however, was mostly on content learning rather than on teaching for processing. In the preconference, she turned Heidi's attention to the idea of text demands to set the scene for talking about teaching for processing. Heidi had an implicit sense of the demands of texts on readers. The following is a portion of her introduction to the text:

> *Heidi:* You are going to read a very interesting book today. It's called *Five Brave Explorers.* Look at the cover. What are you thinking it might be about?
>
> *Miguel:* Some people who go out and have adventures?
>
> *Latisha:* There is a spaceship, so someone is going into outer space. There's also a person who is dressed, like, for the arctic.
>
> *Parker:* This is a woman here who has NASA on her suit. She's an astronaut. But the others look kind of old-fashioned.
>
> *Heidi:* You'll find that these explorers lived in very different times, but all of them were adventurous, as Miguel says. They went to distant places that were dangerous. They were *explorers.* There are five of them. Do you notice anything else?
>
> *Latisha:* They are all black, African American.
>
> *Heidi:* Yes, in the old days, the history books didn't tell us much about the accomplishments of African Americans, but this book tells about black people who were explorers even as long ago as the 1500s.
>
> *Miguel:* That's about 300 [sic] years ago!
>
> *Heidi:* The first chapter is about Esteban Dorantes. He sailed to Florida from Spain in 1527—that's almost 500 years ago. Esteban was a slave in Spain. Do you remember studying about slavery in this country?
>
> *Students:* Yes.
>
> *Heidi:* Well, this was in Spain. Esteban went with the a man named Cabeza de Vaca to Florida. What do you know about Florida?
>
> *Kali:* It's where the beach is.
>
> *Austin:* It's on the east coast.
>
> *Heidi:* Florida is on the east coast. Look at the map on page 13. Do you see where it says Havana, Cuba? Right above that you see Florida. Now take your finger and follow the arrows. That's the territory Esteban traveled during his adventure. It was over 3,000 miles.

Heidi went on to have children locate the difficult names of characters, some place names, and difficult words like *considered, companions, settlement,* and *wilderness.* She asked the children to read the first chapter and to come back ready to discuss whether Esteban was fairly treated or not (he remained a slave in spite of saving the group and was sold).

Children read the story quickly and with accuracy. Afterward, they discussed Esteban and his adventures. There was a discussion of the term *Native American*. Heidi helped them take apart several multisyllable words. She engaged the learners in her introduction and focused their attention on important aspects of the text. She drew their attention to graphic features (such as maps) and also helped students to untangle difficult words.

After the lesson, Heidi and Ann had the following conference in which they discussed the lesson:

> *Ann:* You really engaged children. They wanted to read that book.
>
> *Heidi:* I was surprised at how interested they were. They really like nonfiction.
>
> *Ann:* What do you think they learned today?
>
> *Heidi:* They learned about Esteban, that an African American was doing something important even back then.
>
> *Ann:* I agree that they were really engaged there and did learn something about history. I'm thinking that you also helped them learn that it's important to use the graphic features of the text—like the map.
>
> *Heidi:* They haven't really had a lot of experience with maps, so I didn't know if it would work, but they read it well. I still don't think they really understand the idea of so many years of time.
>
> *Ann:* That takes a lot of experience at their age, but you helped them develop perspective. You did a really great job of describing what this text demanded of them. Do you think they learned anything that they can take into reading other books?
>
> *Heidi:* Yes, they had to think back in time about what it might have been like to be a slave but also to be so smart. Also, they had to take different points of view—like the Native Americans whom these Spanish people were killing.
>
> *Ann:* That's a really good focus for your thinking about guided reading lessons. They are learning from their reading, that's a given, but they are also learning to process a text. This book is giving them a great chance to learn about how to read biography and also how you make connections.
>
> *Heidi:* I think they'll also learn as they start to compare the adventurers in each chapter.
>
> *Ann:* How can you help them to make those connections?

> *Heidi:* Maybe I could do a comparison chart where they show how the people were the same in some ways and different in others.

Together, Ann and Heidi planned the next lesson. Ann suggested that Heidi have children read more than one chapter to speed up the process, and she agreed that making a compare-and-contrast chart would be an excellent extension. The conference ended with an agreement on another time for coaching.

The coach began with a compliment, but not an empty one. We have learned that if there is always a statement like "great lesson" or "good job," teachers learn to listen for the "but"; in fact, they are their own most intense critics. Ann made a statement based on observation that students wanted to read the book, and Heidi agreed. Ann kept the session focused on the children's behavior, and both coach and teacher were able to share what they had observed along with their interpretations. They engaged in collaborative planning for students' learning based on observations. A sense of "right" and "wrong" in terms of teacher behavior does not permeate this coaching conversation. Instead, there is a sense of collaboration and problem solving.

Coached Reflection on One-to-One Tutoring

The teacher leader, who is the coach, visits each trained Reading Recovery teacher at least four times a year to provide more tailored professional development. Just like the group professional development sessions, their work is grounded in actual teaching experiences. The school visit typically goes like this:

- *Before the lesson:* The teacher leader gathers information about the student and the teacher. What is the student able to do in reading and writing? What must the student learn today? What specific feedback does the teacher want on his or her teaching?

- *During the lesson:* The teacher leader observes as unobtrusively as possible, taking detailed notes about the teacher-student interactions. These notes will provide specific examples to return to later during the debriefing. The teacher leader thinks about shifts in the teacher's understandings or about instructional practices that must be achieved during this school visit.

- *After the lesson:* The teacher leader guides the teacher's analysis of the teaching and learning, being sure to return to the questions that the teacher raised before the lesson began. Often, as teachers become more proficient with teaching procedures (the how-to), the reflection after the lesson becomes a more shared "puzzling out" together.

In this personalized context, the teacher leader's role is primarily to coach or guide the teacher's reflection on the teaching. This kind of debriefing is qualitatively different from simply telling the teacher what to do differently. An example is as follows:

> *Teacher:* Peg [*the student*] is too flexible in her visual analysis of words. She just samples the print.
>
> *Teacher Leader:* What do you mean by sampling the print?
>
> *Teacher:* Did you hear her say when she figured out the word *need* that it was just like that word *green* that she knows? She said she didn't even know that she knew the word *need* and that it was just like *green.* So she must have been looking at the middle of the word.
>
> *Teacher Leader:* Is this getting in the way of her making progress in reading?
>
> *Teacher:* Well, she has to look at the beginning of words to figure them out—not anywhere she feels like.
>
> *Teacher Leader:* Okay, you gave one example of Peg's visual analysis of words. Can we find some other examples so we can build a good picture of how this student problem-solves when she's reading? Let's look at the running record and also how she read the new book. I've got some notes here, and you wrote down some things on your lesson record. Let's see what examples we can pull together.

The teacher leader and teacher came up with the following substitutions that Peg made while reading (the second word in each pair is the actual word in the text):

> pulled / put
>
> gave / give
>
> helped / had
>
> going / good

As soon as the teacher saw all of Peg's substitutions, she realized that her characterization of Peg's visual processing as "sampling" the print was unfounded. In fact, Peg seemed to be consistently noticing the beginnings of words and needed to learn to use more than the first part. The teacher revised her theory of what Peg was able to do and continued to consult with the teacher leader about how to teach Peg to use more visual information.

Independent Reflection

Independent reflection is the ultimate goal of reflective inquiry, but we do not assume "stages" in the process. Even the most experienced teachers need instruction and coaching while taking on new instructional techniques. As research provides more information, inevitably all of us are required to engage in new behaviors or acquire different insights on learning and development. We have learned from our work in Literacy Collaborative and Reading Recovery that instruction is dynamic, always adjusting to children's needs, to new texts and materials, and to new information as we grow in our understanding. Most discussions of coaching focus on preservice or new teachers, as if when one becomes experienced, a high level of support is no longer needed. That is simply not the case. Truly expert teaching is built as individuals expand their understanding over time, learning from each child or group of children. Assistance and collaboration accelerate the process so that even very experienced and expert teachers can continue learning. Accordingly, we advocate a balance of collaborative inquiry, coaching, and independent reflection, with all three ways of learning available to teachers as they acquire new understanding.

Independent Reflection on Classroom Teaching

Carol, a literacy coach, had been working for several years with a group of second-grade teachers who were implementing guided reading. They had developed a high level of expertise in using the instructional framework and were focusing their attention on using extension to deepen students' understanding (Pinnell, 2001). In fact, teaching for comprehension was the focus of this year's work across the literacy framework.

Soledad had introduced *The Stories Julian Tells* by Ann Cameron to a group of second graders, and the children had finished this short chapter book in three days. Carol had observed the second lesson using this book, and together she and Soledad had planned the extension activity she would implement. She asked Soledad to reflect on the experience after it was over and to bring a short piece of writing to class (along with the chart the children made) to share with colleagues.

The Stories Julian Tells is a collection of short stories told by a young boy about seven years old. Each chapter is a different story; the central characters are Julian, his little brother Huey, and his dad. Soledad had introduced the text by discussing the characters and pointing out how both text and illustrations show their ability to imagine things. She also showed children several places where the writer used metaphor to make the book interesting. Children found these places and read them aloud, discussing their meaning. There was no formal study of "metaphor," but they got the idea.

Soledad's observation of the children's reading indicated high accuracy and good phrasing on the part of most of them. After reading, they discussed the meaning of the story and again revisited some of the interesting (but literary) language of the text.

Soledad then asked them to talk with their partners about something they imagined when they were little, or they could share something that a little brother or sister or cousin imagined. They talked for about three minutes and then the teacher asked for one or two examples from the group. Next she turned the discussion to what Julian and Huey were like. In some ways the two boys are alike and in some ways they are different. She generated ideas from the group and got comments like the following:

> They both got imaginations.
>
> Julian is big and Huey is littler.
>
> Huey gets Julian in trouble.
>
> Julian is bossy.

She then guided the children to record their ideas on a comparison chart. This chart could be added to as the group read more stories in *The Stories Julian Tells*. If the children read more books in this series, they can always return to the chart and add more comments.

Soledad's self-analysis of her work reflected Carol's coaching support as well as her own independent reflection, of which an excerpt follows:

> I was really glad that I didn't do this extension until they had read most of the book, because I think they had a lot to bring to it. It didn't take much time, but they had a lot of ideas. Carol helped me to think this through and be sure that I did a lot of oral language before I had them tell me what to write. Also, I was going to have them do this in pairs, and I think that would have been a mistake. There was a lot of conversation when we did it together on the chart, and they learned from each other. I was amazed at what they had been attending to and came up with. I couldn't have done a better job by myself. This process also helped some of the kids who had trouble remembering everything they needed to about characters and other details. The chart helped them keep it in their minds. If we read another Julian book, we can add to it or add characters. This would also be a good thing to do in other lessons. I think they might be able to do this in pairs after more practice, and then they can report to each other. I'm

going to try other graphic organizers, but I agree with Carol that they shouldn't just be like a worksheet. It's the oral language that matters.

As this excerpt shows, Soledad had captured an important aspect of using extensions to support reading comprehension, that oral language discussions are a key to expanding understanding. Her insights reflected coaching and would feed back into the collaborative reflection she engaged in regularly with colleagues. Others would learn from her individual analyses.

Independent Reflection on One-to-One Tutoring

Janice, a Reading Recovery teacher with five years' experience, has been teaching Alan for three weeks. She noted on his running records that Alan's reading errors often preserved meaning and structure (the errors made sense and could be read that way), but he usually neglected to use visual information. For example, in a recent running record of his reading he read as follows:

> *Text: The girl looks at the hippo.*
> *Alan:* The girl looks at it.
>
> *Text: The boy looks at the hippo.*
> *Alan:* The boy looks at it.
>
> *Text: Can you see the hippo?*
> *Alan:* Can you see it?

Alan's substitution of *it* for *the* and *hippo* suggests that he is taking meaning and structure into account when reading, but he is neglecting much of the visual information. In fact, he never notices the visual mismatches and makes no attempt to correct them. Janice decides that she must teach Alan to monitor his reading to notice these visual mismatches independently. In the following excerpt, Janice reflects on her teaching interaction with Alan after his most recent Reading Recovery lesson:

> When Alan said, *not up* for *asleep,* I should have just asked him to go back and check, to see if he would notice the mismatch by himself. That's what I've been trying to teach him to do—to monitor on his own. Instead I asked him to say *not* and to check the first letter of the word *asleep.* So *I* found the error for him and didn't give him a chance to learn how to check. I don't know why I didn't have him go back first and check on his own.

Janice's reflection is about her teaching moves, how they relate to the student's present abilities, and what he needs to learn next.

She questions what she did, what she could have done instead, and why. Janice looks for and uses evidence from the lesson to support her analysis, just as she would in the more supportive settings of coached and collaborative reflection. We suggest that those supportive experiences aid Janice in doing the kind of independent reflection described in the next example.

In the following excerpt, after a lesson with Polly, Janice again reflects on her teaching moves. Unlike Alan, Polly neglects to incorporate meaning into her attempts but uses visual information almost exclusively. When she encounters difficult words she tries to sound them out and neglects to think about what would make sense.

> I tried to give Polly just a general teaching prompt after she read that page, because I had a feeling she could find the error, so I just said, "Something's wrong on that page. Can you find it?" I'm still trying to prompt her to think about the meaning, think about the story. Then I want her to use two ways of checking when she's reading—to think if her attempts make sense *and* look right, so hopefully she can do that on her own.

In this example, as in the previous one with Alan, Janice demonstrates her ability to reflect on her teaching moves. She is highly analytical and uses a specific example from the teaching episode to ground her reflections about her teaching. She reflects on her teaching moves, not solely on the student's responses. Janice poses theories about what the student is able to do and needs to learn how to do next, and, most important, what she, the teacher, is doing that may be helping or hindering this progress.

Characteristics of Reflective Inquiry Across Settings and Teachers

The multifaceted model of professional development that we describe provides opportunities for reflective inquiry in three different contexts: collaboratively with a group of teachers, individually with a coach, and independently. Across both settings, classrooms and one-to-one tutoring, we find that reflective inquiry is most powerful when the following features are present:

1. *A balance of support is maintained.* We do not prescribe a sequence of experiences characterized by less supportive professional development until the teacher is able to reflect independently. Instead, we suggest that a balance of support

be maintained. The goal is always independent reflection, but because we recognize that reflective inquiry is made more effective through collaboration with peers and a coach, we do not want to remove either element from this model of professional development. We assume that collaboration with peers and with a coach is necessary if teachers are to expand present understandings, take on new learning, and gain new insights.

2. *There is a focus on student learning.* Our experience with both classroom teachers and tutors suggests that effective reflective inquiry, perhaps the kind that John Dewey had in mind, requires opportunities for collaborative problem solving with peers, with a focus on children's behavior as evidence of learning. At the very least, videotapes are helpful, but actual learning experiences provide real learning and real teaching in real time. Teachers gain experience in closely observing children, gathering evidence, posing theories, and reflecting on teaching decisions in real time, but because they are viewing the lesson and not actually teaching, there is space for reflection.

3. *There is a focus on "next steps."* Collaborating with peers or a coach also provides support to teachers for planning the next step with that child or children, and this seems to be at the very heart of reflection. It's not so much about thinking carefully about the teaching (What happened, what did I do?), but thinking about what comes next and how to adapt behavior based on that reflection (Schon, 1983) that makes reflection a powerful tool for professional development.

All three contexts of reflective inquiry—collaborative, coached, and independent—inform each other as teachers learn from group discussion and coaching and then bring their own new ideas back to the group. This describes a learning community, which a school must become if teachers are to continue their development.

Implications for Teacher Education and Professional Development for Teachers of Reading

How can we incorporate reflective inquiry into preservice education and professional development? These two goals pose quite different problems.

Preservice Teacher Education

It would be a challenge to incorporate reflective inquiry into preservice education as it is now designed; however, that is exactly what should happen. In elementary education, preservice teachers are on a "fast track" to learn a great deal in a very short time. They are simultaneously trying to take on knowledge of the school as an organization, management of people and materials in classrooms, theories of learning and teaching, and an array of instructional approaches for a variety of children of all ages.

Reflective inquiry should focus on simple, practical problems, giving students many opportunities to discuss their initial classroom experiences. We have successfully used videotape analysis for students who are participating in classrooms by keeping the focus narrow (for example, working with one child or with a small group over several weeks) and being very specific about the tasks and highly supportive of the analysis. In these experiences, preservice teachers were gaining skill in the particular instructional technique but also beginning to observe themselves. The development of reflective inquiry as part of preservice teacher education would set the scene for further learning after graduation.

Professional Development for Inservice Teachers

The real promise of reflective inquiry is its incorporation into ongoing professional development. For decades we have tried to improve literacy education by giving teachers new materials or prescribing programs. Introducing highly structured and scripted programs may have a small initial benefit, but in the long run teaching is the factor that makes a lasting difference. Through reflective inquiry, teachers constantly improve their thinking about teaching; moreover, they continually renew their enthusiasm for their work because they increase their success.

We hear a good deal today about implementing research-based practices in classrooms to improve literacy learning. No matter how well founded the practices may be, they will not result in greater student learning unless they can be established in classrooms. Furthermore, having only one or two effective teachers in a school will not make a difference for larger numbers of children. Today's students need year after year of effective instruction in the elementary years. The delivery of research-based reading practice must be nested within a comprehensive school reform effort that brings teachers together for further learning and enlists their commitment to the process. The National Reading Panel (NICHHD, 2000), in fact, has stated the following:

> Few if any studies have investigated the contribution of motivation to the effectiveness of phonics programs, not only the learner's motivation to learn but also the teacher's motivation to teach. The lack of attention to motivational factors by researchers in the design of phonics programs is potentially very serious…. Future research should be…designed to determine which approaches teachers prefer to use and are most likely to use effectively in their classroom instruction. (p. 29)

When teachers have the opportunity to look deeply into their teaching, reflect on teaching, and live within a learning community, taking on new practices is continual and automatic. Reflective inquiry has important potential for creating those communities.

References

Darling-Hammond, L. (1997). *The right to learn: A blueprint for creating schools that work*. San Francisco: Jossey-Bass.

Gomez-Bellange, F. X. (2001). *Reading Recovery and descubriendo la lectura national report, 2001–2002*. Columbus, OH: National Data Evaluation Center.

Jaggar, A. (1997, March). *Do Reading Recovery children sustain their gains?* Paper presented at the annual meeting of the American Educational Research Association, Chicago.

Juel, C. (1988). Learning to read and write: A longitudinal study of fifty-four children from first through fourth grade. *Journal of Educational Psychology, 80,* 437–447.

Lindfors, J. (1999). *Children's inquiry: Using language to make sense of the world*. New York: Teachers College Press.

Lyons, C. (1993). The use of questions in the teaching of high-risk beginning readers: A profile of a developing Reading Recovery teacher. *Reading and Writing Quarterly, 9,* 317–327.

Lyons, C. (1994). Reading Recovery and learning disabilities: Issues, challenges and implications. *Literacy, Teaching and Learning, 1* (1), 110–119.

National Institute of Child Health and Human Development (NICHHD). (2000). *Report of the National Reading Panel. Teaching children to read: An evidence-based assessment of the scientific research literature on reading and its implications for reading instruction*. (NIH Publication No. 00-4769). Washington, D.C.: U.S. Government Printing Office.

Pinnell, G. S. (2001). What does it mean to comprehend a text? In G. S. Pinnell & P. Sharer (Eds.), *Extending our reach: Teaching for comprehension, grades K–2.* Columbus, OH: Ohio State University.

Rodgers, A. (1999) *Teacher and teacher-researcher classroom collaboration: Planning and teaching in a secondary English classroom using process-oriented drama approaches.* Unpublished doctoral dissertation, Ohio State University, Columbus, OH.

Rodgers, E., Fullerton, S., & DeFord, D. (2001). *What does it take to reform instructional practices?* In J. V. Hoffman, D. L. Schallert, C. M. Fairbanks, J. Worthy, & B. Maloch (Eds.), *50th yearbook of the National Reading Conference* (pp. 519–532). Chicago: National Reading Conference.

Schon, D. (1983). *The reflective practitioner.* New York: Basic Books.

Sprinthall, N. A., Reiman, A. J., & Thies-Sprinthall, L. (1996). Teacher professional development. *Handbook of research on teacher education* (pp. 666–703). New York: Macmillan.

Zeichner, K. M., & Liston, D. P. (1996). *Reflective teaching: An introduction.* Mahwah, NJ: Erlbaum.

Chapter *12*

Professional Development
at Benchmark School

Irene W. Gaskins

Key Ideas

✓ The knowledge and skills that teachers need to help children fulfill their potential cannot be achieved in the short time that professors have with preservice teachers.

✓ If we want all students to receive the education they deserve, it is imperative that professional development be part of the fabric of the school and that a menu of professional development opportunities be available at each school.

✓ To ensure that this happens, it is the job of the instructional leader of the school to recognize and understand classroom expertise, to keep current on instructional research and theory, and to know how to orchestrate meaningful opportunities for teachers to collaborate and grow.

For

• K–12 teachers

• Administrators

It is widely accepted among educators that the crucial factor in determining student progress is the teacher. Because there is not one way of teaching that works for all students, teachers need to be aware of a variety of instructional approaches that might be used to accomplish a specific learning goal. Making decisions about the best practice for a particular student and situation requires judgments based on a knowledge of pedagogy, learning theory, and research, as well as on careful reflection about classroom experiences. Such knowledge is impossible to acquire in a few short years of preservice education. Acquiring the knowledge to make instructional decisions that are in the best interest of students requires classroom experience in conjunction with lifelong learning. School leaders have an obligation to foster this lifelong learning by providing school-based, long-term, collaborative professional development that is related to teachers' practice and features ongoing and reflective professional dialogue.

New teachers, especially, deserve and desire support and professional development as they face the complexities of daily classroom life, including the need to choose and adapt curriculum, plan and implement lessons, and manage a classroom. New-teacher induction programs, beginning several weeks before the start of the school year and continuing at least throughout a teacher's first year, should acculturate new teachers to the mission and philosophy of their school, promote unity and teamwork, and guide teachers in establishing effective classroom management procedures, routines, and instructional practices. All teachers, but particularly early-career teachers, appreciate the availability of experienced colleagues with whom they can collaborate on an as-needed basis as they deal with the daily dilemmas of classroom teaching. In addition, a school needs to have structures in place that provide opportunities for teachers to plan lessons and hone their skills in collaboration with other teachers, as well as to visit one another's classrooms, discuss students with supervisors and teachers, and receive effective feedback about their instruction. The goal of these professional development opportunities should be to improve student outcomes.

At Benchmark School, which is dedicated to developing methods for teaching struggling readers, we have endeavored to create an environment rich in opportunities for professional growth. Over the years, by studying the research on classroom instruction and collaborating with one another and top researchers in the field, the staff and I have grown in our knowledge of teaching. In the process, we have confirmed that a key to improving student outcomes is professional development. We have also confirmed that professional development is a lifelong journey, best traveled in collaboration with colleagues.

Professional Development Options

Just as students learn differently, teachers also learn differently. Thus, the most successful professional development programs provide teachers with options. In this chapter, I discuss the options for professional development that we implement at Benchmark, as well as provide a few examples that describe some of these options. These options include being apprenticed to a master teacher; collaborating with staff to improve instruction and develop curriculum; attending seminars, meetings, inservice programs, and retreats; reading books and articles and viewing videotapes from a professional library; participating in the development and maintenance of curriculum initiatives; cultivating partnerships with local universities; and writing about one's practice.

Apprenticeship

The model for professional development at Benchmark has always been "each one teach one." As Benchmark's first teacher, I was ensconced in a large classroom in a church basement that I shared with two newly certified teachers and several volunteer assistants. It was our own one-room schoolhouse for 17 struggling readers, ages 6–14. Each day we observed one another teach and spent considerable time after school reflecting on our instruction and discussing how we could better meet the needs of our students. We pored over the professional literature in search of answers to teaching dilemmas. These times of reflection and collaboration were exhilarating, and the result was almost always better instruction for our students.

Today a staff of 90 works at Benchmark to meet the needs of nearly 200 struggling readers in grades 2–8. The informal apprentice model begun at the school's inception has, over the years, become more defined. Novice Benchmark teachers are more formally apprenticed to master teachers. This is accomplished in several ways. For example, most often a new staff member begins at Benchmark as a support teacher: someone who assists the head classroom teacher in such ways as teaching small groups, interacting with students about their written responses to literature, and assisting in other ways that the teacher may request. After a year or two the support teacher may become a co-teacher, sharing more fully in instructional responsibilities and interactions with parents. In another instance, a support teacher may be assigned to spend a year in the classroom of a master teacher who has been designated a teacher trainer. The teacher in training shadows the master teacher throughout the school day for an entire school year, including participation in the staff development opportunities at the school. Susan North's experience is an example of an apprenticeship at Benchmark.

Susan came to Benchmark School as a newly trained reading specialist who had begun graduate study after her four children entered school. Her first position at Benchmark was as a teacher in Benchmark's five-week summer program, a teaching assignment for which she prepared by participating in a week of inservice at Benchmark. At the conclusion of the summer program, Susan was hired for the school year as a support teacher. For the two weeks prior to the opening of school, Susan participated in Benchmark's induction program for staff members new to their positions.

It happened that the classroom to which Susan was assigned was one in which I was piloting a new word identification program. Throughout the year there was much conversation among the head teacher, co-teacher, Susan, and me about how the word identification program was working with this class of new Benchmark students. On most days I taught and Susan observed. On other days, when I could not be present in the classroom, Susan or the co-teacher taught and gave me feedback about the word identification lessons I had written. On other occasions, I observed Susan teach and gave her feedback. The result of all this observation and collaboration was improved lessons and an increasingly competent teacher. Susan also read professional articles and attended the weekly support teacher seminars where these articles were discussed. In addition, she participated in Benchmark's monthly inservice programs.

The following year Susan moved to a different classroom to gain experience with another veteran teacher and younger children. At the conclusion of her second year at Benchmark, Susan was selected as a teacher in training, which meant that she would fill a head-teacher position the following year if one became available. Susan's third year at Benchmark was spent shadowing and teaching with teacher-trainer Theresa Scott. Susan also spent one to two hours a day meeting with Theresa to discuss why Theresa made the decisions she did in teaching her students. Theresa also systematically taught Susan how to prepare for, manage, and carry out the many duties of a head classroom teacher. To further Susan's professional development, the school sponsored Susan's attendance at the annual conference of the International Reading Association and at local conferences. Now in her fourth year at Benchmark, Susan is a competent head teacher who has earned the confidence of her students, their parents, and the staff. There is no doubt that she is well prepared for her job. Nevertheless, Susan knows she can still continue to learn, and she takes advantage of many of the opportunities for professional growth at Benchmark.

Collaboration

Collaboration, which is clearly an important key to the success of professional development, can take many forms besides apprenticeship. For example, teachers collaborate with their supervisors, who are charged with the responsibility of working with teachers in any way necessary to ensure that teachers have the knowledge and resources to provide students with the instruction they need to make satisfactory academic progress. Teachers are also encouraged to collaborate among themselves. A third form of collaboration at Benchmark is with the psychologists, counselors, and social workers who make up our Support Services Department. A fourth type of collaboration is the collaboration that occurs to develop curriculum.

Teacher-Supervisor Collaboration

At Benchmark, where there is a supervisor for every three classrooms, supervisors regularly spend time in their supervisees' classrooms. They teach model lessons, provide feedback to teachers about their instruction, and teach diagnostic lessons to help teachers determine the strategies, tools, and approaches to instruction for specific students. In the Lower School (grades 2–6) teachers have regularly scheduled, individual meetings with their supervisors at least once a week, as well as frequent informal sessions, to collaborate about students, instruction, and curriculum. In the Middle School (grades 7 and 8), teachers prefer weekly group meetings with their supervisor and other teachers who teach at the same level.

A common form of teacher-supervisor collaboration is for a teacher and supervisor to plan a unit of instruction together, then alternate teaching the lessons while providing feedback to each other. For example, supervisor Sally Laird likes to plan with her teachers and then co-teach a six-week writing unit in the classrooms of her supervisees as a way of developing curriculum and as a vehicle for becoming acquainted with the students in the classes she supervises. Another instance of collaboration centers on developing conceptually appropriate content area lessons for our bright students who are reading significantly below their conceptual level.

Supervisor Joyce Ostertag collaborates with teachers to plan science and health lessons. She also helps teachers to select books that are written on an appropriate reading level for each student and that are appropriate for students' conceptual levels. Another collaborative task involves guiding support teachers in ways to assist the head teacher. Supervisor Colleen O'Hara, for example, helps her head teachers to develop a plan for introducing and scaffolding instruction in a particular comprehension strategy, then she trains the co-teachers and support teachers to teach the strategy. Middle School supervisors Linda Six and Eleanor Wiley-Gensemer collaborate in similar ways. On some occasions they co-teach a reading, social studies, or science lesson with a teacher. On other occasions, they respond to a lesson a teacher is teaching by writing in an interactive journal that is passed on to the teacher for his or her response.

Teacher-Teacher Collaboration

Teachers collaborate informally with one another in the planning of units. They also collaborate regularly to discuss ways to design lessons more effectively. Sometimes they observe one another to see a different approach to presenting similar strategies and concepts. Teachers also collaborate in level meetings to establish standards, to determine the sequence of strategy instruction, to discuss ways of teaching a concept or strategy, and to share information about students. They also use collaboration for problem solving. For example, when a student's behavior is particularly problematic, several teachers may brainstorm possible solutions, perhaps including a system for rewarding the student for appropriate behavior.

Teacher–Support Services Collaboration

An important component of professional development is supplied by our Support Services Department. The psychologists, counselors, and social workers in this department have an average caseload of two classrooms per person. One responsibility of the members of Support Services is to get to know the students and parents in the classrooms to which they are assigned and to collaborate with teachers about how best to meet the academic, social, and emotional needs of each student. As a result of this collaboration, teachers acquire deep knowledge about students and families. Based on that knowledge, teachers are able to choose from a variety of ways to help students achieve success in the classroom and on the playground.

Curriculum Development

Curriculum development is ongoing and collaborative. The staff's attitude is that we can always improve our programs. The impetus for curriculum change comes from several sources. Sometimes it is from an analysis of an assessment completed by staff at the end of each school year. For example, in the late 1970s we were concerned about how little our students wrote when asked to write an expository paragraph or even when asked to write a sentence in response to what they read. We explored the professional literature in search of ideas about writing instruction and discovered the work of Donald Graves. He was invited to Benchmark to work with our students and to present an inservice program. What he had to say about teaching writing made such sense that we wondered why we had not thought of it ourselves. A new staff member, Rebecca Hemphill, was particularly excited about Graves's ideas and began developing a writing curriculum for her class based on Graves's theories. Within six months, Becky's students were producing more writing than any other class in the school. Her students literally plastered the classroom walls with their writing. Other staff members observed and were impressed. They asked that we invite Donald Graves back for another visit. By the end of Graves's second visit, the staff was even more interested in developing a schoolwide writing curriculum based on the concepts they had learned. For several years thereafter, written composition was the focus of collaborative curriculum development at Benchmark.

On other occasions, curriculum development has resulted from focusing on a particular idea heard at a conference or workshop. For example, in the early 1980s, we were searching for some way to teach decoding more effectively. The many published programs we had tried were generally too synthetic or too fast paced for our purposes. Researcher Jim Cunningham visited Benchmark and mentioned that his wife Patricia Cunningham would be presenting a talk at an upcoming local conference on the topic "Decoding Big Words Using Little Words." Two of us attended the conference and learned more about that nugget of an idea, which ultimately launched the development of the Beginning and Intermediate Benchmark Word Identification Programs and later the Word Detectives Programs.

On another occasion, curriculum development resulted from two significant events: first, learning about a body of research based on cognitive science that seemed especially relevant to struggling readers, and second, receiving a grant to develop a program related to that research—a program to create learners, thinkers, and problem solvers (Gaskins & Elliot, 1991). We studied the professional literature on metacognition and strategy instruction; attended conferences to hear researchers Richard Anderson, Gerald Duffy, Laura Roehler, Scott Paris, David Pearson, Michael Pressley, and others talk about the instructional methods they were developing based on cognitive theory. We also held inservice programs at Benchmark where experts in cognitive science presented instructional possibilities. Based on this abundance of information, we held weekend retreats at which staff volunteers turned ideas about cognitive science into a program of strategies across the curriculum. The ideas generated at these retreats were electrifying. Those who collaborated in developing the initial strategies across the curriculum program shared their ideas with the rest of the staff.

More recently, the staff has collaborated, based on the work of Linnea Ehri, to revise and update the Benchmark Word Identification Program. The staff has also collaborated to develop a conceptually based approach to teaching mathematics, social studies, and science. Currently we are beginning a staff collaboration, led by Benchmark Middle School teacher Eric MacDonald, to turn our philosophy of "computer as tool" into classroom practice. None of us alone would have been able to develop the curriculum and instruction that exist at Benchmark. The secret to our students' successes rests primarily on the collaboration among the Benchmark staff and with our consultants.

Seminars, Meetings, and Inservice Program

Research Seminar

Since the founding of Benchmark, research seminar has been a major source of ideas for honing curriculum and instruction. Attendance at research seminar is voluntary. Each year we select a topic that will be the focus of our reading and discussion. For example, five years ago we spent the year reading articles about conceptual development and how it could be fostered in the classroom. We revisited that topic last year and continued to refine our thinking. In the late 1990s we explored and compared the concepts of temperament and style. We discussed how they could impact learning and how we could teach students to identify and take control of temperament and style if either seemed maladaptive. This current school year we are once again looking at children's traits and how they can impact learning. As a result of our study of children's traits and how children learn, we are developing an interactive learning profile that will guide us in assessing our students' strengths and challenges more systematically.

Based on a review of the research about the current year's topic, I select articles, chapters, or books that are distributed several weeks before each session of research seminar. Distributed with each article is a set of questions to focus our discussion. Sometimes all the members of research seminar choose to read the same article or chapter; sometimes two or three participants read and report on the same piece; at other times, each individual reads a different article, chapter, or book and reports on his or her reading and its relevance for teaching at Benchmark.

For many years, the 20–25 staff members who usually attend research seminar met at the same time each week. However, in the past several years we have scheduled research seminar at three or four different times throughout the week so that staff members can choose the time that best suits their schedules. The advantage of three or four groups is that more people are engaged in the discussions.

Induction Seminars

In addition to the two-week induction seminar held in August, Colleen O'Hara, a Lower School supervisor, meets weekly with Benchmark's support teachers. During each of these 45-minute sessions the group discusses a different topic related to teaching at Benchmark. One week the topic may be classroom management, whereas another week the topic may be how to conduct a reading group. The goals of the seminar include providing professional development on curriculum and instruction and increasing support teachers' general knowledge of the school, its students, and classroom routines. Two additional goals are to get to know each other and to provide a forum for support teachers to share their struggles and victories with one another.

Team Meetings

Another opportunity for professional development occurs at the biweekly Lower School and weekly Middle School team meetings. The agenda for these meetings may include writing trimester reports, communicating with parents, solving issues of common concern, or planning events that affect all members of the team, such as Grandparents' Day or Back-to-School Night. Refining instruction may also be a focus of the meetings, as it was several years ago when, for six consecutive weeks, 40 minutes of the Middle School team meeting was devoted to a discussion of *Turning Points, 2000* (Jackson & Davis, 2000), a summary of research about teaching middle school students.

Level Meetings

Our 16 Benchmark classes are grouped into six different levels based on students' reading level and age. Teachers at each of the six levels meet to discuss such areas as curriculum, standards and rubrics, and traits of good writing. In the Middle School, teachers alternate the focus of each weekly level meeting. One week is devoted to discussing the students they share and the next week to discussing curriculum.

Inservice Program

On the first Monday of each month we dismiss our 197 students at 1 p.m. so that all staff can attend a two-hour inservice program. About 75% of our inservice programs are conducted by university-based researchers. These researchers visit Benchmark classrooms for the first two hours of the school day, then conduct a late-morning discussion with teachers who are freed from other responsibilities in order to attend. In the afternoon, after students have left for the day, the guest speaker presents a two-hour program to the entire staff that usually features research findings and their implications for classroom teaching.

The other 25% of our inservice programs are led by Benchmark faculty. For example, on some occasions teachers may meet by level, as they did recently to develop standards for writing. Each of the six level meetings was planned and led by a Benchmark supervisor. On other occasions, I present the inservice program.

The term *inservice* can mean many things to many people. To some, for example, it may connote a half-day of being talked at, rather than participating in an engaging, collaborative process. In order to convey to the reader the type of inservice we find most productive, a brief description of a typical in-house inservice follows.

During the 2001–2 school year, I led a two-hour workshop for the staff on the topic "Thinking About Thinking." I chose this topic because research suggests that our students' success ultimately rests on their knowing how, and being willing, to think. The focus of our inservice discussion was the teacher's role in developing good thinkers.

I began the inservice with a 10-minute review of the practices we already have in place, based on what we have learned about how the mind works and how thinking can be fostered. I also reviewed the thinking styles we encourage students to develop (i.e., attentiveness, active involvement, adaptability, reflectivity, and persistence). Next, I gave the staff a problem to solve individually and

asked them to write notes to share with the group about their thinking processes and affective responses as they wrestled with the
problem. After the staff had spent about 10 minutes working individually, I asked them to spend 5 more minutes collaborating with
a partner to discuss how to solve the problem and to reflect on
their approach and affect while attempting to solve the problem.
The problem was as follows:

> The Benchmark Parent Association has a problem. Can you help? A
> committee of Benchmark students visited the pizza shop that fur-
> nishes our Wednesday pizza and requested that students be allowed
> to choose toppings for their pizza. For a small extra charge, the pizza
> shop manager agreed. Up until one week before the first delivery
> day, Benchmark students may place orders for pizza, selecting from
> five different toppings: green pepper, mushrooms, olives, sausage,
> and anchovies. Students may select no topping and thus have a plain
> pizza (sauce and cheese only), or they may order one, two, three,
> four, or five toppings. How many different kinds of pizza will Bench-
> mark parents need to keep track of on Wednesdays now that stu-
> dents can order their pizza slices plain or with any combination of
> five different toppings?

The group seemed to enthusiastically embrace the challenge
posed by the problem as well as the comfort of collaborating with a
partner. Next, the staff, as a group, discussed the thinking processes
and affect they experienced in attempting to solve the problem.
Some staff members commented that the problem stirred up many
emotions, giving them firsthand knowledge of how frustrated our
struggling readers must feel if they are assigned tasks for which
they do not have the necessary background information or skills
and strategies.

For the next activity, I gave the staff a discussion guide (Table
12-1) and summaries of research articles related to thinking and
how the mind works. The staff met in small groups to answer the
discussion question each group was assigned. After 30 minutes of
small-group discussion, the total group reconvened and a reporter
from each group gave a 3-minute summary of his or her group's
thoughts about thinking. I concluded the workshop with a 15-minute
summary. The staff was actively engaged for the entire two hours
and, at the conclusion of the inservice, seemed eager to more deeply
involve their students in authentic thinking activities.

Table 12-1.   Thinking About Thinking Discussion Questions

In answering the questions below,
you are welcome to use the attached summaries of research.

A. State your opinion about the statement: "Good thinking is one of the primary goals of schooling."

1. How would you define thinking?
2. What are the characteristics of a good thinker?

B. State your opinion about the statement: "Intelligence is learnable."

1. What would you predict are a few of the thinking keys to becoming more intelligent?
2. What strategies, attitudes, and habits of the mind should we teach students so that they will be better thinkers, thus more intelligent?

C. In some instances collaborative learning activities do not encourage good thinking. How might a teacher orchestrate a learning situation so that collaborative learning, class discussions, and projects encourage good thinking?

D. Some educators argue that thinking strategies are no substitute for knowledge in particular subject areas. What is your opinion?

Retreats

The purpose of retreats is to give staff uninterrupted time to develop a unit of instruction or to research an instructional topic of interest. Retreats at Benchmark are most frequently scheduled for an assigned half-day when a "floating support teacher" covers the teacher's responsibilities. Throughout the school year, Benchmark's floating support teacher moves from classroom to classroom every two days. The first day she spends in the classroom observing the teacher, getting to know the students, and learning the teacher's routine; the second day, the floating support teacher assumes the teacher's responsibilities while the teacher is on retreat. Each teacher takes about three retreats a year. Teachers appear to love their retreat days, which they claim rejuvenate them.

Workshops and Conferences

As the school receives announcements of local workshops that seem well suited for the level or curriculum of particular teachers, we pass these announcements on to the appropriate teachers or supervisors, encouraging them to attend the workshop with one or two Benchmark colleagues. There are many benefits to sponsoring the attendance of two or three staff members at a workshop. Perhaps the chief benefit is the dialogue the workshop stimulates among those staff members. In addition, Benchmark usually sponsors the attendance of two to five staff members at the annual conferences of the International Reading Association and the National Reading Conference. Staff who attend conferences or workshops write a brief summary of the major ideas they learned and share these summaries with the staff.

Some teachers at Benchmark find it especially rewarding to make presentations at professional conferences. Typically, these teachers choose an area of instruction or curriculum that has been a focus of their school year. Teachers write about their experiences, often collaborating in this effort with supervisors or other staff. For practice, teachers present their programs to the entire Benchmark staff. Thus we all profit from the learning of these teachers.

Professional Library

The Benchmark professional library includes approximately 1,300 professional books published since 1990, as well as some classic texts. It also contains approximately 35 monthly or quarterly professional journals about literacy, content areas, elementary education, middle school education, leadership, technology, and other topics. At the beginning of the school year, staff members sign up for the journals they wish to read. Upon the receipt of each book or journal, I usually review it, often highlighting parts that I find particularly relevant to instruction at Benchmark. Journals are then circulated among interested staff members. Also included in the professional library are videotapes of instruction and inservice presentations.

Development and Maintenance of Curriculum Initiatives

As noted earlier, the staff is continually collaborating with experts in cognitive psychology and education to develop curriculum that is appropriate for our struggling readers. Because we are a school in which the curriculum is continually evolving, it is a challenge to maintain the curriculum initiatives we put in place. The responsibility for this stability is placed largely on supervisors, as they work side by side with teachers each day. Their goal is to ensure that the research-based core of each initiative is maintained. At the same time, supervisors and teachers are constantly honing these curriculum initiatives based on experience and new research findings.

An example of this process is illustrated by the Benchmark Word Identification Program. The initial development of this program took place in the 1980s with the consultation of Patricia Cunningham, Richard Anderson, and Robert Gaskins and in collaboration with the Center for the Study of Reading at the University of Illinois. After three years of experimentation, data collection, and analysis, we thought we had a good program in place (Gaskins, Gaskins, Anderson, & Schommer, 1995). We made no change to the word identification program for the next six years as we turned our primary attention to developing a strategies-across-the-curriculum program. However, during this time we became aware of the need of some of our beginning readers for instruction in phonemic awareness and phonemic segmentation. We felt the need to develop a level of word identification below that which was included in our 1980s program. Thus, with the consultation of researcher Linnea Ehri, our curriculum development for the next six years involved revamping our word identification programs to include more emphasis on fully analyzing words. At the same time we added a revised spelling component. These new components resulted in programs that, for our students, have produced significantly improved decoding and spelling compared to the decoding and spelling of previous students taught by the same teachers (Gaskins, Ehri, Cress, O'Hara, & Donnelly, 1996–1997).

We are constantly on the lookout for research-based ideas that will guide us in improving our programs. Nevertheless, there is always the temptation to want to believe that a program is good enough. This is especially true in view of the fact that change can be painful and take years. We have learned that seemingly small changes, such as fully analyzing a word, can make a tremendous difference in children's success in school. Such improvements are definitely worth the time and effort.

Collaborative Partnerships With Local Universities

Throughout our history we have had a collaborative relationship with one or more local universities in the greater Philadelphia area. Such relationships keep us on the cutting edge with respect to thinking and practice. For example, each summer for the past decade, a professor from West Chester University has taught a reading practicum course at Benchmark. The 15 or 16 students in the course assist Benchmark summer program teachers from 7:45 a.m.–12:45 p.m. each day for five weeks, then meet with their professor in the afternoon. We enjoy and learn from our role in developing these teachers.

Occasionally I have the privilege of being a member of a doctoral committee for a local university. The student is frequently conducting his or her research at Benchmark, and the staff and I gain from interacting with this researcher on his or her topic. In addition, a staff member may be asked to teach a course at a local university or to supervise an independent study. All of these interactions stimulate new ideas about curriculum and instruction and how to foster our goals with students.

Professional Writing

Perhaps unique to Benchmark is the fact that the staff and I do a lot of writing about how we are adapting research-based findings to teaching at Benchmark. This process usually begins by searching the professional literature for research that could be relevant to curriculum and instruction for our students, then sharing these articles and books with the members of our research seminar. After applying the ideas in classrooms and collaborating with the staff about how to refine them, I often draft a manuscript that is co-authored by interested staff members. The draft is circulated among the entire staff for feedback, and those who are particularly interested in the project read and edit multiple drafts right through to submission. This is one of the primary ways in which we codify the curriculum and instruction being developed at Benchmark.

For example, one of my early writing collaborations with staff described the development of the Benchmark Word Identification Program (Gaskins et al., 1988). This paper was the result of four years of drafting, editing, rewriting, and, most of all, learning from one another. It was exciting to have our joint venture published. The value of this project, however, was not so much in the document as it was in the learning that took place by writing about our practices.

The staff and I have also participated in collaborative learning and writing about teaching cognitive strategies and developing a strategies-across-the-curriculum program at Benchmark (Gaskins, Anderson, Pressley, Cunicelli, & Satlow, 1993). Some of us also wrote about our collaborative efforts to develop a conceptually based science program (Gaskins, Satlow, Hyson, Ostertag, & Six, 1994). Another collaborative writing project, mentioned earlier, entailed the addition of fully analyzing words to our word identification program (Gaskins et al., 1996–1997). About the same time that we were refining our word identification program, a group of us shared ideas and wrote about scaffolded instruction at Benchmark (Gaskins et al., 1997). More recently we have written about aspects of instruction that we have been refining in both our Lower School and Middle School classes (Gaskins, Gensemer, & Six, in press; Gaskins, Laird, O'Hara, Scott, & Cress, 2002).

In addition to the writing that has taken place within Benchmark, it has been an exciting learning experience for the staff to collaborate with university-based colleagues in the development of the transactional-strategies instruction model (Pressley et al., 1992). This process has been a productive reciprocal collaboration that has included university researchers interviewing and observing in Benchmark classrooms as well as Benchmark staff reading and responding to written drafts. Whether in-house or in collaboration with researchers in the university community, we are convinced that writing about practice, and involving the staff as creators and editors, is a powerful form of professional development.

Conclusion

Teachers determine the quality of instruction that children receive. Yet we know that neither an undergraduate degree in education nor a teaching certificate is evidence that a teacher is prepared to deliver the excellent instruction that students deserve. Degrees and certificates are starting points. To teach well and meet the diverse needs of students, teachers must have a variety of classroom experiences and engage in high-quality professional development activities throughout their careers.

Therefore, if we want students to receive the education they deserve, it is imperative that professional development be the foundation for a school's curriculum and instruction and that a menu of professional development opportunities be available where teachers teach. To achieve the mission of helping all children to fulfill their potential, schools and the public must acknowledge that, in the end, it is their responsibility to provide the resources that are necessary to develop highly knowledgeable, well-trained teachers. It is not possible for preservice programs to achieve this goal in the short time that professors have with potential teachers. Without the foundation provided by high-quality, school-based professional development, improved student outcomes will not become a reality. Increasing school budgets for professional development is necessary. However, spending money on professional development does not ensure that high-quality professional development will result—and it is the quality that counts. High-quality professional development is much more than a one-shot inservice program. It is ongoing learning that is part of the fabric of the school.

In this chapter, I have shared some of the professional development options that we have found valuable for improving instruction for the struggling readers at Benchmark School. As the instructional leader of the school, I realize that it is my job to recognize and understand classroom expertise, to keep current on instructional research and theory, and to know how to orchestrate meaningful opportunities for teachers to collaborate and grow. This role in helping good teachers to become even better is exciting, fulfilling, and exhilarating.

References

Gaskins, I. W., Anderson, R. C., Pressley, M., Cunicelli, E. A., & Satlow, E. (1993). Six teachers' dialogue during cognitive process instruction. *The Elementary School Journal, 93,* 277–304.

Gaskins, I. W., Downer, M., Anderson, R., Cunningham, P., Gaskins, R., Schommer, M., & the Teachers of Benchmark School (1988). A metacognitive approach to phonics: Using what you know to decode what you don't know. *Remedial and Special Education, 9,* 36–41.

Gaskins, I. W., Ehri, L. C., Cress, C., O'Hara, C., & Donnelly, K. (1996–1997). Procedures for word learning: Making discoveries about words. *The Reading Teacher, 50,* 312–327.

Gaskins, I. W., & Elliot, T. T. (1991). *Implementing cognitive strategy instruction across the school: The Benchmark manual for teachers.* Cambridge, MA: Brookline Books.

Gaskins, I. W., Gensemer, E. W., & Six, L. (2003). Tailoring a middle school language arts class to meet the needs of struggling readers. In R. McCormack & J. Paratore (Eds.), *After early intervention, then what? Teaching struggling readers in grades 3 and beyond.* Newark, DE: IRA.

Gaskins, I. W., Laird, S. R., O'Hara, C., Scott, T., & Cress, C. (2002). Helping struggling readers make sense of reading. In C. Block, L. Gambrell, & M. Pressley (Eds.), *Improving comprehension instruction.* San Francisco: Jossey-Bass.

Gaskins, I. W., Rauch, S., Gensemer, E., Cunicelli, E., O'Hara, C., Six, L., & Scott, T. (1997). Scaffolding the development of intelligence among children who are delayed in learning to read. In K. Hogan & M. Pressley (Eds.), *Scaffolding student learning: Instructional approaches & issues* (pp. 43–73). Cambridge, MA: Brookline Books.

Gaskins, I. W., Satlow, E., Hyson, D., Ostertag, J., & Six, L. (1994). Classroom talk about text: Learning in science class. *Journal of Reading, 37,* 558–565.

Gaskins, R. W., Gaskins, I. W., Anderson, R. C., & Schommer, M. (1995). The reciprocal relationship between research and development: An example involving a decoding strand for poor readers. *Journal of Reading Behavior, 27,* 337–377.

Jackson, A. J., & Davis, G. A., with Abeel, M., & Bordonaro, A. (2000). *Turning points 2000: Educating adolescents in the 21st century.* New York: Teachers College Press.

Pressley, M., El-Dinary, P. M., Gaskins, I. W., Schuder, T., Bergman, J. L., Almasi, J., & Brown, R. (1992). Beyond direct explanation: Transactional instruction of reading comprehension strategies. *The Elementary School Journal, 92,* 513–555.

Chapter 13

Distributed Leadership for Instructional Improvement: The Principal's Role

Michael Aaron Copland

Key Ideas

✓ The essence of educational leadership is the improvement of learning.

✓ School leadership that improves learning is a shared enterprise, distributed across many actors, not the sole domain of the principal.

✓ An analysis of two school cases illustrates the nature of leadership practices employed by principals who seek to improve learning, including (1) a persistent, public focus on learning, (2) the use of inquiry, (3) the development of enabling structures, (4) shared responsibility for decision making, and (5) personal participation as a learner.

For

• Pre-K–12 school and system leaders

• Pre-K–12 policy makers and those who prepare pre-K–12 educational leaders

Leadership is the guidance of instructional improvement.

—Elmore, 2000, p. 13

Simply and eloquently, Elmore puts his finger on the most central task facing school leadership today. Gone are the days of school leader as CEO, plant manager, or mere "agent of the board," who worried little about instructional matters and more about making sure the buses ran on time. Effective school leadership today is increasingly embodied by a persistent and public emphasis on improving teaching and learning; in no content area is this need more insistent than literacy. High-quality literacy instruction is fundamental work for educators. School leaders are ever more accountable for guiding continual instructional improvement and for demonstrable progress in outcomes for students.

Increasing, too, is the realization that one person sitting in a formal leadership role cannot reasonably accomplish all that is expected in terms of promoting improvement in any instructional domain (Copland, 2001). Those studying and thinking about the distribution of leadership in schools are clear that the responsibility for improving teaching and learning rests with multiple actors in the school (Elmore, 2000; Sergiovanni, 1984; Spillane, Halverson, & Diamond, 2000). Leadership that seeks to promote high-quality instruction necessarily extends beyond the school principal to include many other "leaders" in the school community: assistant principals, teacher leaders, coaches, professional development specialists, parents, and teachers in classrooms.

The relatively recent shift in emphasis toward models of shared leadership signal a coming sea change in education that is only now emerging across schools engaged in systemic efforts to improve teaching and learning. What does it look like and what are the challenges, in practical terms, for leaders working on continual improvement in instruction? How do we conceive of distributing leadership for instructional improvement and for sustaining high-quality instruction? What do successful principals do in such arrangements? How does the broader distribution of responsibility for instructional improvement shape the principal's role? This chapter is an effort to contribute clarity about distributed leadership practice that aims to promote high-quality instruction—who leads, what challenges leaders face, how leaders enter, and illustrations of strategies that leaders employ to focus professional learning in context.

First I will briefly summarize the key challenges facing leadership efforts to improve teaching and learning today. A brief review of research on distributed leadership follows; it attempts to capture the essence of conceptions of instructional leadership for addressing the challenges. Two cases of school leadership in action, drawn from schools within a recent research effort, are presented next. They highlight professional development work focused on literacy instruction and provide illustrative examples of the practice of distributed leadership that responds to the challenges inherent in improving instructional practice. The cases spotlight quality approaches to leadership, each centered on different aspects of improving literacy instruction and each incorporating multiple actors in leadership roles. Finally, a cross-case discussion distills some common essential practices that principals employ to meet the challenges in context.

The Challenge of Leading Instructional Improvement

Within schools today, the demands of leadership faced by principals and others form an incredibly complex set of challenges. School leaders juggle instructional, managerial, and political functions, framing and solving problems that emerge within their particular contexts, while trying to make sense of new initiatives that come from outside the school—from the district, the state, or even the nation. This is particularly true in the area of literacy; virtually all state accountability initiatives have literacy learning as a cornerstone. This current environment tremendously heightens expectations for school leaders while creating new possibilities and directions for improving teaching and learning.

School leadership today faces an expanded and public sense of accountability for results at the level of the school, often enforced through standardized assessments mandated by states. Principals and other leaders are challenged to ensure that their schools "measure up" in a climate of heightened expectations, inspection, choice, and criticism. In communities around the country, it has become commonplace for leaders' heads to roll, so to speak, when the school test results hit the local paper. Media focus and the climate of high-stakes accountability make it very difficult for schools and school leaders to remain out of the spotlight; this is particularly true for those schools where achievement levels in the basics of reading and writing are not up to standard.

Compounding the accountability pressures, school districts increasingly have come to view the school as the center of change, and divert responsibility to principals and others at the school for acquiring and directing human and financial resources on behalf of their organizations. The standards-based reform movement that began in the 1980s focused on setting the bar; the responsibility for figuring out how to get over that bar has been delegated largely to schools, in many settings. As a result, school leaders currently exist in a world in which creating better schools is an absolutely integral part of their work; leaders have no choice but to attend to the work of instructional improvement. Not only is the work of instructional improvement a school-level leadership responsibility, it is also increasingly understood as an "inside-out" process, occurring in a particular context and accomplished by particular actors inside the school community. This view stems from a growing recognition that externally mandated fixes to instructional concerns, fixes that have largely ignored context, have rarely resulted in positive, sustainable improvements in teaching and learning.

Adding to the complexity, the aforementioned trends are causing evolution and expansion of leadership roles and opportunities for others at the school, swelling the boundaries of responsibility and accountability for leadership action beyond the principal's office. Leadership in schools today is not about creating a teaching culture of compliance or adherence to rules. Teachers and other school community members are viewed as partners in decision making and as fully vested players in leading the improvement of instruction. Principals are expected to work collaboratively with others at the school to create systems and structures that encourage teachers and others to think deeply and creatively about their practice. Questions of "who takes orders from whom" give way to a focus on fostering and building communities of learners, which create the possibility for sustaining positive work at the school beyond the transient tenure of the formal leader.

Though in some ways creating new stresses and demands for schools, these trends also provide a unique set of circumstances for the exercise of distributed leadership, specifically focusing on providing high-quality instruction. In the next section, a brief review of the scholarship on the current thinking on leadership distribution in schools provides a deeper conceptual understanding of what it is and how it works, and sets the stage for the presentation of cases that follow.

Rethinking Instructional Leadership

The sheer scope of expectations associated with the challenges facing school leaders has prompted significant rethinking in scholarship and practice. This is particularly evident in new conceptions of ways in which leadership for instructional improvement can be distributed. Although a noteworthy body of very recent work is developing on the topic of distributed leadership, conceptual forays that stake out new directions, away from role-based conceptions of leadership and toward functional or organizational views, are not all new.

A few notable scholars have been productively engaged in this thinking for nearly twenty years. In an early treatise, Sergiovanni (1984) argued that leadership is an artifact or a product of organizational culture, and that the particular shape and style of leadership in an organization is not a function of individuals or of training programs; rather, it has to do with the mixture of organizational culture and the density of leadership competence among and within many actors. Sergiovanni posited a fundamental shift, discerning leadership less as a set of management techniques and more as a set of norms, beliefs, and principles that emerge, and to which members give allegiance, in an effective organization. In a complementary vein, Murphy's (1988) comprehensive analysis of the first decade of instructional leadership literature devoted considerable attention to analyzing problems that emerged from a general failure in the scholarship on that topic to consider both the micro and macro levels of contextual issues in school leadership. Murphy criticized what he viewed as errantly placed attributions of causality in the literature—that improvements in teaching and learning were due to the efficacy of actions performed by persons in formal roles of authority rather than by organizational conditions. Such early work underpins the recent emergence of broader considerations of leadership in schools.

Recent efforts to reframe leadership in schools are rooted in notions of distribution. In an important contribution, Elmore (2000) sets out a framework for understanding the reconstruction of leadership roles and functions around the idea of distributed leadership in the service of large-scale instructional improvement. This new way of seeing is rooted in principles of distributed expertise, mutual dependence, reciprocity of accountability and capacity, and the centrality of instructional practice. Elmore identifies five leadership domains—policy, professional, system, school, and practice— each encompassing multiple actors, and develops a robust understanding of leadership functions associated with each domain. In this way, Elmore pushes the field to relocate the authority and responsibility for improving teaching and learning, separating it from the sole control of those "up the chain" of the administrative hierarchy, and embedding that authority and responsibility in the daily work of all those connected to the enterprise of schooling.

Similarly, Spillane et al. (2000) suggest that school leadership is necessarily a distributed activity "stretched over" people in different roles rather than neatly divided among them, a dynamic interaction between multiple leaders (and followers) and their situational and social contexts. Lambert (1998) also understands leadership as broad concept, separated from person, role, and a discrete set of individual behaviors. Rather than being primarily centered on the principal, the capacity for leadership resides within and among all members of the larger school community—administrators, teachers, parents, and students—suggesting shared responsibility for a shared purpose and requiring the redistribution of power and authority. Complementary to this understanding, others offer the view that leadership is an organizational quality, originating from many peoples' personal resources and flowing through networks of roles (Ogawa & Bossert, 1995; Pounder, Ogawa, Adams, 1995).

Scholarly work on leadership distribution is not confined strictly to the theoretical realm. Empirical evidence is also surfacing in support of the notion that within school communities that achieve excellent results in improving teaching and learning, the capacity to lead is not principal-centric by necessity, but is rather embedded in various organizational contexts. McLaughlin & Talbert (2001), for example, examined organizational context effects on teacher community, teaching, and teachers' careers and found no instances of administrative leaders who created extraordinary contexts for teaching by virtue of their own unique vision; nor did the study reveal any common patterns in strong principals' personal characteristics. Successful principals were men and women with various professional backgrounds who worked in collaboration with teacher leaders and in respect of teaching culture. They found a number of ways to support teachers in getting the job done. The leadership of these principals was not superhuman; rather, it grew from a strong and simple commitment to making the school work for their students, and to building teachers' commitment and capacity to pursue this collective goal. Perhaps most important, the responsibility for sustaining instructional improvement was shared among a much broader group of school community members rather than owned primarily by formal leaders at the top of the organizational chart.

So what, in concrete terms, does distributed leadership for instructional improvement look like? What do principals do, specifically, to improve instruction in a distributed leadership arrangement? On a practical level, how might the broader distribution of responsibility for instructional improvement alter the principal's role as the "formal" leader in the school? The next section highlights two examples, drawn from literature, of distributed leadership practices that specifically touch on improving aspects of literacy instruction.

The Practice of Distributed Instructional Leadership: Two Cases

No school is exactly like the next, yet virtually all school leaders face challenges similar in nature to those described earlier. Teachers and administrators are being asked to implement research-based practices that require dramatic shifts in the ways they help students learn. The two cases that follow provide examples of leadership that is focused on improving instruction through one or more of the key challenges noted above. The cases highlight different ways that quality professional development, focused on aspects of literacy learning as well as other content areas, can become an integrated part of teachers' and administrators' routine work, contrasted with the typical "drive-by" workshops that occur on one or two inservice days per year.

Case 1: Building Accountability for Teaching and Learning in an Elementary School

The first example, summarized below, describes a school I will call Slattford Elementary (a pseudonym), which has evolved a way of directing its professional development efforts to the improvement of literacy instruction. The case, which incorporates the work of Post (2002), highlights the improvement of language production for second-language learners in the primary grades, guided by various leaders across the entire school community. The principal's role in this school, while vitally important, blends into the fabric of other leaders' interactions.

Slattford Elementary School is the largest of eight elementary schools in the Oak Valley School District. The school was built in 1947 and currently houses approximately 870 students in grades

K–5. *Student centered* is a term often used to describe the many programs and learning opportunities that define Slattford. The school's vision and mission states it this way: "All students reaching high standards—no matter what it takes." Staff, parents, and community are active partners in working to achieve this goal. The school's population is a heterogeneous mix of students: approximately two-fifths Hispanic and roughly equal proportions of Filipino, Caucasian, African American, and Asian/Pacific Islander children. Oak Valley is a middle-class community in a densely populated region of the country.

Student achievement at Slattford is measured in a variety of ways. The SAT-9, given in the spring to all students in grades 2–5, provides one gauge of effectiveness of instructional programs. Every September, the Concepts About Print (CAP) test is administered to all kindergarten students. The Developmental Reading Assessment (DRA) is given to all students twice a year. Slattford's Spanish bilingual students are given the Spanish Assessment of Basic English (SABE) test in grades 2–5.

Beyond evidence collected through these sorts of measures, Slattford also works hard at accountability from the ground up. At Slattford, Principal Tom Phillips and the school leadership team have structured a half day set aside every two weeks for teachers to meet in grade-level teams and conduct cycles of inquiry—time when teachers inquire together about their own practice in relation to school goals for improving learning. The content of the kindergarten team's February 2001 meeting reflects the development of their inquiry practices and their commitment to one another and to accountability to their students over time. Their focus at the February meeting is on English language learners. The kindergarten teachers have been wrestling with the best way to deliver literacy instruction to their second-language students. They designed an inquiry plan the previous November, when another grade-level team in the school shared findings on equity issues that led kindergarten teachers to believe that language production among English language learners, particularly those of Cantonese and Vietnamese descent, was an area on which they needed to focus. One teacher observed that these students, who often entered school speaking little English, "seemed to have the same vocabulary five years later" and "needed to be targeted for language development."

In the meeting, teachers immediately pick up on the agenda established at the conclusion of last month's meeting. Principal Phillips participates as a learner in the meeting, and the kindergarten team brings him up to date describing their strategy. Teacher Marguerita Sturgis says, "We're each observing two English-learning students every month in the classroom and in the yard, talking about what we're seeing and looking for commonalties and how we can better serve them." Phillips's presence in the grade-level professional development meetings is routine and expected; he makes it a regular commitment.

The teachers are using a systematic approach to data collection by keeping a chart of students' progress that they update at these monthly meetings. Each teacher discusses his or her target students while another records. Though only in their fourth month of inquiry into this problem area, the teachers have already found ways to implement changes in their practice based on what they learn by comparing observations.

To enhance their work with students, teachers collaborate to develop games and lessons that, based on their observations, are conducive to language production. They compare schedules and determine ways to redistribute students periodically for more intensive work in homogeneous language groups. Later in the year, based on what they conclude from their analysis of target students, they determine criteria for assigning students to first-grade classes based on language and ethnicity.

The work of the kindergarten team is organized around generating new, practical knowledge. Their charts of students' academic and social progress are a relevant source of data for their young students. The charts allow teachers to make informed changes in practice and respond to their students' specific needs. New knowledge, constructed through joint activity, is the basis upon which teachers transform their practices for teaching English language learners.

As teachers build a community that challenges traditional norms of independence and autonomy, trust is a key condition. The high level of trust that the kindergarten community shares allows teachers, as well as Principal Phillips, to challenge one another. In addition, Phillips works with individual teachers to develop evaluation criteria focused on the improvement of literacy instruction, and he makes this an area of focus for his classroom observations and feedback to teachers. Through the process of inquiry, the community breaks down social barriers that increase its capabilities for collaborating to formulate and achieve goals and to develop appropriate practices. Individual teachers benefit from this joint work and have moved beyond acquiring knowledge alone to jointly constructing knowledge. Through collaboration, teachers individually and collectively take a consistent, critical stance toward their work. Through the process of inquiry, teachers develop mutual accountability and a shared professional identity.

The Slattford case highlights the comparative advantage of a strong professional community in sharing and sustaining accountability for good student outcomes in literacy learning. The combined use of a cycle of inquiry and teacher-developed, teacher-led professional development promotes a clear and present focus on the continual improvement of literacy instruction. The principal's role in this effort is several-fold: to understand the needs of students in context, to guide and structure teacher leadership activity in service of those needs, to support teacher leaders' efforts with ample allocation of time for teachers to meet, and to participate as an active learner in the process of inquiry with teachers.

In analyzing the exercise of leadership at Slattford and its connection to improving literacy instruction, some obvious focuses come to the fore. Teachers work from data and coherently link their focus on content and assessment of instructional practices to individual student learning needs. Principal Phillips and the leadership team have worked out structural supports to provide teachers a regular time and space to meet as a team. The school has allocated a small but significant chunk of time each month that the kindergarten team can devote to their ongoing inquiry process. There is evidence that teacher groups in the school engage in data collection and analysis in the service of planning and goal setting that is focused on improving student outcomes. They received training and coaching in their inquiry process, initially organized and provided by the principal and the leadership team at the school.

The team's work is primarily led by the teachers themselves, but it is observed and reinforced by the principal through his conversations with teacher leaders and participant observation of the practices they develop. The principal also coordinates opportunities for teams to meet and talk with one another. With a prompt from another grade-level team, the kindergarten team recognized the need for extra attention to a group of children with special learning needs. They took steps to establish an inquiry plan that focused their collective attention directly on helping these students to achieve comparable standards that the school holds for all children. Also in evidence is careful attention to student placement and assignment, a responsibility delegated by the principal to the grade-level teams. Teachers developed in-house assessments to collect data related to the identified learning issue. The kindergarten team's emphasis on individual and collective accountability for individual students transcends the typical standardized-testing paradigm. Teachers' own professional learning over the course of an entire school year is a function of their inquiry work on the identified problem. Assessment of their own practice and accountability for learning among their English language learners is a primary focus of their professional development.

As a result of these conditions and the shared commitment to accountability, the Slattford kindergarten team has reinvented the meaning of professional development within their community. Their case reveals that learning in an inquiring community needs to be understood as progress made by both individual teachers and the community of teachers through their professional interactions. In this sense, one can see high-quality literacy instruction being built within this professional community. The development of new knowledge of practice is constructed and held accountable on a communal level. At the same time it is put to use as knowledge for practice in individual classrooms.

Case 2: Treating Teachers as Professionals and Nurturing Schoolwide Capacity in an Elementary School

In a second school case, described below, the work of another school principal can be seen nurturing a vibrant schoolwide professional community, which in turn focuses energy on continual improvement in learning and teaching. I call this school New Harbor Elementary (a pseudonym), and the case draws on the work of Curtis (2000) and Meier (2002).

It's 11:30 a.m. one Wednesday at New Harbor Elementary, and not a teacher is to be found in a classroom or on the lawns and pathways outside. Nevertheless, the teachers are doing some of their most important work. Every school day, between 11:30 a.m. and 1 p.m., Principal Terry Barton and all New Harbor teachers gather in the teachers' room for 90 minutes of professional development, a "midday block." The teachers debate instructional theory and practice, try to solve problems that have come up or are likely to come up in their classrooms, discuss curriculum, commiserate, seek advice, offer encouragement, quietly reflect, or refine a lesson plan.

"It's always wonderful stuff—things that get your brain stretched," says teacher Barbara Loren of the content of the midday block. "I feel like a professional." Although the format of the daily meeting is always open to revision, last school year two of the five weekly midday blocks were set aside for personal planning. Three of the five were scripted, with formal agendas and case-study analyses, in which each teacher documented the literacy or math progress of two students, sharing and analyzing work samples with other teachers.

Bilingual teachers confer about what's working and what's not and plan for refinements in the instruction. The literacy specialist leads workshops on reading curriculum, and the math specialist does the same for math. Conversations about whether practices in existence should be modified or eliminated often lead to consensus before the topics are brought up on formal agendas. For example, frequent informal discussions about Exhibition Nights, in which students present their work to parents and other members of the community, led to an agreement that their frequency should be reduced from three times a year to two.

Before one midday block, teachers were asked to diagnose a piece of student writing with the idea of determining the next step in instruction. Using samples of work from the two students they had decided to use for yearlong case studies, they analyzed the pieces and offered suggestions on how best to improve that particular student's writing. Now that she has experienced such stimulating collegial interaction plus the time for reflection and planning that is taken for granted in many other professions, Loren says she could not go back to the isolation that is often the fate of teachers. "I need to be able to talk to adults. I treasure that time of sharing ideas. It's a time to bond, which other teachers don't get to do."

Although many school administrators say that building time for teachers to join together as professionals during a jam-packed school day is practically impossible, Principal Barton, who seldom takes no for an answer, says it was easy. Teachers meet while students have lunch, study hall, and a recreation period. Paraprofessionals— usually parents—come in during that time and oversee the children. "It's simple, inexpensive, and it makes all the difference," Barton says.

Barton's style and philosophy prevent her from stepping in with a prescription for the best way to solve a problem, both at midday block sessions and when she formally evaluates teachers, which she does every other year for each teacher. "I don't think suggestions are too useful," Barton says. For evaluations, Barton focuses on teachers' literacy and math instruction. She comes into a classroom with a blueberry iBook, takes laptop notes on what the students are doing and the teacher's interaction with the students, and then immediately turns those notes into questions for the teacher and prints them on the spot. "I leave them with questions," she explains. When a follow-up discussion is scheduled, Barton talks through the questions with the teachers and allows them to reflect on their classroom actions. "Ordinarily, they get back to what they need to do next." If they're really stuck, Barton may refer them to another teacher.

"If they learn from each other, it's so much better. You're fostering that whole sense of interdependence and independence." No teacher should be dependent on one source for answers, just as no student should be dependent on one source for answers, Barton states. That philosophy has also been transferred to the classroom, where teachers encourage students to seek help from each other.

New Harbor teachers like Shirley Valadez praise Barton for demonstrating morale-boosting respect for the staff in many ways, not the least of which are giving them an equal voice in decisions and allowing them to attend outside professional development conferences of their choice. Through keeping an eye out for what her teachers would be interested in, letting them decide what conferences or classes would best benefit their teaching, employing an on-site, full-time substitute teacher, and taking advantage of grants, Barton has created a system in which professional development is valued and regularly and advantageously used.

"The people you have on your staff will make or break you," Barton insists, which makes the hiring process—in which a team of teachers interviews each candidate—all the more critical. The hiring process is unique, and prospective New Harbor teachers cannot be shy about being in a fishbowl. Candidates are asked to solve a classroom problem or come up with an idea to improve teaching at the school—with fellow teacher applicants. The domineering problem-solver who imposes his or her ideas on others is hastily rejected because collaboration is so important at New Harbor.

Establishing a close relationship with the students is at the top of Barton's list of practices that make a difference for their learning. "The kids have to know you care about them," she says. One way she expresses care is by making an effort to visit every classroom in the school at least once a day. "It gives me a connection with the kids," she says, and signals learning as a priority. Although other needs sometimes intervene, she does manage to accomplish this goal on most days.

New Harbor Elementary exemplifies the comparative advantage of school leadership conducted by a strong and committed principal who has clear beliefs about learning—for students, for teachers, and for the school as a whole—that drive her work. Although Barton is centrally important to the school's ongoing efforts to improve instruction, she clearly recognizes that she cannot and should not try to be everything to everyone.

The school incorporates a collaborative approach to leadership, in which many people from many vantage points in the system share in the work of improving teaching and learning. Well-established workplace and systems structures, such as the 90-minute midday block, serve continual professional growth among the staff, and that growth maintains a specific and laserlike focus on improving teaching and learning for children. Accountability is evident at a ground level; Barton's frequent presence in classrooms and her questioning approach to supervision and evaluation of instructional practices in literacy contribute to a climate of openness to scrutinizing practice that extends beyond conversations between teachers and principal to include much interaction between teachers focused on the growth of their practice. The teacher selection process that the school employs acts as a strong quality control measure that ensures that new faculty share a commitment to New Harbor's established mission and vision. Curriculum and classroom assignment decisions are rooted in data about how well the processes serve children.

Leadership Lessons

The cases presented here showcase schools with leadership that might be called "high functioning" in terms of promoting high-quality instruction. Each example touches in some way on specific leadership action for improving aspects of literacy teaching and learning, and a cross-case analysis suggests more global lessons regarding strategies and approaches the principals employ to improve teaching and learning generally in these schools. Five key themes emerge that capture the essence of how these principals promote and distribute leadership for learning: (a) a persistent, public focus on learning, (b) the use of inquiry, (c) the development of enabling structures, (d) shared responsibility for decision making, and (e) personal participation as a learner.

A Persistent, Public Focus on Learning

A persistent, public focus suggests three things. First, principals need to work to establish norms, beliefs, and goals within the school community that are learning focused, both for students and for professionals, and then "walk the talk" in every way possible. Such a focus gives meaning and direction to the school's efforts to improve. In the school cases, Principals Phillips and Barton maintain a public focus on aspects of literacy learning, tied to the mission and vision in the school, and suggest through their words and actions with students, teachers, and parents that high-quality literacy teaching and learning matters.

Second, principals need to work with others to identify the primary focus of the professional learning agenda. For each of the case schools, literacy instruction is a consensus area of focus for instructional improvement and learning assessment. Teachers at Slattford and New Harbor are centrally involved in decision making and in planning their professional development agenda around literacy and other key content areas. In both cases, teachers do more than simply offer input; they see the big picture and share a common vision for instructional excellence. Their ongoing professional development work is built into routines at the school; their daily work with students is characterized by steady progress based on advances in knowledge and understanding. Most important, teachers and administrators work together to co-construct this clear focus; it is not imposed from above through the exercise of formal power.

Finally, principals must use the evaluation process to evaluate teaching practices in the consensus areas of content focus. Both Principals Phillips and Barton take advantage of the annual evaluation process to make the improvement of literacy teaching and learning a focus of classroom observation and discussion. Rather than leaving this to chance encounters, the principals seek out regular opportunities to observe and provide feedback for teachers engaged in literacy instruction.

The Use of an Inquiry-Based Process for Instructional Improvement

The principals' introduction of inquiry processes as a means for ongoing improvement brings a powerful tool to bear on professional growth and student learning. Both Slattford and New Harbor employ approaches to ongoing inquiry that have principals and teachers immersed in examining student achievement data that is collected from various sources and focused on particular content areas or student populations targeted for improvement. Inquiry processes that become integrated into the daily or weekly routine also offer a vehicle for leadership distribution. Although experts from outside the school community may provide help with identified teacher learning needs, the primary means for instructional improvement are conversations among the teachers and principals themselves. Accountability is not strictly defined by an externally imposed set of standards or assessments; rather, teachers hold each other accountable to the vision and mission that they all share.

In defining and revisiting these efforts, particularly in the area of literacy instruction, members of the school community are not just recipients of someone else's vision for what important work is to be done. Rather, they are an integral part of creating this understanding. The use of an inquiry-based approach gives voice and merit to the views of all school community members in the development, implementation, communication, and evaluation of a focused effort that defines the school's most important work.

The case school principals also attend to the learning skills that teachers will need in order to carry out a cycle of inquiry. In an effort to foster teachers' capacity and comfort in generating knowledge of practice, teachers receive ongoing professional development in asking questions and understanding problems, in developing accountability frameworks to guide cycles of inquiry, and in constructing standards against which to measure their school's progress in their focused reform effort. Furthermore, principals structure opportunities for practice and continual attention to these skills, so that they may eventually become a regular part of teachers' professional repertoire.

In working from data at Slattford and New Harbor, teachers have stepped into new leadership roles and responsibilities, planning and leading inquiry, examining the practice of others through the lens of student work, and continually holding their own practice up for scrutiny by others. Once established, as is the case in both of these schools, inquiry becomes a means by which trust builds across a school community and barriers to improvement come down.

The Development and Implementation of Structural Supports

Perhaps more than any other aspect of principal leadership, the creation of structures that enable teachers to have concentrated time together focused on teaching and learning issues is key. Mobilizing time and people around organizational purposes is a big part of creating a work environment that motivates and sustains continual effort toward identified goals for improving teaching and learning.

Both Phillips and Barton have figured out ways to make use of available time and resources to carve out regular, recurring time for teachers to meet in an inquiry mode. The daily 90-minute block at New Harbor and the grade-level team meeting structure at Slattford each focus clearly on instructional improvement and offer ongoing time for teachers to conduct cycles of inquiry, to discuss and debate key issues related to teaching and learning, and to open their practices up to scrutiny. Principals coordinate schedules, time structures, and personnel resources to make these conversations possible.

Shared Responsibility for Key Instructional Decisions

Principals who are successful in building leadership capacity and promoting instructional improvement do not exercise authority by telling others what to do. Rather, they focus on asking questions, exploring data, and engaging faculty and the broader community in questions that can move the school forward. They also recognize expertise in others and provide ways to enhance it. For example, those who have expertise in literacy teaching and learning take leadership in that area. In some cases, this means that principals have to be willing to let go, or share leadership functions traditionally associated with the role. Tom Phillips gave over responsibility for the design of inquiry plans to grade-level teams; Terry Barton left teachers with questions, not prescriptions, after her classroom visits for evaluation purposes.

Although a willingness to share responsibility appears key, the cases suggest that the principal's role in leading instructional improvement remains a necessary and crucial one. Both Phillips and Barton play prominent roles as catalysts for change, protecters of vision, and leaders and organizers of inquiry. Yet the process of engendering shared leadership does require principals to involve others in meaningful decision making, letting go of some of the formal responsibility in order to share it with others.

Principal Participation as a Learner

Principals who continue to make their own learning a priority through participation in classrooms and professional development accomplish important objectives on at least two levels. First, principal participation as a learner in the school sends the message that learning is important. This is, in a sense, an aspect of "walking the talk," part of making learning a persistent public focus. Principal participation in classrooms and professional development sends a clear signal to students and teachers that learning matters for everyone in the school.

Second, principals who participate deepen their own understanding and ability to contribute to the important dialogue about improving instruction in particular content areas. In seeking to promote high-quality literacy teaching, for example, the ability to lead is rooted in the leaders' thinking, beliefs, and understanding about literacy and literacy instruction. As the cases suggest, both Terry Barton and Tom Phillips participate in literacy-focused professional development alongside their teachers. Developing knowledge of good literacy instruction and how to speak the language of instruction with teachers by actively participating in professional development efforts builds their credibility and trust and focuses their ability to scrutinize instructional practices.

Conclusion

In the current landscape of challenges facing school leadership, improving teaching and learning emerges as the principal's primary responsibility. His or her role in fulfilling this remains crucial. Yet consistent with current notions of leadership distribution, principals cannot accomplish all that is expected without the careful and thoughtful leadership of teachers and others in the school. The building of such partnerships requires principals to focus clearly and consistently on a vision for learning and to promote inquiry into practice through the construction of structures that support collaborative work focused on improving teaching and learning. By sharing ownership and distributing leadership for instructional improvement and taking seriously their own ongoing professional learning, principals can work in concert with others to accomplish great results for students.

References

Copland, M. A. (2001). The myth of the superprincipal. *Phi Delta Kappan, 82* (7), [n. p.].

Curtis, D. (2000). Treating teachers as professionals. George Lucas Educational Foundation [On-line]. Available: http://www.glef.org

Elmore, R. F. (2000). *Building a new structure for school leadership.* Washington, DC: Albert Shanker Institute.

Lambert, L. (1998). *Building leadership capacity in schools.* San Francisco: Jossey-Bass.

McLaughlin, M. W., & Talbert, J. E. (2001). *Professional communities and the work of high school teaching.* Chicago: Chicago University Press.

Meier, N. (2002). *Case study notes—New Harbor Elementary.* Stanford, CA: Stanford University Press.

Murphy, J. (1988). Methodological, measurement, and conceptual problems in the study of instructional leadership. *Educational Evaluation and Policy Analysis, 10* (2), 117–139.

Ogawa, S., & Bossert, S. (1995). Leadership as an organizational quality. *Educational Administration Quarterly, 31* (2), 224–244.

Post, L. (2002). Leadership caselette notes—Slattford Elementary. *BASRC evaluation study*. Stanford, CA: Stanford University Press.

Pounder, D., Ogawa, R., & Adams, E. (1995). Leadership as an organization-wide phenomena: Its impact on school performance. *Educational Administration Quarterly, 31* (4), [n. p.].

Sergiovanni, T. J. (1984). Leadership as cultural expression. In T. J. Sergiovanni & J. E. Corbally (Eds.), *Leadership and organizational culture* (pp. 105–144). Urbana, IL: University of Illinois Press.

Spillane, J., Halverson, R., & Diamond, J. B. (2000). Investigating school leadership practice: A distributed perspective. *Educational Researcher, 30* (3), 23–27.

. . . .

The two schools referred to in this chapter were studied at the Center for Research on the Context of Teaching at Stanford University, focusing on an evaluation of the Bay Area School Reform Collaborative (BASRC), a large-scale school reform effort funded jointly by the Annenberg Foundation and the Hewlett Foundation.

Part IV

Professional Development
Ideas That Make a Difference

Coaching School Leaders in Literacy

Lillian A. Augustine

To improve student performance in literacy and to ensure that all students will be able to read on grade level by the end of third grade, according to the New Jersey Governor's Reading Initiative, we proposed an intense new professional development design in Coaching the Principal Model. We provided professional development for school leaders in grades K–6. We contracted with a retired language arts supervisor to conduct workshops for this target population and to schedule site visitation to each participant's school to assist administrators in continuing their observation and evaluation of literacy lessons. The consultant served as a coach.

Having participated in this project, administrators will be able to do the following:

1. Identify essential components for the instruction of literacy
2. Recognize them in lessons
3. Provide feedback to teachers
4. Develop suggestions and/or action plans for teachers in need of improvement

All of these are set in the content of our Framework for Effective Teaching, as based on Charlotte Danielson's *Framework for Teaching*. At the conclusion of the school year, we had a closing evaluation session with the coach and administrators to determine our needs for the future. We also met with the district's Peer Review Committee of Administrators and Supervisors to analyze the teachers' observations and evaluations through blind readings to note changes in the review of evaluating elementary lessons in literacy.

Principals expressed an appreciation for these workshops and school visits. They felt the effect of the observations, and a coach confirmed that they were focused on the critical elements of instruction as they relate to literacy development.

The International Reading Association's Literacy Study Group Initiative

Matt Baker

The International Reading Association has developed a professional development initiative entitled IRA Literacy Study Groups. IRA believes that quality information is essential to effective professional development and that knowledgeable teachers are the most important factor in improving children's achievement in reading and writing. IRA Literacy Study Groups have been developed to help teachers gain access to the best professional literature available in the field of literacy education and to provide a flexible structure for teacher discourse based on the concepts of professional exploration, collaboration, and application. Groups of educators assume responsibility for their own professional growth by creating and sustaining collaborative networks in which they read, write, and reflect on their practice.

The concept behind IRA Literacy Study Groups is simple: Give teachers a collection of research-based resources that will help them to grow as professionals in their field; allow them time to read and write about what they are learning; and suggest proven ways that they can share and explore what they have learned with one another and, ultimately, with their students. The aim of the study groups is to put teachers in charge of their own learning, allowing them to play a larger role in determining what they need to learn in order to strengthen their own professionalism.

IRA Literacy Study Groups are organized around themed collections, or modules, of materials selected from IRA books and journals. All materials have been peer reviewed and reflect theoretical and/or research perspectives. Each module includes a facilitator's guide, at least one recently published book, at least five journal articles with a discussion guide, position statements or other related brochures, and a journal for recording ideas and personal reflections. These modules provide all the resources necessary to make professional development a manageable and effective option for educators and schools.

The study groups are made up of literacy educators who share interests about their professional learning. The individuals come together regularly to read and discuss materials on a topic they wish to study in depth. The composition of the study group is determined by participants and may be organized formally within a school or school district, or organized informally by colleagues with comparable job responsibilities.

IRA has created modules on the topics of adolescent literacy, beginning reading, reading comprehension, and vocabulary and has plans to offer modules on more topics. See http://www.reading.org for more information on IRA Literacy Study Groups.

Professional Development Through a University-School Partnership: Implementing Balanced Literacy Instruction

Pamela Chase

So often when I go to a workshop I come away pumped up and eager to try out the ideas. Then I get back to my classroom. There is no time to prepare the materials or to make the changes; the new techniques just end up being a dream. The best professional development experience I ever had was uniquely different. It resulted from a yearlong partnership between my school and a nearby university. A primary goal of the professional development was to help K–3 teachers in my school implement balanced literacy instruction with guided reading; after the training, the university would also benefit by having a site where students could observe effective practices, such as small-group instruction, in action.

Leveled books and professional materials were ordered with grant money, but what made the experience exceptional was the fact that I was actually given the time, space, and support to implement all of the ideas. A reading professor from the university was in our school almost weekly for a full day. She held study group meetings before or after school, modeled lessons for teachers as needed, observed our teaching, and conferred with us. She was my mentor and guide: We discussed learning techniques and strategies, literature choices, classroom management, and lesson planning. She provided immediate feedback and answers to questions or problems and was there to hold my hand through the stress of change.

Having a year to learn a new teaching method enabled me to get past the preview stage and change my mindset. I realized I didn't have to jump in and do the whole thing immediately; I could take things slowly and sort of evolve over time. As the university professor introduced new challenges, I took ideas home, digested them, and prepared the materials needed. Making the change from whole-class instruction to flexible grouping practices with guided reading entailed a great deal of work and a solid commitment, but I found the process invigorating. This was particularly so as the year went on, and I felt more comfortable with the format and saw improved reading success for my students.

I gained so much from this experience. My teaching is more intimate. Through the small-group format I've come to know the children better and they me; they interact with one another more and take a more active role in our discussions. I've learned to group and regroup children according to their needs and to focus more closely on the skills they need as readers when I plan. It's working. This year has been a struggle, a time of change, and a good time of growth.

Teaching Reading Strategies at the Secondary Level

Gayle Cribb

For the last 14 months, I have been part of a Strategic Literacy Initiative (SLI) network, where I have been participating in professional development for the teaching of academic literacy in the content area at the secondary level. I teach history and Spanish. One of the things that has changed for me as a result of this experience is my understanding of what reading is. As I went into SLI, if you had asked me what reading was, I would have said that it was all about getting the message from the author. The more the reader, the better the reader understood exactly what the author meant to communicate.

One of the strategies we learned at SLI was Think Aloud, a metacognitive strategy aimed at making thinking more "visible." The facilitators had been careful to choose a compelling piece, a chapter from *Sula* by Toni Morrison entitled "1919." They gave us copies of the chapter, which had been divided into chunks, and we worked in pairs. One person read a sentence aloud to the other and then said his or her thoughts about that sentence, especially explaining how he or she made sense of the text. The listening partner noted each time that the reader made a prediction, visualized a passage, made a connection, identified a problem in understanding, or set about solving a problem. The pair traded roles after each chunk, usually a paragraph or two, so that both people experienced being both a reader and a listener. Then we shared our experiences and observations in a larger group.

What surprised me in this activity was how differently we each made sense of the text. After all, this was a group of college-educated people, and if I had walked into the room cold I would have known it was a group of teachers with just one visual sweep of the room. These folks knew how to get things organized, to take charge and reach out for people. They bubbled with the liveliness that distinguishes teachers from the average room full of adults. Moreover, we were secondary teachers who had chosen to participate in an intensive yearlong professional development series on literacy, a pretty select group. Yet we were quite diverse in terms of what understandings we were bringing to the text, how we approached the text, how easily we paid attention to it, what we were distracted by, and what we found challenging. I remember noticing, for example, how anxious my partner was to figure out "what happened," whereas I was taking a leisurely stroll through the text, enjoying the language and being patient with the development of the plot.

Next we watched a video, a case study in which a ninth-grade girl, enrolled in an academic literacy class in a public high school in San Francisco, was doing the same task we had just finished doing, using the chapter from *Sula*. Here was another mind going after a challenging text. She did some of the things we had done as well as some new things all her own. Yet the process, the struggle to make meaning, was immediately recognizable as what we had just done.

Later, back at my school, when I helped to teach my faculty this strategy of Think Aloud, the differences among us were even more striking. In addition to everything I'd noticed at SLI, we diverged widely in how comfortable we were with reading itself, in how intimidating it felt to reveal our thought processes and in what we believed the purpose of reading to be.

Thus, my understanding of what reading *is* has shifted. I now think that reading is thinking—that it is the interaction between the author and the reader, that the meaning is constructed by the reader in active relationship to the text. It matters just exactly what the reader brings to the reading, in terms of experience and prior knowledge, as well as what the reader expects to get from the reading and his or her own processes for doing so. As adults we sometimes say, "I read that book 20 years ago. I just reread it, and it was a completely different book!" *We* are different, so the book is different. Classic literature and historical documents resonate differently and take on different meanings in different eras, to even the most highly respected intellectuals of an era. Consider, for example, the interpretations of the Constitution by people as learned as Supreme Court Judges.

What this shift in my understanding means in my classroom is, perhaps, subtle but important. I find that I am more curious than I used to be about what exactly my students are thinking when they are reading. I listen more closely for how they are trying to make sense of the piece and ask them more questions about their process. I am less urgent about identifying and providing that missing piece of information or logic. I am more expectant about learning something about my students or the text or life from their particular reading of the text. I notice that they no longer look like "young," "unskilled," "immature," or "inexperienced" readers to me. Instead, they look like readers, just like me, just like my colleagues, who have their own challenges and struggles and fascinating selves to bring to the text. I can't help but think that my students feel this shift toward peerness, however subtle, and respond in kind.

Project STARS: A Professional Development Program for Intermediate Grade Teachers

Christy J. Falba

My role in the 2002–3 school year is to oversee implementation and evaluation of Project STARS (Strategies To Accelerate Reading Success). The instructional model was created by literacy specialists in the Clark County School District in collaboration with literacy faculty at the University of Nevada, Las Vegas.

As director of K–12 literacy and elementary technology in a large western school district, I was charged with the oversight and implementation of Project STARS, which provides an instructional model for our district's intermediate teachers to use in an intervention process for students who are demonstrating difficulty in reading. A 45-hour Professional Development Education (PDE) course provides the opportunity for intermediate teachers to learn effective reading and writing instructional strategies. The teacher training model and instructional strategies are based on current research in the areas of staff development and literacy intervention.

Project STARS was developed to support regular education third-, fourth-, and fifth-grade students who need additional instruction in reading. Teachers assess students, identify individual strengths and needs, and provide daily, 30-minute Project STARS lessons in small-group settings. Lessons place an emphasis on the development of student-applied phonics skills, comprehension skills, reading and writing fluency, and student independence and confidence in reading.

Appropriate instruction is determined by using a combination of measures including the Reading Inventory for the Classroom, Qualitative Spelling Inventory, the Motivation to Read Profile, informal assessments, and previous school records. These assessments identify reading and listening comprehension levels, word knowledge, spelling, writing skills, and student self-confidence in reading. Project STARS–trained teachers plan and implement instruction in a structured, 30-minute, small-group lesson. The components of the lesson include rereading, running record, word study, guided reading, and independent reading and response. In addition, teachers learn how to establish an effective literacy environment.

The effectiveness of Project STARS is based on systematic, data-driven decisions made by classroom teachers. It is a reading intervention program targeting middle grades that focuses on assessment and proven teaching strategies.

Block Scheduling: A Means for Providing Planning and Professional Development Time in Elementary Schools

Kathy Ganske

Lack of a common time for grade-level teams to meet to discuss students, plan, and engage in professional development activities is a frequent lament among elementary teachers and administrators alike. So, too, it was when I was a second-grade teacher in central Virginia. However, a little ingenuity, collaboration, and educational leadership changed all of that. My four-teacher team, and all of the other grade-level teams in this K–5 school, went from minimal common planning time to a half-day a week. For the second-grade team, the change meant that every Thursday afternoon was nonteaching time. We planned units of study, revamped the existing report card, conferred with parents, provided information sessions about curricular issues, and engaged in myriad other activities that necessitated time during the school day. How was this minor miracle achieved?

Before the change to block scheduling, all students in the school were slated for a half-hour of physical education every day (teachers' planning time) and a half-hour for lunch. In addition, once a week the students were scheduled for a half-hour each of library, music, and art, specials that usually fell on different days for a given teacher. In order to provide teachers with a common time, these three classes were rescheduled back-to-back on the same day, along with the physical education period, creating a block of time. Grade-level teachers whose block was in the morning took students to their first "special" and then picked them up after lunch, two and a half hours later. In the interim, the specials' teachers rotated the classes from one special to another and then delivered them to lunch. Those of us who had an afternoon block walked students to lunch and picked them up at the end of their fourth special, again two and a half hours later. The block schedule not only provided a much-needed common time for grade-level teams, it also had other benefits. For example, it limited instructional interruptions to one day (with the exception of physical education), and because the specials were held one after another on the same day, it enabled specials' teachers to collaborate and focus their instruction on a common theme, often one that integrated with classroom study. It was definitely a win-win situation, one well worth exploring.

The Use of Videotape in a Classroom Setting

Diane M. Lane

One of the ways that we as educators learn new techniques and teaching strategies is to view exemplar teachers teaching lessons on videotape. We watch and visualize ourselves in our classrooms imitating or adjusting the technique to fit our students' needs. Besides viewing well-trained teachers in their classrooms, teachers need to view their own teaching on videotape.

As a mentor to a first-year teacher (FYT), the veteran teacher must help to facilitate the FYT's experience in the classroom. In the state of Ohio, the FYT takes the Praxis 3. In the spring of the first year, an out-of-district educator will be evaluating the FYT's progress in the classroom using the four domains from Pathwise (Educational Testing Services). In preparing for this, the FYT constructs a lesson plan for her students. A videotaping of the lesson takes place. After the lesson, the mentor and teacher will analyze the lesson by watching and discussing the videotape, examining each domain for strengths and weaknesses in the lesson. Working together they can plan new lessons using the information that the video provides. In turn, if the FYT is having a recurring concern, the mentor can be videotaped teaching a lesson. Both will analyze the situation and make appropriate adjustments to the FYT's lesson.

For a mentor to be a constructive coach, the use of video is an excellent reflective tool. Using a video will help the FYT to better understand teaching and classroom organization. It is an eye-opening experience to view oneself and become aware of what is really transpiring in the classroom.

Changing the Course of Professional Development Through Differentiation

Gail L. Robinson and Shannon Riley-Ayers

The Context

"I'm your new literacy specialist and I'm here to help." These are the words that teachers in New Jersey hear when reading coaches, who are part of a statewide literacy initiative, join the staff in schools that are selected to receive additional instructional support to raise literacy rates. The role of these coaches is to provide high-quality professional development that connects teachers to best practice through collegial discourse, demonstration lessons, in-class coaching, teacher study groups, and professional resources. This model is grounded in research that suggests that sustained contact with teachers in the context of the school environment is a valuable way to enhance teacher learning and thus improve student performance. Yet, for many educators, neither help from literacy specialists nor state initiatives are enough to convince them to engage in an approach that departs from practicing teaching and learning as a private solitary endeavor. To convince educators to participate in this kind of professional development, specialists use a strategic plan that enables them to build relationships, differentiate support, and scaffold teacher learning. The use of such coaching strategies continually produces success in more than 70 schools throughout the state.

The following is an example of how professional behavior can be changed when there is purposeful interaction around the common goal of improving teaching to advance student learning.

The Approach

To gain entry into professional practices of teachers, specialists begin by earning the teachers' trust. Valuing the worth and expertise of each teacher, being a nonevaluative resource and active listener, identifying with the teacher's strengths and needs through the use of a literacy survey, and presenting relevant research are all part of coaching strategies that have opened doors and diminished the reluctance of many teachers.

The Results

The trust of several reluctant teachers was gained in a school when a literacy specialist offered to help one teacher who wanted to rearrange the desks in her classroom. After doing so, the specialist recommended using the additional space that rearranging the desks provided to establish literacy centers around the room. The students in this class are beginning to improve academically and work more cooperatively. The teacher attributes the change to switching from presenting whole class instruction almost exclusively to providing more focused instruction to smaller groups of students while the rest of the class engages in meaningful literacy activities. The reflected, "I listened to what the teacher thought she needed to do, and then I used moving the desks as a way to establish a relationship. That enabled me to coach her toward teaching practices that would benefit all of her students. I knew she would be motivated once she saw that her decisions resulted in improved student performance." The seemingly small task of rearranging a classroom generated a change in philosophy for this teacher. The teacher commented to the coach, "You changed the way I teach. Your help gave me the courage to do something different."

This teacher's success piqued the interest of colleagues in her school to request assistance from the literacy specialist, who is now coaching many teachers throughout the school in various aspects of literacy instruction.

Schoolwide Study Groups

Barbara Taylor

From 1999 to the present, I have been helping high-poverty schools engage in study groups to improve reading instruction. This work was part of the CIERA School Change Project in 1999–2002 (Taylor & Pearson, 2001; Taylor, Pearson, Peterson, & Rodriguez, 2002a) and the Minnesota Reading Excellence Project in 2002–2004. We began with the work of Murphy and Lick (2001) to guide our efforts, and over the years our School Change in Reading approach to study groups has evolved. The concept of study groups is simple, but the act of achieving effective study groups is not.

We ask teachers to look at data on their students and to reflect on research on effective reading instruction to decide where to focus efforts. A study group should take on a research-based, substantive aspect of reading instruction in which improvement is needed. This may be refining one's ability to ask higher level questions related to text, learning how to teach comprehension strategies, improving one's ability to coach students in strategies to decode words while reading. Teachers then meet once a month for five to nine months to improve their teaching abilities in their area of focus. During the monthly meetings teachers may learn a new teaching technique related to their topic, read a relevant research article, reflect on how instruction related to the new technique has been going within their classrooms, share data on students' growth in the focus areas, share data or reflections on their improvement in teaching, or share videotapes of their own teaching related to the focus area. The point of the study group is to learn new teaching techniques within an area of focus and to reflect on one's actual practice to help students achieve greater growth in reading. The model has been found to be effective in improving students' reading achievement (Taylor, Pearson, Peterson, & Rodriguez, 2003).

To be effective, study groups have a rotating leader, a note taker, and a timekeeper. Every study group has an action plan to guide its efforts. Action plans and meeting notes are shared with other study groups in the building at a monthly large group meeting. Teachers are strongly encouraged to meet in study groups that span more than one grade level.

References

Murphy, C., & Lick, D. (2001). *Whole-faculty study groups: Creating student-based professional development* (2nd ed.). Thousand Oaks, CA: Corwin.

Taylor, B. M., & Pearson, P. D. (2001). The CIERA School Change Project: Translating research on effective reading instruction and school reform into practice in high-poverty elementary schools. In C. Roller (Ed.), *Learning to teach reading: Setting the research agenda*. Newark, DE: International Reading Association.

Taylor, B. M., Pearson, P. D., Peterson, D. P., & Rodriguez, M. (2002). Looking inside classrooms: Reflecting on the "how" as well as the "what" in effective reading instruction. *The Reading Teacher, 56,* 270–279.

Taylor, B. M., Pearson, P. D., Peterson, D. S., & Rodriguez, M. (2003). *The CIERA School Change Project: Using research, data, and study groups to improve classroom reading instruction and increase students' reading achievement.* Ann Arbor, MI: University of Michigan, CIERA.

The Power of Teacher-Led Professional Development

Eleanor Wiley-Gensemer

Several years ago when I was teaching a seventh-grade language arts class composed of struggling readers, I facilitated a study group for teachers who wanted to join me in investigating the importance of fluency instruction and ways to implement fluency instruction into our already busy language arts classes. There were four elements to this professional development opportunity that made it both effective and memorable.

First, we were interested in improving our practice based on research. I had read some of the current research on fluency, and I wanted my colleagues to read the same articles and talk with me about them. The goal was to explore how fluency instruction fit the needs of our students and also how it fit into the research-based instruction that already existed in our classrooms.

Second, the participants *chose* to be involved in researching the topic. Participation was not mandated. I offered to facilitate a group of teachers who would meet to discuss current research on fluency and who would be willing to try some of the research-based ideas and report back to the group. Eight of my colleagues elected to join me for this professional development opportunity.

Third, we met on a regular basis, approximately once a month. During our meetings we discussed fluency research and talked about our attempts to implement these research-based ideas. We had multiple opportunities throughout the year to refine our understanding of the research based on classroom experience and additional readings and discussions within our group.

Fourth, this professional development opportunity led to immediate and productive changes in our classrooms. We saw fluency instruction help our students to gain confidence in their reading, improve their comprehension, and become aware of an element of reading that they had previously ignored. In addition, students' self-esteem as learners and readers grew as teachers from elementary school classrooms agreed to form partnerships with my middle school class. Thus, my students had an authentic reason for developing fluency.

This model of professional development is one that matched the philosophy of the school, that instruction is research-based, and met teacher needs for choice in what they studied. There were multiple opportunities to meet and talk about what they had read and tried in their classrooms, and there was evidence of improvement in instruction accompanied by positive changes in their students.

Forging a Common Literacy Experience

Deborah W. Allen

It is important for early childhood teachers to understand that when young children start school they have aalready had a variety of literacy experiences. Those opportunities for the development of literacy have come from informal interactions with family members, neighbors, other children, and community institutions. It is also important for preservice teachers to reflect on how their own personal experiences as well as their professional preparation influence the ways they will interact with their future students.

I decided that I could get preservice teachers to understand these two factors in a concrete way. In order to use literature that would allow us to have a common experience, I selected chapter 2 of *To Kill a Mockingbird*, by Harper Lee. In that chapter, the heroine, Scout Finch, enters kindergarten and her teacher, Miss Caroline, begins her teaching career. The author descriptively provides the reader with insights about the community and its residents, the educational preparation of the teacher, and detailed information about the two protagonists.

Through the use of this well-crafted text, I can facilitate discussion that focuses on literacy development from the perspectives of the child, family, school, and community. I have found that the discussions range from literal to critical analysis of the factors that influence early learners. The students can make connections with their own experiences as well as the experiences of others. I have found that the most successful way to use the text is to ask the preservice teachers to read the chapter in advance and to prepare a one-page response. At the next class session, I divide the students into literature circles to discuss the reading. In the past, I asked students to read the chapter in class, but they found it difficult to have in-depth discussions. This effective activity is generally done in the second class meeting for the language arts methods courses I teach.

Editors

Dorothy S. Strickland is the Samuel DeWitt Proctor Professor of Education at Rutgers, the state university of New Jersey. She was formerly the Arthur I. Gates Professor of Education at Teachers College, Columbia University. A former classroom teacher, reading consultant, and learning disabilities specialist, she is a past president of both the International Reading Association and the IRA Reading Hall of Fame. She received IRA's Outstanding Teacher Educator of Reading Award. She was a recipient of the National Council of Teachers of English Award as Outstanding Educator in the Language Arts and the NCTE Rewey Belle Inglis Award as Outstanding Woman in the Teaching of English. She has numerous publications in the field of reading and language arts. Her latest publications are: *Preparing Our Teachers: Opportunities for Better Reading Instruction*; *Beginning Reading and Writing*; *Administration & Supervision of Reading Programs*; and *Supporting Struggling Readers and Writers: Strategies for Classroom Intervention 3–6*.

Michael L. Kamil is a professor of education at Stanford University. He is a member of the Psychological Studies in Education Committee and is on the faculty of the Learning, Design, and Technology Program. He received his B.A. from Tulane University and his M.A. and Ph. D. from the University of Wisconsin. His research explores the effects of computer technologies on literacy and the acquisition of literacy in first and second languages. He has been editor of *Reading Research Quarterly*, *Journal of Reading Behavior*, and *The Yearbook of the National Reading Conference*. He

co-edited the *Handbook of Reading Research*, Vols 1, 2, and 3. He was a member of the National Reading Panel and the Rand Reading Study Group. He is currently a member of the National Literacy Panel and chairman of the Framework Planning Committee for the National Assessment of Educational Progress.

Contributors

Deborah W. Allen is a professor at Kean University, where she teaches undergraduate and graduate level courses in language arts, children's literature, research methods, and multicultural curriculum. She also serves as coordinator of a U.S. Department of Education teacher recruitment grant. Prior to her appointment at Kean University, Dr. Allen was director of an early childhood center in New York City serving 175 children and taught kindergarten and second grade in New York City public schools. Dr. Allen has published in numerous journals and is a contributor, editor, and reviewer for others.

Donna E. Alvermann is Distinguished Research Professor of Reading Education at the University of Georgia and a former teacher in Texas and New York. She co-directed the National Reading Research Center in 1992–1997, was past co-chairwoman of the International Reading Association's Commission on Adolescent Literacy, and currently edits *Reading Research Quarterly*. Her co-authored books include *Content Reading and Literacy: Succeeding in Today's Diverse Classrooms*; *Reconceptualizing the Literacies in Adolescents' Lives* (1998); and *Adolescents and Literacies in a Digital World* (2002).

Lillian A. Augustine received an Ed.D. in educational administration from Teachers College, Columbia University. She holds a B.A. in elementary education from Newark State College, now Kean University, and an M.A. in early childhood education from the same institution. Currently she is the assistant superintendent for Learning and educational services in the Perth Amboy Public Schools in Perth Amboy, New Jersey. She is a former New Jersey Teacher of the Year, Carnegie Teacher Fellow, and recipient of numerous educational grants. As principal of Schoenly School in Spotswood, New Jersey, Dr. Augustine coordinated the review and recognition of her school as a National School of Excellence by the U.S. Department of Education.

Matt Baker is editorial director of books and special projects for the International Reading Association in Newark, Delaware. He manages the Association's book publishing program, which produces more than 20 books a year in all literacy disciplines. Among other responsibilities, he leads acquisitions efforts and develops book projects from proposal to final manuscript. Baker joined the IRA staff in 1995 and has managed the book program since 1998.

Jennifer Berne is an assistant professor of reading and language arts at Oakland University in Rochester, Michigan, where she teaches courses in children's literature, wrtiting, and teacher education. Her current research investigates the connection between teacher's literacy practices and their student's literacy learning.

M. Susan Burns is an associate professor at George Mason University. Her main activities include teaching and research on language, literacy and cognition as it applies to young children (birth through grade 3) who are living in poverty, are from multilingual or multicultural contexts, or have disabilities. Prior to this position she served at the National Academy of Sciences, directing the projects that produced *Preventing Reading Difficulties in Young Children, Starting Out Right: A Guide to Promoting Children's Reading Success,* and *Eager to Learn: Educating Our Preschoolers.* Most recently she is coauthor of *Preparing Our Teachers: Opportunities for Better Reading Instruction.*

Pamela L. Chase is an elementary teacher for the Haddon Heights School District in Haddon Heights, New Jersey. She has taught first through sixth grades in the past 15 years. She is currently teaching third grade at Glenview Avenue School.

Michael Copland teaches in Educational Leadership and Policy Studies at the University of Washington. His research interests include work conceptualizing learning-focused leadership, leadership in the context of school reform, the principalship, and research and development of problem-based instructional materials for use in preparing educational leaders. Recent publications include "The Reform of Administrator Preparation at Stanford: An Analytic Description," in the *Journal of School Leadership,* and "The Myth of the Superprincipal," in *Phi Delta Kappan.* Dr. Copland holds a Ph.D. from Stanford University and was formerly a teacher and school administrator in the Bellingham (WA) Public Schools.

Gayle Cribb has taught middle school and high school in a small agricultural town in California's Sacramento Valley for 24 years. Her students include the children of farmers, farmworkers, cannery workers and commuters to the Bay Area. She teaches Mexican students who have just arrived in the United States for the first time as well as Chicanos who have lived in Dixon all of their lives. Always interested in the issues of language acquisition, culture, and equity in education, she teaches honors U.S. History, U.S. history in Spanish (for those students who have not acquired enough English to succeed in a mainstream class), and Spanish 3.

Janice A. Dole is currently on the faculty in the Department of Teaching and Learning at the University of Utah. Her current research interests include reading and school reform in high poverty schools and professional development in reading education. Dr. Dole has been on faculties at the University of Denver, the Center for the Study of Reading at the University of Illinois, and Michigan State University. She is the author of numerous articles and books and a past member of the Reading Development Panel of the National Assessment of Educational Project. She does frequent consulting to states on Reading First.

Gerald G. Duffy is a former elementary and middle school teacher and a professor emeritus from Michigan State University, where he served for 25 years as a reading educator and researcher. His many articles, research reports, and books focus on the effective teaching of literacy with an emphasis on strategy instruction, teacher effectiveness, and exemplary professional development. He is a former president of the National Reading Conference and a member of the Reading Hall of Fame. He continues to write and consult from his home in Deer Park, Washington.

Christy J. Falba is the director of K–12 literacy and elementary instructional technology in the Clark County School District (Las Vegas), the sixth largest district in the country. Dr. Falba's areas of expertise include curriculum development, literacy, technology integration, and teacher education. Research interests focus on reading intervention strategies for struggling readers and the integration of technology in teaching and learning. Dr. Falba received her Ed.D. from the University of Nevada, Las Vegas, and has served as the school district liaison for several university-school district collaborative projects. In 2002, Dr. Falba was honored as the College of Education Alumna of the Year.

Susan Florio-Ruane is professor of teacher education at Michigan State University. Her research includes studies of "Schooling and the Acquisition of Written Literacy," "Reading Culture in Autobiography," and "Re-engaging Low Achieving Readers by Innovative Professional Development." Her paper "The Social Organization of Classes and Schools" won the Division K Research in Teacher Education Award of AERA. She publishes in journals including *American Educational Research Journal, Research in the Teaching of English, Language Arts,* and *English Education.* Her book, *Teacher Education and the Cultural Imagination,* won the NRC Frye Outstanding Book Award. In 2003, she received the MSU Distinguished Faculty Award.

Kathy Ganske is an associate professor of reading education at Rowan University, New Jersey, where she teaches graduate and undergraduate courses in literacy and supervises the reading clinic. A former classroom teacher with more than 20 years of experience, she has taught primary through upper elementary grades in various regions of the country. Through her research and consulting work Dr. Ganske continues to be actively involved in classrooms. She has written numerous articles, is the author of *Word Journeys: Assessment-Guided Phonics, Spelling, and Vocabulary Instruction,* and co-author of *Supporting Struggling Readers and Writers: Strategies for Classroom Intervention 3–6.*

Irene W. Gaskins is a school administrator who particularly enjoys her roles as teacher and instructional leader. Prior to earning her doctorate in educational psychology from the University of Pennsylvania, Gaskins taught in public and private schools. In 1970, while teaching at the University of Pennsylvania, and sparked by her interest in children who have profound difficulties learning to read, Gaskins founded Benchmark School. It is a school for struggling readers, as well as a laboratory for designing instruction that works for all students. Gaskins has received IRA's William S. Gray Citation of Merit for lifetime achievement and was honored as a Distinguished Educator by *The Reading Teacher*.

Cynthia L. Greenleaf is co-director of the Strategic Literacy Initiative at WestEd. Her work focuses on building knowledge, in collaboration with teachers, to address the literacy learning needs of young people. She leads a team of researchers in an integrated program of research and development initiatives to promote high-level literacy for diverse youth. Dr. Greenleaf earned her Ph.D. in language and literacy education from the University of California, Berkeley. She is co-author of *Reading for Understanding: Improving Reading in Middle and High School Classrooms* and publishes scholarly writings in such journals as *Harvard Educational Review* and *Teaching and Teacher Education*.

Kathy Highfield received her B.A. in elementary education and French and her M.A. in literacy instruction from Michigan State University. She is currently working on her doctorate in reading and language arts at Oakland University, specializing in literacy instruction, teacher learning and test preparation. She has 13 years of classroom teaching experience with students from second to sixth grades at Rose Pioneer Elementary School in Holly, Michigan. She is a frequent presenter at local, state, and national reading conferences, sharing her research on student learning in Book Club, effective instruction for test preparation, and teacher learning.

James V. Hoffman is professor of language and literacy studies at the University of Texas at Austin, where he directs a reading specialization program at the undergraduate level and teaches graduate courses in reading and research. He is the chairman of the Association's National Commission on Excellence in Elementary Teacher Preparation for Reading Instruction. Hoffman served on the board of directors of the International Reading Association from 1996 to 1999. He is a former elementary classroom teacher and reading specialist and has served as president of the National Reading Conference as well as editor of *Reading Research Quarterly* and editor of the *Yearbook of the National Reading Conference*. His major research interests are in the areas of teacher preparation, beginning reading instruction, and the texts used in reading instruction.

Diane Lane is an intervention teacher in the Hilliard City School District in Hilliard, Ohio. She has been an educator in elementary schools for 23 years. Her training has included a master's degree in reading education, Reading

Recovery teacher, and literacy coordinator. As well as educating young minds, Diane has coached and mentored teachers in her district. She has had the opportunity to present and instruct teachers at conferences and workshops. Diane believes that working with teachers will ultimately reflect in the success of students' achievement.

JoAnn B. Manning is the Executive Director of the Laboratory for Student Success (LSS), the Mid-Atlantic Regional Educational Laboratory at Temple University. She received a Doctorate from Temple University, and has more than 30 years in education, as teacher, supervisor, principal, Assistant Superintendent, and Superintendent for school districts in the state of Pennsylvania. She has been a contributing author to six edited volumes, and serves on several professional boards, including the National Advisory Board for *The School Community Journal*; the Leadership Team for the Collaborative for Academic, Social, and Emotional Learning (CASEL); and for the Philadelphia Chapter of the Black Alliance for Educational Options (BAEO).

Joanne K. Monroe is the director of curriculum and instruction for the Clinton Township School District in Annandale, New Jersey. She previously worked as a language arts and social studies supervisor, served as an instructional specialist for the New Jersey State Department of Education, and taught primary grades and high school English. Joanne is a past president of the New Jersey Reading Association and the Tri-County Reading Council. She has taught as an adjunct at the Graduate School of Education at Rutgers and at Rider University.

Allison U. Nealy is currently a special education teacher concentrating on adolescent literacy in both resource and collaborative classes. She teaches several college-level courses in these areas. She currently works at the high school level and has formerly taught in both middle schools and psychoeducational centers for children with severe emotional disturbances. She holds a master's degree in special education and a doctorate of education in reading.

Jean Osborn has worked in a variety of educational settings. She began her career as a preschool and kindergarten teacher in a program for at-risk students at the University of Illinois. Next she worked as a field representative of the Direct Instruction Model in the U.S. Department of Education's Follow Through Program. She then joined the staff of the Center for the Study of Reading at the University of Illinois and became its associate director. During the past five years she has served as a consultant to the Texas Education Agency, the Reading and Language Arts Center at the University of Texas at Austin, the Illinois State Board of Education, and the U.S. Department of Education. Her most recent publications include "Put Reading First," a booklet written for teachers and based on the findings of the National Reading Panel.

Elizabeth S. Pang received her B.A. in English from the University of Oxford. She has an M.A. and Ph.D. in educational linguistics from Stanford University. She was a research assistant to the National Reading Panel, synthesizing research on the education and professional development of reading teachers. She has publications on children's reading and comprehension of hypertext, literacy teacher education, and second-language reading. A researcher and language specialist at the Ministry of Education in Singapore, her current research examines the cross-linguistic transfer of reading skills in bilingual children.

Gay Su Pinnell is a professor in the School of Teaching and Learning at Ohio State University. She has received the International Reading Association's Albert J. Harris Award for research in reading, the Ohio Governor's Award for education, the Charles A. Dana Foundation Award, and is a member of the Reading Hall of Fame. With Irene Fountas, she is co-author of *Guided Reading: Good First Teaching for All Children* (1996), *Guiding Readers & Writers, Grades 3–6* (2000), and a number of other books and articles. She also has co-authored *Systems for Change: A Guide to Professional Development,* with Carol Lyons.

Taffy E. Raphael is a member of the curriculum and instruction faculty in literacy education at the University of Illinois at Chicago, teaching courses related to methods of instruction, teacher research, and related topics. Prior to joining the UIC faculty, Dr. Raphael taught and conducted research at the University of Utah (1980–1982), Michigan State University (1982–1997), and Oakland University (1997–2001). Dr. Raphael's work in teacher education was recognized by her receipt of the Outstanding Teacher Educator in Reading Award from the International Reading Association in May 1997. Dr. Raphael's research has focused on question-answer relationships and strategy instruction in writing, and, for the past decade, Book Club, a literature-based reading program. Throughout these research projects, she has studied teacher learning and professional development through teacher study groups. She received Oakland University's Research Excellence Award in September 2000. She has published in the leading research journals and has co-authored and edited several books on literacy instruction, including *Book Club: A Literature-Based Curriculum* (Small Planet Communications 1997, 2002), with Kathy Au, *Literature-Based Instruction: Reshaping the Curriculum* (Christopher-Gordon, 1998), and *Super QAR for Testwise Students* (Wright Group, 2002). She was selected for the International Reading Association Reading Hall of Fame in 2002.

Shannon Riley-Ayers is currently a program coordinator with the New Jersey Department of Education, where she manages the reading coach program and implements key components of the Governor's Early Literacy Initiative. She holds a master's of education in language and literacy and a doctorate in educational psychology from Pennsylvania State University. Her practical experience includes teaching kindergarten and serving as an elementary reading specialist in New Jersey public schools. She has also worked with preservice teachers at The College of New Jersey and continues to work on current literacy issues with inservice teachers by conducting professional development workshops.

Gail L. Robinson is a coordinator in the Office of Early Literacy with the New Jersey State Department of Education. Her work there includes program design and implementation of the Reading Coach Program, a professional development model to support K–3 teachers. She has taught literacy education in early childhood classrooms for 20 years and has mentored teachers, collaborated with administrators and peers to create standards-based curriculum, and presented staff development seminars focusing on balanced literacy education in K–12 classrooms. Robinson has conducted numerous family education seminars that promote the love and joy of reading along with effective strategies to encourage student reading beyond the school day. She is a certified nursery, elementary, and Reading Recovery teacher.

Emily M. Rodgers taught for 10 years in Newfoundland prior to joining the faculty of Ohio State University. Her research focuses on the professional development of teachers and the nature of effective scaffolding of literacy learning. Her paper "Language Matters: When Is a Scaffold Really a Scaffold" won the National Reading Conference's Outstanding Student Research Award in 1999. Emily is co-editor, with Gay Su Pinnell, of "Learning From Teaching in Literacy Education: New Perspectives on Professional Development."

Cathy M. Roller has been director of research and policy at the International Reading Association since 1998. Roller develops policy statements with the board of directors, develops relationships with professional partners, and oversees the traditional role of the research division—disseminating reading research to many different audiences through print and electronic media, annual conference activities, and responses to inquiries. She spearheaded a research commission that explored elementary teacher preparation for reading instruction and has recently presented the highlights *Prepared to Make a Difference* from the Report of the National Commission on Excellence in Elementary Teacher Preparation for Reading Instruction.

Ruth Schoenbach is co-director of the Strategic Literacy Initiative (SLI) at WestEd in Oakland, California and co-author of *Reading for Understanding: A Guide to Improving Reading in Middle and High School Classrooms* (Jossey-Bass, 1999). Since 1990, Schoenbach has worked collaboratively with SLI Co-Director Cynthia Greenleaf to build a multilevel research and development program focused on supporting increased literacy learning for adolescents through teacher professional development. Schoenbach holds an Ed.M.

from the Harvard Graduate School of Education. Her key areas of interest include professional development design and curriculum design for accelerating access to high-level literacy for underperforming youth.

Robert Stechuk is a doctoral student at George Mason University in Fairfax, Virginia, where he received a Keller Fellowship from the Helen A. Keller Institute for Human Disabilities. His research interests include: typical and atypical child development; language and bilingual development; and early literacy. From 1999–2002 he was an administrative faculty member in the Graduate School of Education at George Mason University. Prior to working at GMU he was employed for 15 years in Head Start and early intervention programs.

Barbara M. Taylor is Guy Bond Chair in Reading and Professor of Reading Education at the University of Minnesota where she has been on the faculty since 1978. She works extensively with elementary teachers in year-long professional development related to the effective Early Intervention in Reading program she developed in 1989. Her research interests focus on early reading intervention and on school and teacher factors contributing to children's success in reading. She directed a CIERA study of schools which are beating the odds in teaching children to read. Currently, she is the principal investigator of another CIERA study on school reform in reading in high-poverty schools.

Herbert J. Walberg is University Scholar and Research Professor of Education and Psychology at the University of Illinois at Chicago. Holding a Ph.D. from the University of Chicago and formerly Assistant Professor at Harvard University, he has written and edited more than 55 books and written about 350 articles on such topics as effective teaching, educational productivity, accountability, creativity, and exceptional human accomplishments. Among his latest books are Psychology and Educational Currently Walberg serves on the board of the Chicago International Charter School, which serves 4,900 largely inner-city students on six campuses. He also serves on several other non-profit boards.

Eleanor Wiley-Gensemer is a middle school teacher and language arts supervisor at Benchmark School in Media, Pennsylvania, a school for bright students with learning differences. She is responsible for training new teachers in the classes she supervises, and also facilitates ongoing professional development for veteran teachers in those classes. She is a doctoral student in the reading and language arts program at Widener University in Chester, Pennsylvania. She is a board member and past president of the Delaware Valley Reading Association and is Director of Membership Development of the Keystone State Reading Association, Pennsylvania's state affiliate of the International Reading Association.

Index